THE V&A ALBUM 2

THE V&A
ALBUM 2

Templegate Publishing Ltd
in association with
The Friends of the V&A

COVER: Autumn, tile decoration in the old Grill Room (now Poynter Room), lead-glazed earthenware painted in colours. Designed by Sir Edward Poynter and painted on Minton blanks by the ladies of the South Kensington School of Art.

FRONTISPIECE: The Temple of Pan in the grounds of Osterley Park House.

ISBN 0 946345 03 1

Published by Templegate Publishing with The Associates of the V&A
Photographs Crown Copyright unless otherwise stated
Essays © 1983 the authors

Edited by John Physick
Designed by Roger Huggett and Sharon Ellis-Davies/Sinc
Printed in England by Raithby, Lawrence & Company Ltd, Leicester and London

Contents

CONTENTS

ONE OF THREE SURVIVING COPIES OF THE FIRST ENGLISH TRANSLATION OF THE CATHOLIC MASS.

The disclosi[n]g of the Canon of the Popish Masse. Wyth a sermon annexed unto it of the famous Clerke of Worthie memorye D. Marten Luther [colophon;] Imprynted have at all Papistes, By me Hans Nitpricke. (Probably 1547].

This violent attack, backed up by Luther's sermon on the "blasphemy" of "readyng thys Antechristian Canon in Theyr Masses", contains the first printing of the Roman Catholic mass in English, with side notes explaining the actions and gestures of the priest.

Rare books and manuscripts from the sixteenth to the twentieth century in English Literature and History, Music, Economics, Politics and Philosophy, Science and Medicine, Travel. Please write for catalogues.

PICKERING & CHATTO LTD

ANTIQUARIAN BOOKSELLERS, FOUNDED 1820

17 PALL MALL, LONDON SW1Y 5NB

01-930 2515

The 217th Meeting of the Advisory Council on 15 June 1983. Round the table, from the right: Lady Casson, Countess Spencer, Lord Harlech, H.R.H. Princess Michael of Kent, Sir Alexander Glen (Chairman), Sir Roy Strong (Director), John Physick (Secretary), Anthony Burton (Assistant Secretary), Robin Holland-Martin, Barry Till, Sir Nevil Macready, Professor John Russell Brown, Professor J.B. Trapp, Professor Richard Gombrich, Professor Christopher Frayling, Victor Margrie, Jean Muir, John Last.

THE ADVISORY COUNCIL
1913–1983

Sir Alexander Glen

The last eighteen months have been the most momentous since the foundation of the V&A 130 years ago. In this brief period the constraints of Whitehall control are now history, the challenge of the great freedom – and greater responsibility – of Trustee status lie immediately ahead. Inside the Museum much is stirring, and outside, Bethnal Green and the Theatre Museums are assured an exciting future. But legislatively it was a close run thing.

The late 1970s had been a despairing time, but throughout a good part of the last 130 years the governance of the Museum has been indeed somewhat ambivalent. In early days of course the position was clear enough. Henry Cole ran the place, assisted, it is true, by Richard Redgrave and J.C. Robinson, but holding power absolutely in his own hands and consolidating this in his dual role as Secretary to the Department of Science and Art and at the same time as Superintendent of the South Kensington Museums.

This turbulent, hard-driving man created not only the V&A but much of South Kensington as well. It is particularly fitting that this memorable year of 1983 has seen renewed tribute to him in the opening on 17 March by Her Majesty The Queen of the magnificent Henry Cole Wing.

With his retirement, change was profound, sadly so, as the nineteenth century neared its end, when concern as to how the South Kensington Museums were being run led to the setting up of a Select Committee. Its *Report* in 1897/1898 was highly critical. There was even mention of the possibility of moving the Museums out of government control and establishing them instead as Trustee Museums similar to the British Museum. The proposal was discarded however, first in the *Report* itself which came down in favour of a new Board of Visitors to

advise the Lord President, and finally in 1906 by Lord Londonderry, as first President of the new Board of Education, on the ground that the connection between the Art Museum and the Royal College and the Art Schools throughout the country was so important that the Board of Education itself must continue to hold executive responsibility.

In the correspondence and minutes of the time there was much sound thinking. One outcome was the separation by 1909 of the V&A into the V&A Art Museum and the V&A Science Museum. There was recognition, interestingly, that excessive Departmental control could make it difficult to attract the services of a Director of the quality required and that this could equally militate against a Council desirous of exercising effective responsibilities. For it had been accepted that a new body was required and the decision already taken in 1906 that a permanent Advisory Council be appointed.

Indeed, much correspondence deals with the need for the proper constitution of this body and even more concerning its secretary. Treasury approval was sought for a salary scale of £400 p.a. rising by £25 to £800, indication of the senior status required when it is remembered that the salary scale of the Director himself was £700 by £25 to £800. Confirmation of this lies in the appointment to the post in 1910 of Mr Paul Oppé, CB, and his almost immediate elevation to the new but very temporary status of Deputy Director.

What, however, was happening during these years to the Advisory Council? There was a secretary, even a Deputy Director, but there was no Council. It was not until 1913, seven years after Lord Londonderry's decision, that an Advisory Council held its first meeting on the 24 January with

Lord Reay in the Chair, nine members present and two absent.

So the Advisory Council was to have a life of 70 years from 1913 to 1983, with eight Chairmen. Well over one hundred distinguished men and women have given time and thought to its deliberations, and the V&A owes much to them. The role of the Council was never clear, however, so long as the V&A remained within the structure of Whitehall. That it had no executive power was proper, but in the event of dispute had it any specific responsibility and was it primarily advisory to the Director or to the Minister? That its influence was to vary throughout the years largely as personalities changed, both in Whitehall and in the Museum, was inevitable.

The financial constraints of the late 1970s finally forced the weaknesses inherent in the status of the V&A to be faced. The closing of the Museum one day a week because of limited resources, the termination because of the same reason of the greatly valued Regional Services, the curtailment of public enjoyment of individual galleries – sometimes at short notice because of lack of staff – all these outside the control of the Museum were enough to cause serious public and political concern.

What was fortuitous was that these problems and their aftermath coincided with the time in office of a young Director, Roy Strong, clear in his mind where the Museum should go and determined to build within it a collegiate form of delegated authority. That this, coupled with the resolve to balance this executive structure with a well-judged constructive and monitoring role for the Advisory Council, enabled the Museum as a whole to plan the strategy required to meet the challenges and opportunities in a difficult period. As the last Chairman of the last Advisory Council I thank my colleagues for the robust manner in which they have acted during these critical days. In particular we all owe a very special debt to John Physick who achieved outstanding liaison with all concerned and who now, in his last year in the V&A, has been appointed Deputy Director, the first to hold this office since 1913.

That the V&A must be moved at long last out of government control was self evident. The initial response of government had been uncertain. However, Trustee status was recommended strongly by the Rayner Scrutiny under Mr Gordon Burrett, CB, in 1982. This was accepted by the Minister of the Arts, Mr Paul Channon, put to Parliament early in 1983 as an important part of the National Heritage Bill, which received its final reading and Royal Assent a matter of hours before Parliament was prorogued on 13 May.

After 130 years it was indeed a close run thing.

Much else, however, had been happening. The Henry Cole Wing now provides outstanding facilities for conservation and a new home for the Sheepshanks and Ionides Collections and the Constables. This in turn has made possible major improvements which are being effected in the Primary Galleries. Better housekeeping, too, is

being achieved on lines usefully set out by the Burrett Report. Especially welcome was Mr Channon's decision endorsing the importance of the Theatre Museum to be established in Covent Garden.

This far-reaching programme could not have been achieved without the whole-hearted support and understanding of Mr Paul Channon and his staff in the Office of Art and Libraries. In consequence, services in danger of being taken for granted have been given a new significance and, still more important, the future potential and duties of the world's greatest Museum of the decorative arts takes on a totally new perspective.

In this, the Boiler House made possible by the generosity of Sir Terence Conran, is providing something very special. It seeks to fulfil the essential objective on which Cole set his mind, education in and promotion of good design. The Ford Sierra exhibition demonstrated the 'how', the hard solid struggle with the endless hours not only on the drawing board, but at home, in the factory, cajolingly, sometimes almost hopelessly, the effort which alone can overcome the depressingly predominant number of mediocre products. Sir Roy Strong and

Sir Terence Conran have placed an implant within a great Museum which – if it can be brave and aggressive enough – could transform a much wider area than South Kensington.

It is an exciting present and even more exciting future that Sir Roy Strong, Lord Carrington and the Trustees and all who work in the V&A have the good fortune to face. We, the Advisory Council, wish them all good fortune which we wish, too, to the Associates and Friends of the V&A, who do so much to help and support the Museum.

Recent Acquisitions

Design by Pablo Picasso for Leonide Massine's costume as
the Chinese Conjuror, in the ballet *Parade*, libretto by Jean
Cocteau, choreography by Massine, costumes and decor by
Picasso. Pen and brown ink. 27.3×19.7 cm. The ballet was
first performed by Diaghilev's Ballet Russes on 18 May
1917, at the Théâtre de Châtelet, Paris. Theatre Museum.

1 Wine Cooler (one of a pair), silver-gilt, London: hallmarks for 1809–10. Maker's mark of Paul Storr for Rundell, Bridge and Rundell. Engraved with the Latin inscription of Rundell, Bridge and Rundell. Accepted by the Government from the estate of the late Marquess of Ormonde in lieu of death duties and allocated to the V&A. The two wine coolers were originally made for James, Earl (later Marquess) of Ormonde (1774–1838), who spent heavily at Rundell's after receiving financial compensation from the government for relinquishing his rights as hereditary chief Butler of Ireland to levy a duty on all wines imported into that country. Department of Metalwork. 2 Crucifix, ivory, by David Le Marchand, Anglo–French, about 1700. A. 42–1983. One of three recorded religious carvings by the leading ivory carver working in England in the early eighteenth century.

Purchased with the assistance of the National Art-Collections Fund. Department of Sculpture. 3 A bookbinding: Turkish, leather over paper pasteboards; exterior covers gold tooled with large circular medallion with scalloped border, blue painted fillets and highlights; interior covers of plain green silk. 312×210 mm, Turkey, probably third quarter of fifteenth century, L. 531–1983. This fine example of early Ottoman bookbinding was formerly in the collection of the late Dr F.R. Martin. It was probably executed for Sultan Muhammad II or Mehmet Fātih ('The Conqueror') in the third quarter of the fifteenth century. The style is inspired by Herat bindings of the early fifteenth century, particularly in the floral motifs of the flap and the flowers on the wide border of the circular medallion. National Art Library.

1

2

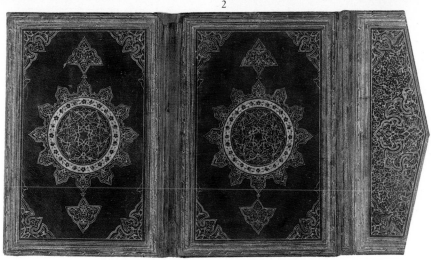

3

DEUTSCHE WERKBUND-
AUSSTELLUNG
KUNST IN HANDWERK,
INDUSTRIE UND HANDEL ⋅ ARCHITEKTUR
MAI CÖLN 1914 OCT.

Opposite: Poster advertising the exhibition *Deutsche Werkbund-Ausstellung. Kunst in Handwerk, Industrie und Handel*, held in Cologne, 1914, by Peter Behrens (1868–1940), printed by A. Molling and Comp. Hannover–Berlin, colour lithograph, 90.2×63.5 cm, E. 279–1980. Department of Prints and Drawings and Photographs, and Paintings. 1 Toy Village, carved wood: five monastic buildings, a windmill and three barns, made by David Jones for the children of Eric Gill, 1922–4. (Misc. 94–1983). Hand Puppets, carved wood, four probably representing the children of Eric Gill and made for them by David Jones (1922–4). (Misc. 95–1983). Bethnal Green Museum of Childhood. *2 Kimono* with hanging sleeves (*furisode*), figured silk with roundels of pine, bamboo, and plum against an overall geometric pattern. The design is reserved in white tie-dye on a red ground. Japanese, early nineteenth century. FE. 32–1982. Far Eastern Department. 3 Poster advertising the exhibition *Le Quatrième Salon de la Libre Esthétique* held at the Musée Moderne, Brussels, 1897, by Theo van Rysselberghe (1862–1926), printed by Monnom, Brussels, colour lithograph, 98×71.5 cm, E. 280–1980. Department of Prints and Drawings and Photographs, and Paintings.

1

2

3

Throne chair with footstool (one of a pair): sheet silver on a teak carcass, Indian, mid-nineteenth century. I.S. 10 & B – 1983. Indian Department.

1 Coloured maquette for the mural on the Pitt and Scott warehouse, King's Cross, 1981, by Graham Crowley (b. 1950), felt tip, 17.4×54 cm, E. 435–1982. One of the most striking innovations in the city scape of this country is the mural painting on the exterior walls of buildings. This is a popular art form often specifically located in deprived areas. Given the present demolition rate, most of the buildings will not survive long, and so it seemed important that the designs at least for some of the major schemes should be preserved in the Museum. Graham Crowley's Pitt and Scott mural is seen daily by thousands of railway passengers three minutes out of King's Cross. Department of Prints and Drawings and Photographs, and Paintings.

2 *The Temple at Philae*, 1858, photograph by Francis Frith, (1822–98), albumen print from wet collodion on glass negative, 360×468 mm, An album of 20 mammoth plate views of *Egypt, Sinai and Jerusalem* published *c.*1860 by William Mackenzie, London, Glasgow and Edinburgh. Frith's views in this publication are the most impressive photographs of the monuments of the Near East taken in the albumen/collodion period (*c.*1851–85) and among the grandest topographical views in the history of photography. Department of Prints and Drawings and Photographs, and Paintings.

1

2

Opposite: Evening ensemble: Renaissance Cloth of Gold crinoline (bodice, skirt, and over-skirt over hoops), English, London, Zandra Rhodes, the Elizabethan Collection, Autumn/Winter 1981. Diadem, glass in resin on metal, English, London, Andrew Logan for Zandra Rhodes, Autumn/Winter 1981. T. 124 to C–1983; T. 125–1983. The ensemble was given by Miss Zandra Rhodes; the diadem was given by Mr Andrew Logan. Department of Textiles and Dress. 1 The Walpole Casket, Limoges, plaques by the master IP. c.1540, gilt metal set with stamped silver foil and enamelled copper plaques. Height 16.1 cm, width 12.3 cm, C. 49–1982. Department of Ceramics. 2 Cabinet, designed by Gio Ponti, with decoration devised by him and the designer Piero Fornasetti, 1950. W. 21–1983. 3 Cabinet, open, Department of Furniture and Woodwork. (Photographs by Sir Geoffrey Shakerley).

1

2   3

N. M. Rothschild & Sons Limited

Merchants and Bankers

Nathan Mayer Rothschild (founder of the London House)
at the marriage of his daughter, Charlotte, in London on 11th September, 1826.

New Court, St Swithin's Lane, London EC4P 4DU
Telephone: 01-280 5000   Telex: 888031

santa fé east™

200 OLD SANTA FE TRAIL
SANTA FE, NEW MEXICO 87501
(505) 988-3103

Although just entering its fourth year in New Mexico, Santa Fe East has established itself as an important gallery of American art with an impressive national reputation. From its conception five years ago, the gallery has continuously explored and defined the "American" in American art.

Santa Fe East has two gallery wings. The North wing of the gallery represents a dazzling collection of jewelry and Native American pottery unique to the Southwest. The South wing proudly displays museum quality American art of the late 19th and early 20th centuries. Important exhibitions, carefully curated, beautifully documented and expertly presented, are organized throughout the year. Often these exhibitions are accompanied by events intended to provide the public with educational opportunities, such as symposiums, lectures, films and demonstrations.

One can always find exquisite works by artists John Marin, Charles Demuth, Charles Burchfield, Thomas Hart Benton, Leon Gaspard, Ben Shahn, Lilla Cabot Perry, Jane Peterson, Bernique Longley and Millard Sheets. Artists from past and present, from New York to California, and from Traditionalists to Modernists, are carefully selected to give meaning and definition to the words "American Art."

Santa Fe East has gone beyond producing catalogues for major exhibitions to publishing books on important American artists. *Ben Shahn: Voices and Visions*, 1981, has won many regional and national awards, and has guaranteed Santa Fe East an important place among art book publishers. Other titles which have gained recognition are *Bernique Longley: A Retrospective* and *Lilla Cabot Perry: Days to Remember*.

For centuries, Santa Fe has been a cultural center on the North American continent. Santa Fe East continues this tradition by bringing together art unique to the American Southwest with fine American art.

Top left: Alexander Brook (1898 - 1980)
Tan Nude *1948. Oil on canvas, 36 x 27½ inches.*

Top right: Lilla Cabot Perry (1848 - 1933)
The White Bed Jacket. *Pastel, 25½ x 31½ inches.*

Center: Maria Martinez and Family
Black on Black San Ildefonso Pueblo Pottery.

Bottom: Marsden Hartley (1877 - 1943)
Still Life with Grapes *1915.*
Oil on canvas, 23¼ x 43 inches.

FIG. 1 Apsley House, Hyde Park Corner.

APSLEY HOUSE AND THE BATTLE OF THE WATERLOO BANQUETS

Elizabeth Longford

I have chosen this rather bellicose title for what ought to be a purely festive article; but I hope my reasons will be adequate. Many conflicts may be seen as focused upon Apsley House and the Waterloo Banquets, some light hearted, others bitter.

The first Battle of Apsley House was fought in 1809 but did not involve Wellington, who at that date was more profitably engaged in fighting the Peninsular War. Apsley House (FIG.1) had been bought by Wellington's eldest brother Richard, the Marquess Wellesley, in 1807 from Lord Bathurst for £16,000 (the mansion at Hyde Park Corner was designed by Robert Adam for Lord Chancellor Bathurst, formerly Lord Apsley, in 1777–8). Wellesley employed James Wyatt the architect to make alterations and moved in with his wife Hyacinthe and family in 1808. But the marriage was breaking up: 'Dreadful scenes' according to Wellesley's biographer Iris Butler took place at Apsley House. The couple were legally separated in 1810. Five years later came the Battle of Waterloo. As the splendid victor, Wellington (FIG.2) was able to help his bankrupt brother by buying Apsley House from him for the very generous sum of £42,000.

Now began the famous Waterloo Banquets held to celebrate the victory over Napoleon on 18 June 1815. The date for the first banquet is thought to be between 1817 and 1819. My own instinct is towards 1818 or possiby the next year. Wellington had not deposited the first £5,000 of purchase money until summer 1816 and the floor of Apsley House was being strengthened in spring 1817 to receive the giant statue of Napoleon by Canova in the hall (FIG.3). (One hopes the floor is still strong, for Napoleon is still there!) Moreover Wellington was in France commanding the allied Army of Occupation until the end of 1818.

We can argue about the date; it was

for Wellington's comrades to argue about the guest-list. Naturally everybody clamoured for an invitation. But the old dining-room at Apsley House would hold only a limited number of heroes. So the Duke with his noted commonsense decided to draw the line at those who had not actually fought on the battlefield. The decision produced some verbal skirmishes. A general officer, for instance, who had been posted far out at Hal guarding the allied right flank and who had remained unengaged throughout the whole of the glorious day, would not be invited to the victory feast.

Those early banquets were not quite the glamorous affairs they were later to become. The dining-room had been left by the Marquess Wellesley in a fairly shabby state. And Wellington's own thoughts about Waterloo were sombre enough. He had wept after the battle and hated conducting visitors – even lovely ladies – over the field. The London mob's enthusiasm for Waterloo rapidly diminished once the war

FIG.2 The Duke of Wellington, 1814, by Sir Thomas Lawrence, P.R.A.

ended and was followed by years of economic depression. There were individual attempts to assassinate the Duke in Paris and again in the Park; while on 23 February 1820 the Cato Street conspirators planned to murder the whole Cabinet, Wellington among them, in Grosvenor Square. In the early 1820s neither the rich nor the poor were enjoying the fruits of victory in peace and quiet.

Wellington by temperament was a genial but never an extravagant host. He was always reprimanding his wife Kitty for wastefulness, and in 1827 we find her writing from the country to the housekeeper Mrs. Cross at Apsley House that His Grace was again complaining about the bills: Butterman 9s.7½d., Fruit 8s., Soda water £1.10s., yet 'he says he never eats butter or cream or fruit and has drunk but one glass of soda water since he went to London'.

Things had been even worse in 1820 when there was a male steward, Thornton. The Duchess accused Thornton of ordering for 42 people at three dinners a total of 298 lbs. of butcher's meat, quite apart from lamb, calves feet and sweetbreads – over £7 per person per dinner, as well as 'fish, fowls, everything'! Kitty pointed out that 'dishes but little touched at one dinner are served up again to a different Party where but one day intervenes between the dinners . . . & that for that reason many noblemen give two dinners immediately following . . .' One can imagine the roast beef left over from the Wellington Banquets being rolled in pastry and served next day as *Boeuf Wellington*.

Despite the bad times Wellington's friends persuaded him that he must have the dining-room redecorated. His friend Mrs Harriet Arbuthnot was a guest the first time he used the embellished dining-room, on 23 April 1820, and she wrote: 'It is magnificent and

FIG.3 Napoleon I, by Antonio Canova, at the foot of the staircase, Apsley House.   FIG.4 The Dining Room, showing the centrepiece of the Portuguese Service, in 1982.

the greatest improvement to the house.' (FIG.4). There were many grand parties in this room beside the Waterloo Banquets. Mrs Arbuthnot describes dining there before the opera and also attending a party at which many Whig grandees were present, of whom the gentlemen professed to believe in the innocence of George IV's repudiated wife, Caroline of Brunswick. If Caroline was innocent, jeered the Tory Harriet, no Whig Lord would ever be able to divorce his wife for adultery!

Another eight years passed and Wellington was Prime Minister. Again his friends told him that Apsley House was still not quite worthy to hold all his artistic treasures – presented to him by grateful sovereigns and peoples – far less to impress potential Waterloo ban-

queteers. The Duke decided to build on to the mansion a new Waterloo Gallery and other amenities, at a cost of £14,000, in which the Waterloo Banquets were to be held continuously until his death in 1852 (FIG.5). He gave the commission to the architect Benjamin Dean Wyatt, another member of the famous family (FIG.6). Alas, this commission caused much warfare between Wellington and Wyatt – but much laughter to posterity in reading their combative correspondence.

As early as 1828 Mrs Arbuthnot was reporting that Wellington and Wyatt had quarrelled, the Duke begging her to handle Wyatt on his behalf. She agreed, saying that when 'his house is the admiration of all London', *she* would claim the credit! In fact she was

to make fresh drawings for the doors and windows of the new Gallery, considering that Mr Wyatt's designs were 'frightful'. She also altered the skirting board and, '*though I say it as should not, it is really beautiful*'. Her only battle was with the Duke himself. He insisted on hanging the walls with '*yellow*' damask, the very worst colour for pictures and which would kill the effect of the gilding. Today the Duke has lost the battle of the damask which is now crimson (FIG.7)

Meanwhile Wellington and Wyatt went on with their accusations and counter-accusations long after the Gallery was finished. By 1830 Wyatt had 'exceeded his estimates three times over'; to which the architect was to retort that his employer had added enormously to his original require-

3

4

FIG.5 The Waterloo Gallery designed by Benjamin Dean
Wyatt. Watercolour by Joseph Nash, 1852.   FIG.7 The
Waterloo Gallery, Apsley House, in 1982.

5

7

FIG.8 The Waterloo Banquet of 1836, by William Salter,
engraved by William Greatbach.   FIG.9 Key.

8

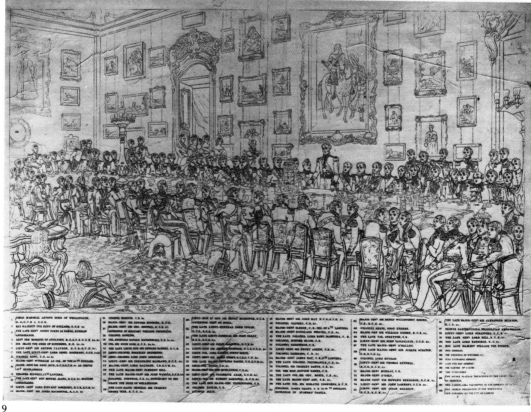

9

ments. There was big trouble in 1839 when Wyatt's clerk of the works stole Wellington's groom's new clothes; and violent recriminations two years later when Wyatt proposed to cure a smoking chimney in the Waterloo Gallery and drawing-room underneath it by sending up a 'Climbing Boy' to sweep it.

'You appear to me to have forgotten, if you ever knew,' thundered the Iron Duke, 'the reason for any of these measures about chimneys.' (The Duke wanted iron doors for inserting machines into the chimneys to clean them.) 'The employment of Climbing Boys is prohibited by Act of Parliament.' Fortunately the Waterloo Banquets, being held each June, were warm enough without fires.

Mrs Arbuthnot had become lyrical over the magnificent parties held in the new Gallery in 1830. King William IV and Queen Adelaide came to breakfast on 11 July, King William and the King of Württemberg on the 25th, and the King and Queen of England again on the 28th, after a review in Hyde Park. Then the wheel of fortune turned once more and the tide of battle flowed round Apsley House in the following year.

The Duchess, frail but spirited, had died on 24 April 1831 in the great ground floor suite. She had pointed with her emaciated finger at the glorious trophies that surrounded her – porcelain services, silver plate, candelabra, batons – and cried out to her friend Maria Edgeworth: 'All tributes to merit – there is the value! and pure! pure! – no corruption – ever *suspected* even.' Three days after her death a London mob demanding parliamentary reform stoned the darkened house of mourning.

A second, more serious attack was delivered by a rioting reform mob on 9 October of that same year. A stone narrowly missed the Duke's own head

as he sat at his desk, and almost every window-pane in the house that stones could reach was broken. The Duke ordered Wyatt to put up iron outside shutters instead of mending the glass. Luckily he had already had the Waterloo Gallery protected with outside shutters, 'or all his fine pictures', wrote Mrs Arbuthnot, 'wd have been spoiled'. Lord Grey of the Reform Bill had taken umbrage at the Gallery's shutters, telling everyone that the house would never be attacked by his followers.

On Waterloo Day itself, 1832, the Duke was followed by a menacing mob from the Mint in the City to St. James's – but he was always a master of retreat and gave them the slip. The guests who sat down to that particular Waterloo Banquet must have been somewhat shaken.

We can end, however, on a less riotous note – or, if the atmosphere was

FIG.6 The Saveall or Economy. Satire on the building activities of George IV and the Duke of Wellington, by Paul Pry (William Heath), c. 1828. Apsley House is seen on the right.

THE SAVEALL or ECONOMY

at all riotous it was of a very different nature. The grand Waterloo Banquet of 1836 was commemorated by William Salter's splendid oil painting (FIGS.8, 9). Salter managed to get some eighty diners round the immensely long table, though as a quarter of them were dead there was not quite such a squeeze as the picture suggests. Plumed hats and sabres were cast in confusion on the carpet, but there was perfect order on the mahogany table, where the splendid centrepiece (FIG.10) and candelabra of the huge Portuguese service occupied their colossal plateau, surrounded with nymphs linked by garlands of real flowers. Inside the Gallery, the mirror-shutters flashed back the gold braid and scarlet uniforms of the diners: outside the broken glass had been mended, but not until 1833 when William IV attended the Waterloo Banquet.

At one end of the Gallery we see the Wellington Shield on view, presented by the City merchants and bankers (FIG.11) and on the *yellow* walls the wonderful pictures captured at the Battle of Vitoria. They had formed part of the Napoleonic loot and had been given back to their owner, the King of Spain, by the Duke to whom they were courteously returned by that monarch. Near the open door stands a female group, the Somerset ladies and the Countess of Westmorland, allowed for once to listen in.

Wellington himself addressed his brother officers. Perhaps with the words of the Younger Pitt that he himself had listened to in 1805 and always found so inspiring: 'England saved herself by her exertions and will, as I trust, save Europe by her example.' More likely the Duke, refraining as ever from boasting that he and his allies had licked the French, reiterated for the eighteenth time that it had been 'the nearest run thing you ever saw in your life'.

FIG.11 The Wellington Shield, designed by Thomas
Stothard, R.A. 1822.   FIG.10 The central ornament of the
Portuguese Service presented to the Duke in 1816.

11

10

S. J. Phillips,
Ltd.
Silversmiths,
Jewels Antique Plate
Bijouterie

*Rare English and Continental Silver, Miniatures.
Antique Jewels, Fine Snuff-Boxes*

XVIIIth century Danish silver casket with concealed compartment, by Niels Johnsen,
Copenhagen, 1733. Length, 10 inches.

*Valuations for Probate,
Insurance and Division*

139 New Bond Street London W1A 3DL

TELEPHONE 01-629 6261/2 TELEGRAPHIC ADDRESS: "EUCLASE LONDON W.1."

𝓑𝓑𝓢

BERNARD BARUCH STEINITZ

Antiquaire

Un des salons d'exposition

4, RUE DROUOT - PARIS - Tél. : 246.98.98

Photography: Jaime Ardiles-Arce

FIG.8 The St. Nicholas Crozier, about 1150–70, ivory,
12×11 cm. 218–1865.

THE SMALL-SCALE ARTS OF ROMANESQUE ENGLAND

Paul Williamson

The twelfth century may rightly be considered a 'Golden Age' for the Arts in England. Following the Norman Conquest in 1066 there was a nation-wide increase in church building, brought about no doubt partly by the new rulers' desire to establish themselves, so that by the first years of the following century most of the great cathedrals of today had been started and were well advanced. These cathedrals and churches needed to be furnished and embellished and there was a concurrent development in the related arts of monumental sculpture and stained glass. But it was in the smaller-scale arts, the misleadingly-titled 'minor arts', that England most distinguished itself: the manuscript illuminations, enamels and ivory carvings produced in this country in the twelfth century were the equals of anything in the same media on the Continent. Between April and July 1984 the most comprehensive display of these precious objects ever seen will be shown at the Hayward Gallery in the exhibition *1066–1200: English Romanesque Art*. The V&A is one of the major lenders to the exhibition: together with the British Museum it has the strongest holdings of this material in existence.

England is more unfortunate than any other European nation in the terrible losses it has suffered to its medieval artistic heritage. When the Normans took control of the country there seems to have been a hostility to the art of their Anglo-Saxon predecessors and many of the most important objects – shrines, altar frontals and crosses – were either destroyed or sent abroad. There are extensive literary descriptions of these Anglo-Saxon treasures, the reading of which cannot fail to produce a certain sadness in the reader that such magnificent objects are now lost to us. The Romanesque treasures of the twelfth century were,

alas, to share the same fate as the Anglo-Saxon: at the time of the Dissolution of the monasteries under Henry VIII there was widespread destruction of many of the most sumptuous creations of the Romanesque and Gothic artists. No church treasuries were spared from the iconoclasts' zeal and one perhaps gains the best impression of how rich the holdings of medieval art were and how tragic the losses when it is revealed in a contemporary source that it took twenty-four carts to transfer the contents of Canterbury Cathedral treasury to London, where the objects crafted of precious metals would be melted down and the others dismantled and destroyed. This is a depressing picture, but we may take some satisfaction by turning to the magnificent survivals of this misguided vandalism and although they constitute only a tiny proportion of the original output we are lucky that we can reconstruct the major developments of the Romanesque period in England. Central to our understanding of the English twelfth-century artistic vocabulary are the manuscripts that have survived in relatively large numbers. These were saved presumably because they could be hidden more easily in times of danger and were not as instantly 'glamorous' as the glittering objects preserved in the church treasuries; the illuminations also survive in remarkably good condition because they have been closed within the books since their creation and have not suffered the fading effect of light – one of the features of the great illuminations of the twelfth century is their ravishing colour. Most important from an art-historical point of view is that sometimes these books can be dated fairly accurately and they therefore act as touchstones for the related 'treasury arts'. It should not be forgotten that there was an intimate inter-relationship between the different branches of

the visual arts in the twelfth century and we sometimes have direct evidence that a particular artist worked in a number of different media. The most famous of the English Romanesque artists is the enigmatic and mercurial Master Hugo of Bury St. Edmunds. We know that Master Hugo was responsible for the illumination of the superb Bury St. Edmunds Bible of about 1135 (to be seen in the exhibition) and we have a unique contemporary document (the *Gesta Sacristarum Monasterii Sancti Edmundi*) which describes how Hugo, unable to find any suitable calf-hide for the Bible in the Bury St. Edmunds area, had to go to Ireland to buy his parchment. Other documents reinforce the impression we gain of Hugo in this reference as a perfectionist and we can only wish that more of his works of art still survived. We learn that the 'double doors in the front of the church (at Bury) were sculpted by the hand of Master Hugo, who in other works surpassed all others, in this magnificent work he surpassed himself', and that he cast a bronze bell in honour of the martyr St. Edmund. Perhaps the most controversial reference to Master Hugo's works, also in the *Gesta Sacristarum*, is the mention that the sacrist Elias, nephew of the Abbot Ording 'commissioned a cross in the choir with Mary and John incomparably carved by the hand of Master Hugo'. Not surprisingly perhaps, this tantalising reference has prompted some authorities to link Hugo with the magnificent Altar Cross now displayed in the Cloisters collection of the Metropolitan Museum in New York (also on view in the exhibition), which is beautifully carved from sections of walrus ivory. Unfortunately it has proved impossible to be conclusive on this point, although the cross and the Bury St. Edmunds Bible are close in style and must also be close in date.

FIG.1 Liturgical comb, St. Albans, about 1120, ivory,
8.5×11.5 cm. A.27–1977.   FIG.5 Head of a Tau-cross,
Winchester (?), about 1140, walrus ivory, 5.5×16.5 cm.
371–1871.

1

5

FIG.3 Oval box, early twelfth century, walrus ivory,
6.5×6 cm. 268–1867.

The vivid descriptions we have of Hugo as a master of many arts are especially fortuitous survivals as they confirm what we would have surmised simply by looking at the extant works of art: even if not all the artists of the twelfth century were as gifted and versatile as Master Hugo, they took note of what was going on in related media. Indeed, it would have been very difficult for the ivory carvers to remain oblivious to the latest styles of the manuscript illuminators as in all probability they worked side by side. Two very different objects in the Museum's collections illustrate how a common style is readily identifiable in different media. The first, an ivory liturgical comb, acquired in 1977, is carved on both sides with scenes from the New Testament (FIG.1): the figures are rather stiff, there is a love of showing the figures in profile, and the whole

crowded composition rewards careful investigation. This distinctive combination of elements can be closely matched in the famous St. Albans Psalter, produced at St. Albans between 1119 and 1123, and we may therefore safely assign the comb to the same centre and to a date of around 1120. Also close in style to the comb are the New Testament scenes in the upper half of a single leaf from a Psalter, probably painted a few years later, perhaps at the end of the 1130s (FIG.2). Here we see again the crowded compositions, full of the same squat figures, many in profile. Although this manuscript is unlikely to have come from St. Albans (it is more likely from Canterbury), there is no doubt that its style derives from the innovations developed there.

The foundations of the Romanesque style in England were laid some years

before the Conquest and a number of the earliest post-Conquest works of art are not noticeably different from those that were produced just before – it is often difficult to be sure whether the ivories and manuscript illuminations of the second half of the eleventh century were executed in 1050 or 1100, and much work remains to be done in this area. A wonderfully-carved small oval box of walrus ivory falls into this rather hazy date-bracket (FIG.3). The scenes around the box have long puzzled scholars and until recently the only explanation offered was that they depicted episodes from a miracle of St. Lawrence, where the saint miraculously restored a chalice that had fallen out of the hands of a deacon on his way to the altar and had smashed; but as the most important scene in this story, the smashing of the chalice, is not shown on the box, there had been misgivings

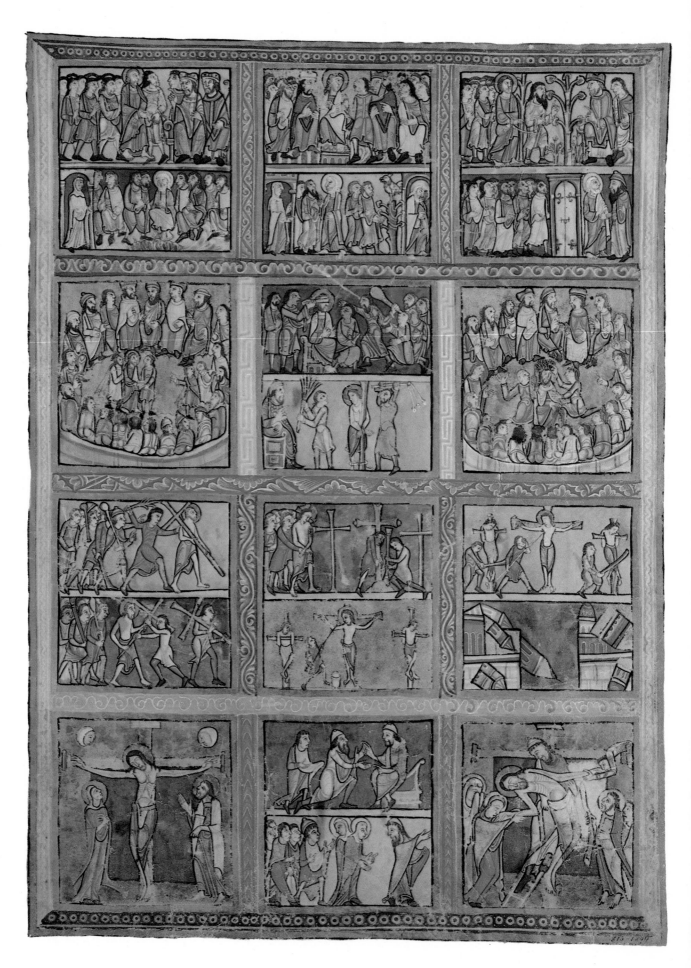

opposite: FIG.2 Leaf from a Psalter with scenes from the New
Testament, Canterbury (?), about 1140, 40×30 cm.
816–1894.   FIG.4 The Gloucester Candlestick, Canterbury (?),
1104–13, gilt bell-metal, h. 51 cm. 7649–1861.

about accepting this interpretation. Recently a new theory has been put forward, that the story is that of the *Visitatio Sepulchri*, the dramatised version of the Maries visit to the tomb, here played by monks. Given this reading, the box is more likely to date from around 1100 than before the Conquest, a dating reinforced by the type of capital on the small canopy (not visible in the photograph).

We can be more sure of the date of one of the V&A's greatest treasures, the Gloucester Candlestick (FIG.4): there is a Latin inscription on the stem which, translated, reads 'The devotion of Abbot Peter and his gentle flock gave me to the church of St. Peter at Gloucester'. As this Peter became Abbot of the Benedictine monastery of St. Peter, Gloucester, in 1104 and died in 1113, we may place the candlestick between those two dates. Probably made in Canterbury, the Gloucester candlestick is one of the most glorious tour-de-forces of Romanesque art. It is cast in gilt bell-metal, in three separate pieces, and is in remarkably good condition. The motifs employed on the candlestick, the animated, clambering figures amongst a dense, fleshy background of foliate ornament were to be remarkably popular and long-lasting in English Romanesque Art, and are to be seen in manuscript illuminations, ivory carvings and metalwork from the end of the eleventh century until well into the third quarter of the twelfth; they were most successfully utilised on the products of the Canterbury and Winchester workshops. From the latter centre probably comes the luxuriant walrus ivory head of a tau-cross (FIG.5), showing Christ blessing in the centre, with St. Michael subduing a dragon to the left, while another figure to the right struggles to free himself from the jaws of a similar dragon. It is a marvellously-conceived piece of sculpture, using every cen-

timetre of the available surface and combining a consummate skill in the depiction of the human form with a magisterial treatment of foliate ornament.

On turning to the art of the enameller in twelfth-century England, it is not quite so clear what is English: many of the enamels associated with England have stylistic traits which are also found on the Continent and the technique of their manufacture is indistinguishable from Mosan (from the valley of the Meuse) products. In addition, it is possible that some of the enamels traditionally ascribed to England were imported from abroad or were made in England by Mosan artists, such as the two 'Henry of Blois' plaques in the British Museum, made just after the middle of the century. There are, however, a number of enamels which can confidently be described as English, several of which are in the V&A. All the members of this group are of *champlevé* enamel, a technique which entails engraving the design on the copper surface, scooping out the areas where it is to be filled with enamel, and gilding the remaining portions. On a plaque of about 1170–80, showing St. Paul being let down in a basket from the walls of Damascus (FIG.6), this technique can be seen clearly, as a section of the enamel between Paul's head and the walls of the city has fallen away, revealing the copper ground (this can also be seen in the top right corner). The plaque is one of seven showing scenes from the Lives of St. Paul and St. Peter, a group which probably formed part of an altar frontal or a piece of church furniture.

Slightly earlier are three *ciboria*, covered vessels for holding the eucharistic wafers, two of which are in the V&A (the 'Balfour' and 'Warwick' ciboria) and the third in the Pierpont Morgan Library in New York (the 'Malmesbury' ciborium). The Balfour

ciborium (FIG.7), like the Malmesbury ciborium, retains its cover with six scenes from the Life of Christ: on the bowl are another six scenes, this time from the Old Testament, which typify those on the cover so that, for instance, the scene of Christ carrying the Cross is balanced by the scene of Isaac bearing the logs for his sacrifice. This sophisticated iconographic programme is surrounded by foliage patterns which give the ciborium a distinctly English look, and once again the closest parallels are to be found in the manuscripts of the time. There can be no doubt that such a magnificent and complex object as the Balfour ciborium was made at the behest of, and probably under the supervision of a senior ecclesiastic and it is likely that only a very small number of these ciboria were ever made.

One is tempted to view the so-called 'St. Nicholas Crozier' in the same light (FIG.8). It is clearly a work of art of the highest quality, made for a discerning patron, and it has a very rare choice of subject matter – for in addition to the Nativity at the tip of the volute there are scenes from the Life of St. Nicholas, which would seem to suggest that it was made specifically for the head of an institution devoted to that particular saint. The unknown craftsman who carved this crozier deserves to rank alongside the finest sculptors of any age: it would be hard to suggest how he could have utilised the awkward surfaces more beautifully, how the narrative flow could be bettered, and how the details could be more finely picked out. Objects such as this crozier and the other small-scale arts of this period have a true monumentality which belies their size and they exemplify the achievement of the English Romanesque in a different, although no less eloquent, way than the major cathedrals of the same era.

FIG.6 St. Paul let down in a basket from the walls of
Damascus, about 1170–80, enamel plaque, 8.5×12.7 cm.
M.312–1926.   FIG.7 The Balfour Ciborium, about 1170–80,
champleve enamel on copper, h. 18.5 cm, diameter at lip of
bowl 15.5 cm. M.1–1981.

6

7

CHRISTIE'S

Pierre Bonnard: L'Indolente, circa 1899, £302,400.
Record auction price for a work by the artist.

Christie's Review for Christmas

Christie's Review of the Season 1983 makes a perfect Christmas present. As always it is a valuable guide for collectors and others interested in the international art market. Lavishly illustrated in colour and with articles by acknowledged experts on all manner of subjects, it will also give hours of pleasure to the general reader and art students will find it an absorbing book. Available at bookshops price £25, or direct from Christie's at the address below. Applications should be made to John Herbert, Public Relations Director.

Christie's. Fine Art Auctioneers since 1766

8 King Street, St. James's, London SW1Y 6QT   Tel: (01) 839 9060 Telex: 916429

THE MARGARET DE FOIX BOOK OF HOURS

Rowan Watson

The manuscript acquired by the V&A with the Salting Bequest in 1910 and known as the Margaret de Foix Hours (Salting 1222; MS.L.2385–1910) is a magnificent example of the kind of luxury hand-written book produced by commercial workshops in fifteenth century France. Books of Hours were the backbone of the book trade at the time, to judge by the number of surviving examples: like the family Bible of 'respectable' Victorian families, Books of Hours were treasured by the citizens of late medieval Europe.

The production of manuscript books in medieval Europe was very largely anonymous. It is very rare that we can name the people who wrote and illuminated any particular book, even though archives such as tax rolls give us the names of those involved in the writing, decorating and binding of such things. Styles of decoration and miniature painting in manuscript books tended to be homogeneous within any province, which makes it difficult to localise any book with certainty. This was a reflection, no doubt, of the mobility of the craftsmen and women concerned, of trade in books in varying states of completion, and of customers who were uniformly influenced by changing fashions.

The Margaret de Foix Hours was made in France at some time in the third quarter of the fifteenth century, but it is difficult to assign it to any particular region either on stylistic or other grounds. What evidence have we to link it with Margaret de Foix, who became the second wife of Francis II, Duke of Brittany, in 1471? The text, which is all in Latin, assumes that the user was a man (case endings in the prayers are for a man), though it is possible that little attention was paid to this kind of detail – the text was that

FIG.8 Hours of the Cross: the Way of the Cross, and Crucifixion scene (fol.125r).

available in the workshop at the time the book was ordered. The only textual evidence for the association with the duke and his wife comes with a number of folios bound onto the end of the book containing a prayer to end the sterility of Francis and his wife Margaret, and to provide offspring. These last folios were written in the same script (*lettre bâtarde*) but by a different hand from the rest of the book; the size of the ruled space for the writing is different, and the parchment is stouter and more shiny than that in the rest of the book. The initial that begins the prayer, a D done in brushed gold on a monochrome red ground, with a realistic sketch of flowers in the bowl of the letter, is the only decorative feature of these folios (a marked contrast to the rich decoration of the rest of the book) and is in a style associated with the last third, at least, of the fifteenth century. So this prayer gives us ambiguous evidence for the original ownership of the manuscript. That it was bound up with the rest of the book at some time in the fifteenth century is shown by the stamps that decorate the leather binding, which date it no more precisely than to the second half of the century.

Duke Francis had two wives, both of them called Margaret: Margaret of Brittany, his cousin, was 12 on their marriage in 1455 but did not bear a son until 1463 (the son died shortly after birth); Margaret de Foix he married in 1471 and their first child, Anne de Bretagne, arrived in 1476. The attribution to the second marriage, childless for five years, rests on the evidence of an erased coat of arms (folios 21 *verso*, 222 *recto*, and, in miniature, 47 *recto*). Neither ultra-violet nor infra-red light is of help in reconstructing the arms. The dexter side may well have been of ermine, the ducal arms of Brittany, and it does seem likely that the sinister side, evidently quite a complicated

coat of arms, included an element made up of thin vertical red stripes on a gold ground, the Foix arms. This is the basis of dating the book to 1471/6.

Many Books of Hours provide clues as to their place of origin in their text, but this is unfortunately not the case with our manuscript. Details of the prayers, antiphons, verses, etc., that make up the text conform to the Paris 'Use', a term signifying the liturgical practices in the church services of a particular province or diocese. This Use was becoming general at the time (like the Sarum Use and the Rome Use, it was followed outside its place of origin), so it provides no guarantee that it was written in Paris or intended to be used there. St. Geneviève is the only saint with Paris connections to be singled out in gold letters in the prefatory calendar; Paris saints like Marcel, Avia and Honorina are given no prominence. Indeed the calendar makes one think of certain documented cases where the scribe seized any saint's name to fill the space on the page with little attempt to provide a reliable guide to their feast days in the diocese. The saints in the Litany similarly give us no clue. The text may have been a standard product of a workshop that supplied illuminators, who in turn finished them to the requirements of a particular customer. Francis II had to have his own prayer written separately in a different workshop and handed to the binder to be bound in with a book bought 'off the shelf'. He would also have had his arms put in a place left blank for the purpose.

A number of features reflect the conditions in which the manuscript was illuminated. Stylistic analysis shows how different tasks were apportioned between the miniaturist, his journeymen and apprentices. The gilding was probably the responsibility of a single workman or woman, who added gold leaf to every page according to a design

45

FIG.1 Calendar for November, with a man knocking down acorns and a woman feeding them to pigs; in the roundel, a figure representing Sagittarius (fol.11r). FIG.2 St. Matthew attended by two angels, at the beginning of the extract from St. Matthew's Gospel (fol.17v).

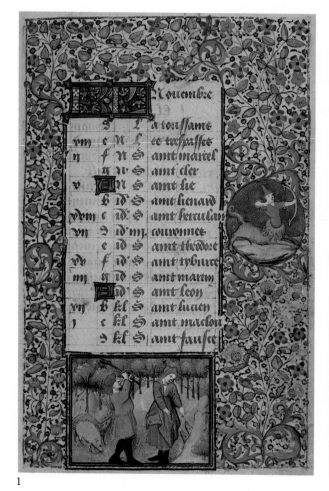

1   2

FIG.3 Matins, Hours of the Virgin: in the largest panel, the
Annunciation. Around this are scenes from the life of the
Virgin's family – the marriage of Joachim and Anne, her
parents, the angel announcing to Joachim in exile that he
could return to his wife, Joachim meeting Anne at the
Golden Gate; the birth of the Virgin (fol.33r). FIG.4 Lauds,
Hours of the Virgin: the Visitation, with smaller scenes
showing the presentation of Mary at the Temple, St. Anne
teaching the Virgin, and the marriage of Mary and Joseph
(fol.47r).

3

4

FIG.5 Tierce, Hours of the Virgin: the Betrayal of Christ, with smaller scenes of the Agony in the Garden, the Judgment of Pilate, and the Scourging of Christ (fol.68r). FIG.6 Sext, Hours of the Virgin: the Adoration of the Magi, with the Adoration of the Shepherds beneath (fol.73v). FIG.7 Compline, Hours of the Virgin: Coronation of the Virgin, with the death of the Virgin beneath (fol.92r). FIG.9 Hours of the Holy Spirit: Pentecost scene, with smaller pictures of Moses receiving the Law, the Baptism of Christ, and the Ascension of Christ (fol.135r).

5

6

7

9

sketched in advance. There is a striking uniformity, one which argues for the involvement of a single craftsperson, in the large 3-line initials throughout the manuscript. These initials, in which blue and orange three-pointed ivy leaves circle within a blue lettershape, the whole upon a gilded ground, do not vary from one end of the manuscript to the other. Nor do the 1-line initials made of a gilded letter shape on a blue and purple ground. Letters of this kind are the hallmark of Franco–Flemish manuscripts for the first three-quarters of the fifteenth century and are to be seen as the basic routine products of workshop apprentices. There is only one 3-line initial which shows the intrusion of a new style: the letter S at the beginning of the St. Luke's Gospel extract (folio 15 *recto*) has a floral pattern in white on the blue body of the letter within which is a colourful spray of realistically painted flowers – this is a feature of decoration first found in the middle of the fifteenth century and which gained momentum quickly thereafter.

Perhaps the most striking feature which reveals the 'mass production' aspect of our manuscript is the border decoration. This is of the highest quality and executed in three styles. The first, confined to text pages and to the calendar (FIG.1), is based on twirling acanthus leaves in blue with brushed gold underleaf – leaves of this kind are thought to have been copied in Paris in the early fifteenth century from Italian ornamental motifs and to have spread from there to France and Flanders. With these acanthus leaves are long stems with leaves and more or less realistically painted flowers and fruit – daisies, sweet pea, hare-bells, red currant, pea pods, strawberries; occasionally a pot of flowers sits at the bottom of the lower margin. We also observe a technique widely practised in

French workshops, one that exploited the slightly transparent nature of parchment: the outline drawing of foliage and flowers used to guide the illuminator on one side of the page was also followed to paint the same image directly behind on the other side of the page. There is therefore a reversed image pattern. The aim was probably as much to prevent the image on one side showing through to the other side of the page as to save time. Flowers and fruit are realistically shown, an important point for dating, since this tendency first became manifest after the middle of the fifteenth century and was to lead to a style based on the meticulous depiction of such subjects painted in *trompe l'oeil* which spread from Flanders after c.1480.

The second border style is associated with the smaller miniatures (FIG.2). To the features of the earlier style, we have added birds, animals (notably a stoat), peacocks, a snail, and a number of monsters, which play in the foliage. Every border of this kind has a strip of garden bed painted at the bottom of the lower margin with flowers planted in it.

A third style of border is more distinct: the foliage is simpler and the pattern painted on a ground of brushed gold. This style is confined to the folios with the suffrages to the saints. Some have birds, animals, monsters and a strip of garden bed at the bottom of the lower margin (FIG.10), while others are plain except for the foliage. A significant point as regards the division of labour is that the plain style is only ever found on one bifolium, and the 'inhabited' style likewise only on another bifolium. So we have to think in terms of artisans, each with a particular style, seated before a pile of bifolia which once completed were assembled into quires or booklets to make up the block of the book. Each quire had a system of numbering, still

visible, which told the binder in what order to arrange the bifolia within the quire, and the quires within the block of the book.

So far we have looked at the 'routine' aspects of our Book of Hours, ones which give some idea of how the work was split up to produce it. When we come to the miniatures, we come to an aspect of the book in which the customer may have had some say. The smaller miniatures are conventional enough compositions for us to think in terms of routine production: the miniatures of the four Evangelists for the Gospel extracts, of the saints for the suffrages, and the labours of the months for the calendar were necessary adjuncts to the texts that they serve. The compositions betray the influence of widely followed models which probably circulated in the form of sketches or, especially after the mid-fifteenth century, in the form of woodcuts and engravings. With the full-page miniatures (FIGS.3–9), we come to scenes which set this Book of Hours apart and make it fitting for an aristocratic patron.

The full-page miniatures are confined to the Hours of the Virgin, the Hours of the Cross and Holy Spirit, the Penitential Psalms and the Office of the Dead. Iconographically they follow established cycles (the Annunciation for Matins, the Visitation for Lauds, and so on) with one striking exception: instead of the Annunciation to the Shepherds for Tierce, we have a résumé of Christ's Passion (the kiss of Judas, Christ before Pilate, the scourging of Christ). If this does not reflect an obscure local tradition, it must reflect the personal wishes of the customer. These miniatures are of two kinds; all have three or four lines of text within them. The first kind is split up into a number of compartments, some by what look like wooden frames, some by more grandiose architectural frames.

Each compartment has its own miniature, so that we are given a pictorial narrative that relates to a central subject.

The other kind of full-page miniature has no compartments and the whole page forms one unified composition, although more than one action may be taking place. Particularly successful is the scene of the Way of the Cross and the Crucifixion (FIG.9): Christ carries his cross from the bottom left of the page in a train that carries us up to the Crucifix at the top.

How does this miniature painting relate to the history of painting in fifteenth century France? Eberhard König has recently identified a group of works by the painter of these miniatures. He describes them as the work of a master working in Rennes under the influence of Jean Fouquet, the artist who spent some time in Italy before 1450 and who became a major channel for the flow of Italian Renaissance ideas into French painting. If this was so, Fouquet's styles were not totally absorbed. The proportion of the figures in our miniatures – small in relation to the whole scene – and their gestures fall far short of the monumental quality

which Fouquet introduced into French miniature painting. The patterning of the drapery in our miniatures bears little relation to the human form underneath; the lively patterns of bright green, orange, blue and red are not part of a considered or controlled scheme. The architectural settings have no hint of Renaissance styles, but are gothic and flamboyant, reminiscent of such early fifteenth century styles as that of the Parisian Bedford Hours Master. The multiple scene miniatures are programmatic in a markedly gothic manner.

However, the freedom to compose a subject on a full page around a few lines of text may ultimately be derived from Fouquet's example. A successful master such as Maître François could adopt this approach in Paris in the 1470s, but managed to retain a monumental quality with the figures. Our miniaturist may well have been working further away from this milieu.

The Margaret de Foix Book of Hours, then, was produced in the early 1470s and was the work of a well organised workshop; it came 'off the shelf' with the exception of the full-page miniatures, which provide an

echo of innovative styles, the coats of arms and the final prayers for the duke and his wife. Who owned it after 1487, when Margaret de Foix died, and 1488, the date of duke Francis's death, is not known. In the late seventeenth century it was owned by Father Claude Dumolinet (1620–1687), a man who became librarian of St. Geneviève abbey in Paris and whose cabinet of antiquities was famous. This abbey was found to have no manuscripts or books on its reform in 1624; Dumolinet died before he could publish his projected catalogue of the library he had assembled. He was given the book by 'Lord D'Argentré': this was evidently a member of the Duplessis d'Argentré family from Brittany, so it is likely that our manuscript remained in that area until this date. By 1890, it was in the possession of Frederic Spitzer (1815–1890), a Parisian dealer who made his celebrated collection into what was virtually a public museum of applied and industrial art. It was at the sale of this collection in 1893, 'la vente du siècle' that it passed into the hands of George Salting, and thence to the V&A.

FIG.10 The Holy Trinity, the usual illustration preceding the
suffrages to the saints (fol.200r).

Large wooden Crucifix Figure on his original wooden Cross, original polychrome.
(probably) Umbria   Second half XIIth century
Measures: Width 113.5 cm., Height 116.7 cm., / Width 136.6 cm., Height 173.5 cm.

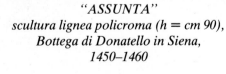

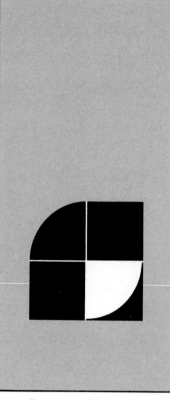

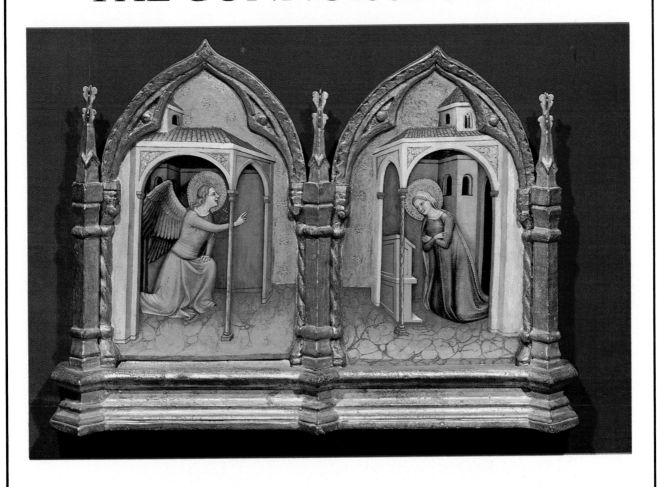

FIG.2 The harem of the Emperor Muhammad Shah (1719–48)
promenading near a country palace, Gentil Album, fol.6.

TWO EARLY COMPANY ALBUMS

Andrew Topsfield

Each of India's invaders has faced the formidable task of comprehending its multiplicity of peoples, religions, castes and customs. Native Brahmin scholars had seldom analysed these phenomena except in mythological terms and from a partial viewpoint. One useful product of the Muslim Sultan Mahmud of Ghazni's irruption into the Punjab in the early eleventh century was the scholar Albiruni's treatise on Indian thought and society. In the sixteenth century the Mughal Emperor Akbar had his court historian Abu'l Fazl compile a great compendium, the *Ain-i Akbari*, which was in part a similar attempt to systematise existing knowledge about the strange land of India. The growth of British power in the second half of the eighteenth century brought a still more fruitful encounter between a small band of East India Company officers, trained in the humanistic scholarship of the European Enlightenment, and the undiscovered riches of India's classical civilisation. The founding of the Asiatic Society of Bengal in 1784 was a landmark in the development of Oriental studies.

Most Company officials of course did not spend their leisure hours translating texts and inscriptions in Sanskrit and Persian. But to live and trade in India they needed at least some knowledge of the main social and religious classes and their customs. Such a knowledge was normally acquired in the course of the daily round. But for some – and their inquisitive families in England – it was also served by the work of local Indian painters who, being deprived of their traditional patronage by the Muslim and Hindu nobility, now turned their hands to various types of documentary painting in a hybrid, Europeanised style which catered for the curiosity of the new rulers of India. Company painting developed wherever there was a Euro-

pean population: first, from about 1770, in southern centres such as Madras, Tanjore and Trichinopoly, then in eastern India, at Murshidabad, Calcutta, Patna and Benares, and in Oudh, Delhi, Agra and the Punjab in the north. In the case of the meticulous natural history studies made for British patrons, the Indian artists' work was of scientific value as well as considerable aesthetic merit. At Delhi and Agra careful but dry architectural studies of the famous Mughal monuments were painted in response to the European taste for the picturesque. But the most common subject matter everywhere consisted of series of paintings depicting the various classes of society, their costumes, trades and crafts, religious festivals and modes of transport, and sometimes also Hindu deities and temples. As a result of mass production these quickly became standardised both in subject matter and style: generally, a representative of each trade or caste appears against a plain background, with his appropriate tools or costume and his wife in attendance (FIG.10). Company painting of this type was seldom individual or original. The British as a ruling class had no real roots in India, and the creative relationship between patron and artist that had prevailed in Mughal times was lacking. Most of the sets that are still preserved in many British homes are simple bazaar work, forerunners of the degenerate modern tourist art. As a vernacular inscription on a nineteenth century set from the Punjab remarks: 'in this book are all Punjabi things . . . all the Sahibs take it to show in England'.

There were, however, at all periods a few outstanding exceptions to this rule. Among the Company paintings in the V&A are two early albums which are of considerable individuality, although in different and contrasting ways. The earlier of the two, the Gentil

Album (1774), is the more unusual in that it is not a random album of curiosities, but a pictorial study of contemporary social and religious life, devised and annotated by a French military officer living at the court of Oudh; a broad use of the term 'Company' is justified in this case by the Europeanised style of its illustrations. The other work, the Boileau Album, was painted at Madras in 1785 for an East India Company official and is a more conventional series of castes and trades. But it is also unusual in the freshness and exuberance of its illustrations, qualities which are lacking in the stereotyped work of later years.

Of these two patrons, Col. Jean Baptiste Joseph Gentil (1726–99) is historically the more important figure. Born of a noble military family, his career in India was interrupted by the collapse of French power in 1761. He then entered the service of the Nawab of Bengal, later moving to Oudh, where he became military adviser to Nawab Shuja ud-Daula from 1763–75. The court of Oudh, which at this time alternated between Lucknow and Faizabad, had become virtually independent of the powerless Mughal Emperor, and it had inherited much of the opulent display and the artistic, literary and musical traditions of the Mughal court. Its wealth had attracted a number of European adventurers, such as the flamboyant Frenchman Claude Martin and the Swiss engineer Antoine Polier, both of whom formed large collections of paintings and manuscripts. European artists such as Tilly Kettle and Zoffany also came seeking the Nawabs' patronage.

Gentil was another collector of Indian manuscripts and paintings, as well as of arms, medals, coins and natural history specimens. He made an early, and as always unsuccessful, attempt to introduce the Himalayan shawl-goat into France. His interest in

FIG.3 The presentation of Col. Gentil to the Emperor Shah Alam by Nawab Shuja ud-Daula in the Angur Bagh garden, Gentil Album, detail of fol.16.   FIG.5 Examples of women's jewellery, Gentil Album, detail of fol.34.   FIG.1 Modes of transport and household servants of the Mughal Emperor, from the Gentil Album, painted at Faizabad in 1774, detail of fol.4, (size of whole page 37×53 cm). I.S. 25–1980.
FIG.4 *Above:* Brahmins perform *puja* before a water-filled vessel during the autumnal festival of Dassehra.
Below: Nobles and ladies celebrate Diwali, the winter Festival of Lights, by playing *chaupar* at a shrine to Lakshmi, goddess of good fortune, Gentil Album, detail of fol.43.

3

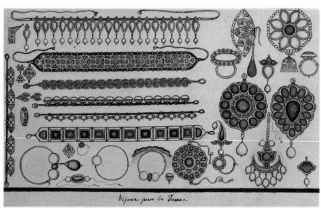

5

1

4

painting is shown by an anecdote from his *Mémoires sur l'Indoustan*, which was published in 1822 by his son. In 1772 Tilly Kettle had painted a portrait of the Nawab, of which Gentil had a miniature copy made for his own use by an Indian artist. However, when the Nawab saw this copy he liked it so much that he kept it, asking Gentil why he should need such a picture: 'mon portrait n'est-il pas gravé dans votre cœur?' Gentil wittily replied that this was indeed so, but he required a picture for showing to his friends; and since the Nawab had already given his copy away to the British Resident, he should be allowed to keep the original portrait by Kettle instead. Gentil later presented this picture to Louis XVI and it is still at Versailles.

Gentil's major commission at Faizabad was a series of illustrated albums which included the one now in the V&A. These were painted over a period of five years by a group of three local artists, including Nivasi Lal and Mohan Singh, who worked under Gentil's close supervision. The series was in effect a pictorial résumé of Gentil's researches into the political and social history of India. It begins with an illustrated atlas of the Mughal empire, dated 1770, which is now in the India Office Library. This was followed by histories of the Mughal emperors (1772), of Indian coins (1773) and the early rulers of India (1773), and a study of the Hindu deities (1774); these four albums were presented to the French monarch and are now in the Bibliothèque Nationale. The V&A album, which is also dated 1774, is mainly concerned with social history, in a somewhat miscellaneous fashion, as its title indicates: *Receuil de toutes sortes de Dessins sur les Usages et coutumes des Peuples de l'Indoustan . . .* This album seems to have been the last in the series. Gentil may have continued to annotate it in his retirement, for in

1775 British political pressure forced him to leave Oudh, and he finally returned to France two years later.

All six albums are painted in watercolour in a similar style, with careful but stiff and schematic drawing and a pallid tonality quite unlike the richer gouache work of Mughal painting. This effect is clearly what Gentil intended. Many of the illustrations have the explanatory simplicity of those found in a modern Larousse dictionary.

The V&A album is a wide volume in a worn leather binding, containing fifty-eight illustrated pages, in most cases with commentary in French on the facing page. These notes are written in more than one hand and some passages appear verbatim in the posthumously published *Mémoires*. Although the subject matter is diverse, it is systematically presented. The first half of the album deals mainly with the life of the nobility and consists of four main sections. The first six folios depict the Mughal Emperor and his court: the ceremonies of the durbar, the legendary Peacock Throne and other royal paraphernalia as well as various modes of transport and members of the household staff (FIG.1) are all shown. A scene of the imperial harem taking the country air (FIG.2) is unusual for the Gentil albums in its use of the traditional gouache technique of Mughal painting. Fols.7–13 record royal hunts at which Gentil himself was present. One page depicts the total of each day's carnage during a ten-day hunt held by Shuja ud-Daula. Another shows the Nawab striking unavailingly with his sword at a curled up pangolin. Fols.14–21 deal with Gentil's own involvement in the recent history of Oudh, including his negotiations with the British following the defeat of the Nawab's forces and his encounter with the Mughal Emperor Shah Alam (FIG.3). Finally, fols.22–26 depict the

sports and pastimes enjoyed by the nobility, such as polo, lance, javelin and archery exercises, chess, cards, *chaupar*, backgammon and entertainments such as snake-charming, acrobats, jugglers, cock-fighting and fights between rams, blackbuck, camels and elephants. Kite-flying, which became a highly developed art in Oudh, is given a page of its own.

The second half of the album is concerned with the doctrines, rites and festivals of the two main religions of the period, Islam and Hinduism. Fols.27–33 and 35 illustrate aspects of Islam, such as the positions used in prayer, the orders of Sufi mystics, Muslim cosmology and birth, marriage and funeral rites. More particular to Oudh are scenes of the royal procession and celebrations at the end of the month of Ramadan, and a record of the Muharram procession held at Faizabad in 1772. Not surprisingly, Hinduism, with its complex mythology and social system, takes up more than twice as many pages as Islam (fols.36–48, 51–52, 54–58). Here Gentil acknowledges a debt to Abu'l Fazl's *Ain-i Akbari*, from which he derives his version of the cosmogony, castes and doctrinal groupings of the Hindus. Other subjects, which are depicted in a generally dry and schematic manner, include the major deities (especially the ten avatars of Vishnu), forms of trial by ordeal, birth, marriage and funeral rites including suttee, the annual popular festivals (FIG.4) and the four stages of human life. Within this overall scheme there are some unexpected interpolations, such as two miniature copies of Tibetan scroll-paintings (*thangkas*), one of them described as having been 'found in a temple in Bhutan'. Fols.34 and 49 also relate to Gentil's collecting interests, as they show weapons as well as careful depictions of contemporary jewellery, which are today of much documentary value (FIG.5). The fas-

FIG.6 A toddy collector and his family, from the Boileau
Album, painted at Madras in 1785, fol.26, inscribed:
Toddyman. Size of whole page 36.3×27 cm. I.S. 75–1954.
FIG.7 *Sannyasis* performing austerities over a fire. Boileau
Album, fol.9, inscribed: *Sannaisey Divine Worships this way*.

6

7

FIG.8 A tribal hunter removes a thorn from his wife's foot, Boileau Album, fol.23, inscribed: *A Chinchao cast or hunters*.   FIG.9 A French officer and his factotum, Boileau Album, fol.11, inscribed: *French officer & his Debash*.

8

9

FIG.10 'A Tadwan or Malabar fortune-teller', Tanjore, early nineteenth century, 28×22 cm. I.S. 0927(6).

cination of the Gentil Album lies as much in details such as these as in its revelation of a cultivated eighteenth century Frenchman's encounter with Indian life.

The album painted for John Peter Boileau at Madras in the following decade contrasts with the Gentil Album in almost all respects. Its plain paper cover is briefly inscribed: *Drawings of Castes &c. made at Madras 1785 for J.P. Boileau Esqre.*, and the captions to its forty-two watercolour illustrations are laconic and sometimes cryptic, having apparently been taken down in dictation from a native informant. It is already a conventional set of trades and castes, for these had developed earlier in the south than elsewhere; the Venetian adventurer Manucci had commissioned comparable paintings to illustrate his racy history of Mughal India while residing at Madras as early as 1701–6.

Little is known of Boileau himself. He came of a Protestant family that had fled France in the previous century, several of whose members were to serve in the East India Company. He became a writer in 1765 and from 1768–74 served as an assistant at Bandarmalanka and Masulipatam, where he returned to serve on the Council from 1778–85. After 1785 there is no trace of his appointments, and it is perhaps possible that he had his album painted at Madras as a souvenir before he sailed for England.

If it is less serious and original in conception than the Gentil Album, the Boileau Album is certainly less restrained in style. Compared with the pedestrian work of Gentil's artists, the anonymous Madras painter works with rude gusto and much wit. His album shows a vestige of the Hindu manuscript tradition by opening with the image of the auspicious elephant-headed god Ganesha. This is followed by a conventional puzzle picture of five tigers with a single head. The remaining forty pages depict the castes and professions, in no discernible order: Brahmins and the nobility mingle with the lower orders such as cowherds, fishermen, potters, collectors of palm toddy (FIG.6) and religious mendicants. A scene of Hindu ascetics performing austerities around a blazing fire is vigorously painted (FIG.7). As so often in Company sets, husbands and wives tend to be shown together. The unpopular *bania* (merchant) and his wife are shown leering unpleasantly. A scene of a leaf-skirted tribal hunter removing a thorn from his wife's foot is especially charming (FIG.8). A debonair Frenchman with a frisky dog perhaps derives from an imported print (FIG.9). Another European is shown lounging on a chair smoking a cheroot while a party of labourers excavate a tank. The freshness of these early renderings of typical Company subjects contrasts with the increasingly mass-produced Tanjore work of a few years later (FIG.10), with its stiff figures and featureless background, although here the artist has still made effective use of the richly patterned girdles with which the fortune-teller sounding his pellet-drum is draped.

INDIAN MINIATURE PAINTINGS

STONE AND BRONZE SCULPTURE

THANGKAS

INDIA
NEPAL
TIBET
SOUTHEAST ASIA

DORIS WIENER

Phone: (212) 772-8631

Cable: WINDOWS

Telex: 649-042 INTERPRO

By Appointment

Rare blanc de chine puppet figure holding a child.
Decorated in famille verte enamels in china.
circa 1675–1725 AD   Height 26 inches

E&J FRANKEL Ltd.
ORIENTAL ART

25 East 77th Street, New York, New York 10021
Telephone (212) 879-5733

Members of The Art and Antiques Dealers League of America,
The Appraisers Association of America and C.I.N.O.A.

EARLE D. VANDEKAR of Knightsbridge Ltd.

Specialising in Fine 18th Century Ceramics

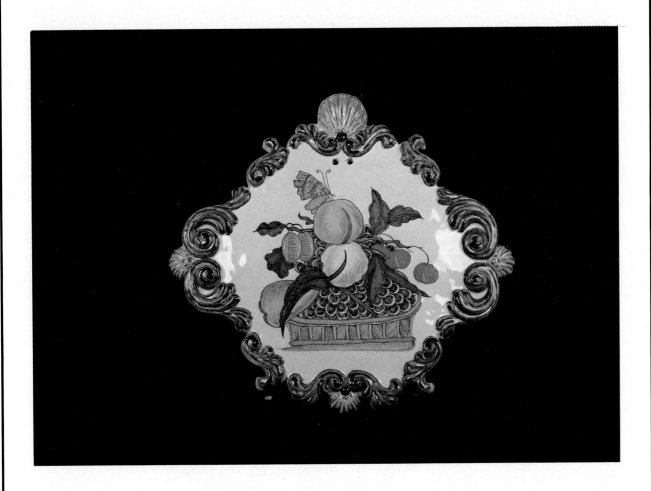

138 Brompton Road
London SW3 1HY, England
01-589 8481/3398

15 East 57th Street
New York, NY 10022
(212) 308 2022

IAN & MARCEL Hand Painted Silks Couture Interiors
Telephone 01-580 1722

HUMPHRIES WEAVING COMPANY
at PALLU&LAKE

Silk and linen brocatelle being woven for the Speaker's bed on an early 19th century Jacquard handloom

HUMPHRIES WEAVING COMPANY
HAND WEAVERS OF FIGURED SILK FABRICS, PLAINS
AND HAND-CUT VELVETS.
SPECIALISTS IN REPRODUCTION OF HISTORIC TEXTILES
MARKETING & TRADE SALES THROUGH PALLU & LAKE

18 Newman Street, London W1P 4AR   01-636 3743

THE SPEAKER'S STATE BED

Clive Wainwright

The Palace of Westminster is one of the most celebrated buildings in the world, but apart from the chambers of the Commons, the Lords and the public spaces such as the Central Lobby which connect them, the interiors are little known to the public. Within the buildings a very wide range of activities connected with the process of government take place. There are for instance committee rooms, libraries, refreshment rooms and the Lord Chancellor's Department, as well as a number of residences in which dwell officials of both Houses. The two most extensive of these residences are those of the Speaker of the House of Commons and the Lord Chancellor; it was for the former that the bed which is the subject of this essay was designed.

But before considering this bed, a little of the history of the building which houses it needs to be told. The mediaeval Palace of Westminster in which our parliamentary system was born and nurtured was continuously adapted to the changing needs of the two Houses of Parliament. During the eighteenth and early nineteenth centuries several of our most famous architects attempted to improve the ancient and overcrowded building. Wren, Wyatt and Soane all made major changes within and without the building, but even after Soane's extensive alterations in the early nineteenth century the accommodation was still considered inadequate for the needs of Parliament. After the passage of the Reform Bill in 1832 and the consequent increase in the attendance of MPs the problem of overcrowding in the Commons became critical. Elsewhere in the building the accommodation was of a very variable quality. There were Soane's splendid

FIG.2 The bed today after restoration. (Photograph: Ken Jackson, copyright Victoria & Albert Museum).

new libraries for both Houses, but the speaker still occupied a subterranean dining room created from what was originally and is now once again the crypt chapel of St. Stephen's. The problem was however solved in October 1834 when the building was consumed by an accidental fire. Only Westminster Hall survived intact. Whilst most people were stunned a few were delighted at the prospect of a modern replacement, these included the young A.W.N Pugin. He watched the fire and wrote 'There is nothing much to regret and much to rejoice in a vast quantity of Soane's mixtures and Wyatt's herasies been effectively consigned to oblivion. Oh, it was a

FIG.1 The bed in the State Bedroom at Speaker's House in about 1903. The hangings are not the original ones, but are made from adapted window curtains. (Photograph: Ken Jackson, copyright House of Lords Record Office).

glorious sight to see his composition mullions and cement pinnacles and battlements flying and cracking . . . . The old walls stood triumphantly midst the scene of ruin'.

The Commons and the Lords were quickly accommodated in two temporary chambers which they were to occupy for some years. The Speaker was moved to a grand house which was especially rented for him in Belgravia, his official residence being in Carlton House Terrace. The story of the competition held to choose a design for the new building has often been told: the winner was Charles Barry who employed A.W.N Pugin to help with the Gothic ornaments of the building. Because of the need to clear the ruins and of the decision to reclaim land from the river, the foundation stone was not laid until 1840, but considering the scale of the building, work proceeded quickly. As soon as there were interiors to be decorated and furnished, Pugin was once again employed to design and control these aspects of the work. From this time until his death in 1852 he was to design and oversee the manufacture of hundreds of pieces of furniture as well as carpets, light fittings, wall papers, even devoting his genius to details like coat pegs and fire irons. The rules of the competition had laid down carefully framed specifications as to the facilities to be provided in the new building. No public building of such a scale had ever been built from scratch in this country before, or probably anywhere in the world. Barry and Pugin had to devise suitable furnishings for rooms of widely differing functions, committee rooms, robing rooms, press rooms and so on, including of course the residences. That they succeeded triumphantly in this objective is testified by the fact that most of these rooms are still in use today, furnished with their original furniture.

FIG.3 The elaborately carved and gilded foot of the bed.
(Photograph: Ken Jackson, copyright Victoria & Albert
Museum).   FIG.4 The new brocatelle and embroidered
pelmet. (Photograph: Ken Jackson, copyright Victoria &
Albert Museum).

3

4

FIG.5 The carver working upon the back posts and the finial.
(Photograph: Ken Jackson, copyright National Heritage
Memorial Fund).   FIGS.6,7,8 The brocatelle being woven
in the hand loom. (Photographs: Ken Jackson, copyright
National Heritage Memorial Fund).

5

6

7

8

THE SPEAKER'S STATE BED

Pugin was to die in 1852 and Barry in 1860 before the building was finally complete. But when Pugin died many major interiors were complete and he left so many designs that many objects and details were posthumously carried out as he intended. He left no drawings for the Speaker's State Bed, so Barry's office was responsible for its design, but the bed as executed betrays Pugin's influence in most of its details.

When the specifications for the new building were devised shortly after the fire the functions which the old Palace had been traditionally required to fulfil had been carefully considered. For instance coronations had, due to the proximity of the building to Westminster Abbey, always been closely linked to its history. The coronation of William IV had been a very economical affair without most of the customary pomp. This was the reaction of a frugal monarch to the excesses of his predecessor. For George IV's coronation had been grand and dramatic with such traditional features as a splendid banquet in Westminster Hall and the appearance of the King's Champion in full armour on horse back. Furthermore he had spent the night before the ceremony at Speaker's House. When Victoria came to the throne the Palace was in ruins. At some stage during the planning of the new building it was specified that a grand State Bed should be provided for Speaker's House so that future monarchs could spend the night before the coronation, or any other night they chose to spend at Speaker's House sleeping in an appropriately regal bed. Charles Shaw Lefevre spent his Speakership from 1839–1857 ensconced in the temporary residences, but must have taken a lively interest in the plans to design and furnish a new and suitably grand abode at Westminster. In the event, Speaker's House was not complete until early in 1859 at which time John

Evelyn Denison, Speaker 1857–1872, at last moved into his new residence.

Luckily a complete record of the furnishing of the Speaker's state rooms survives at the Victoria & Albert Museum in the ledgers of the celebrated cabinet making firm of Holland and Sons who provided the major part of the furniture in the whole Palace. The section of the State Bed Room includes 'June 18 1858 to be furnished in the Mediaeval Style . . . . A walnut & gilt Arabian bedstead 7 feet 6 inches long by 6 feet 6 inches with ornamental carved decorations . . . Silk curtains for bedstead bound wadded & lined with silk with embd valance finished with lace and fringe of full dimensions to enclose bedstead'. The whole contents of the bed room are listed in minute detail including '2 handsome gilt china chamber utensils'. It had, since the middle ages, been the case that elaborate beds such as this had been largely created from textiles with the wooden parts playing a secondary part. This is still largely the case here, where the wooden parts cost £91 8s. whilst the textiles cost £135 15s. 5d. The bed remained in the State Bed Room, but was not used by Edward VII, or as far as I can establish by any subsequent monarch.

In the course of a survey of the furniture of the Palace of Westminster undertaken by the Department of Furniture and Woodwork in 1973 it became apparent that the then location of the bed was unknown. This fact I mentioned in a lecture which I gave at the Victoria & Albert Museum in January 1981 and in which I showed a slide of an old photograph of the bed. This resulted in a newpaper story which led to the rediscovery of the bed in private hands in rural Wales. In 1981 it was purchased by the National Heritage Memorial Fund which also funded its complete restoration. The bed had lost its original hangings by

the beginning of this century, but by the time it was rediscovered even the replacement hangings had vanished. The wooden elements of the bed were in quite good condition, though some parts were missing. The many months of conservation and restoration required were organised and supervised by the museum's department of Furniture and Woodwork with the assistance of colleagues in the Department of Textiles and Conservation. Luckily the Holland & Sons accounts listed in great detail the quantities of textiles and trimmings required and it was equally fortunate that the original contract drawing of the bed was discovered in the Public Record Office. Without this documentation the restoration could not have been undertaken, as no bed of this elaboration of the 1850s exists which could have served as a model.

The accounts showed that the original hangings were of geranium coloured silk brocatelle, a piece of lining material fortunately survived on the head board which gave us the exact colour. No piece of the brocatelle survived, however, to give us the original pattern. We therefore chose the best documented brocatelle of the 1840s, which had been designed by Pugin and made for the celebrated Bond Street upholsterer and antique dealer John Webb. Webb had used this material for hangings in Isambard Kingdom Brunel's Shakespeare Drawing Room which he furnished in 1848. Fortunately research showed that a point paper in the museum's Textiles Department was that for this actual brocatelle, thus the Jacquard cards for the loom could be punched directly from this point paper. Webb's firm in fact made several of the most important pieces of furniture in the House of Lords including the Royal Throne.

The restoration of the woodwork was undertaken by Peter and Frances

FIGS.9,10 The emblems for the canopy being embroidered.
(Photographs: Ken Jackson, copyright National Heritage
Memorial Fund).

Binnington in their workshop in Battersea. The embroidered emblems of the Thistle, Tudor Rose and Shamrock were the result of many months of work by the Royal School of Needlework, whose predecessors also carried out work for Barry in the Palace. The tinned steel rods needed to support the immense curtains were carefully copied by Mr Donald Cooper from those on the Victorian state bed at Arundel Castle. The range of skills needed to carry out all this work fortunately survived in this country, but no loom existed anywhere in England on which the brocatelle could be woven. Rather than order the material on the Continent, the Heritage Fund, seeing the re-creation of lost crafts as part of their role, paid for the old-established

Manchester firm of Devoge & Co to adapt an existing hand-loom to weave the brocatelle. This loom was set up at the De Vere Mill of the Humphries Weaving Company at Castle Hedingham in East Anglia and it was here that the painstaking work of weaving by hand the 92 yards of brocatelle was carried out. As a result there now exists a loom in this country on which brocatelle of any pattern can be woven. The elaborate tassels and trimmings were provided by Messrs Pallu & Lake of London. Finally the long job of combining all these elements into the finished fully dressed bed was carried out by Seymour Furnishings under the direction of Mr Carter and Mr Knibbs.

Perhaps the most exciting and in a way surprising aspect of the enterprise

was the discovery that the whole range of skills needed to carry out such a large and complex project of restoration still survived in this country and furthermore that they are in the hands of people who can work so well together. The completed bed as shown in the illustrations will have been displayed at the Museum during the summer of 1983, but by the time this essay appears it will once more have been installed at Speaker's House. Thus after a somewhat chequered career, this handsome piece of furniture, the grandest and most elaborate surviving Victorian State Bed, can once more rest happily in the building for which it was created.

9

10

The Total Concept

Entrance hall · Living and Dining Rooms · Bedrooms
Furnishings · Columns · Wall and ceiling panels
Fitted Interiors from the one source

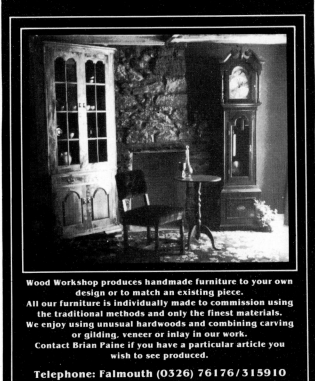

Huntington Antiques Ltd.

Period Oak and Country Furniture, Eastern Carpets and Rugs
The Old Forge, Church Street, Stow-on-the-Wold, Gloucestershire. Tel: 0454 30842

We offer a substantial stock of fine early oak, walnut and country furniture. Always a selection of refectory, gateleg and other tables; dressers and court cupboards; wainscots and sets of chairs; and usually some rare examples of gothic and renaissance furniture.
We would always welcome the opportunity to purchase such items.

Chippendale walnut chest-on-chest, Philadelphia, circa 1760-1780.
Ex-collection Mrs. George Maurice Morris (The Lindens).
Illustrated: *The Magazine Antiques*, January 1956, page 63

Height 92 inches, width 44¾ inches, depth 22¾ inches.

THEATRE MODELS

James Fowler

The Theatre Museum possesses over two hundred models of stage sets as records of past productions dating from the eighteenth century. These are distinct from other types of theatre models that reconstruct lost playhouses, and from children's toy theatres which preserve the décor of many early nineteenth-century dramas.

Modelling scenery goes back at least to the sixteenth century. In his *Il Libro secondo d'Architettura* of 1545, Sebastiano Serlio builds small scale models of cardboard and wood to solve problems of perspective and to help execute scenes in the large. Revels Office Accounts of Queen Elizabeth I also record the making of 'modells' for static scenic pieces before the revolutionary principle of perspective scenes reached the English Court early in the seventeenth century.

The first major designer whose use of set models is well documented in England is Philippe Jacques de Loutherbourg R.A., superintendent of scenes and machines at Drury Lane from 1771 to 1781. He made it his practice to supply the carpenters, painters and machinists with small models and paintings they could copy from speedily and accurately. He constructed models for every scene 'fitted by scale to a small model of the stage of Drury Lane' according to one source of 1831, and used them to test out his effects which often involved dramatic changes of colour. Not having to paint actual scenery himself, de Loutherbourg could devote more time to develop and integrate other elements such as lighting, machinery and costume design which, ahead of his time, he perceived as equally important to the total design.

The model of Kensington Gardens (FIG.1) from the pantomine *Omai* (1785), his last and most spectacular production, is one of six now in the Victoria and Albert Museum to survive from the 380 models and drawings sold after his death in 1812. The pairs of wings showing trees are skilfully profiled to deceive the eye which is attracted to the stronger light upstage. During performance, the holes cut in the backcloth afforded glimpses of gigs and horses beyond in Rotten Row, actually mechanical figures carefully scaled in perspective to maximize the sense of depth. Departing from the formal symmetries of neo-classical design, de Loutherbourg breaks up the stage irregularly with a pictorial technique particularly effective in scenes from nature. That models played a vital role in his ambition to create 'living' pictures is confirmed by his Eidophusikon, the working model theatre six feet high by ten feet wide by eight feet deep he exhibited from 1781. It displayed an extraordinary range of scenes in motion including a ship being wrecked in a storm involving techniques beyond the capacity of theatres of the time but which nonetheless pointed a way to future developments.

Despite his extensive influence, de Loutherbourg's separation of design and execution did not become the norm in the nineteenth century when scene painters such as the Grieve and Telbin families, Hawes Craven and Joseph Harker usually assumed both roles. The drawing by William Telbin the younger (FIG.2) from the *Magazine of Art* XII (1889) shows the scene painter modelling scenery in the paint-shop surrounded by preliminary sketches, scale plans of the stage, reference books and photographs, glue-pot and gelatines. There is a paint-box for rendering distant effects in the model, while in the foreground rocks or trees are represented by coal or birch brooms dipped in plaster, and a raging torrent by floss silk. To him the value of spending time on a model is 'thoroughly to understand from it what

you propose doing – not only the "practicabilities", but also your composition, colour, and scheme of lighting'. When approved by the management, the master carpenter then examines the model to see how scenes can be built, set and struck, before making tracings from it. With these he sets to work while the scene painter begins on the backcloths.

The illustration shows the set being modelled in terms of the proscenium frame of a model of the stage it is intended for. A similar model stage probably used for the same purpose (FIG.3) exists of the Normansfield Amusement Hall at Teddington, a multi-purpose hall privately built in 1879 that miraculously survives with many of its theatrical features intact. The Normansfield model – like Telbin's – adopts the standard scale of half an inch to the foot and contains scene grooves, hanging bars and a system of rings for hoisting cloths, resembling that visible to the rear of Telbin's model.

Edward Gordon Craig's revolt against the pictorial design of the Victorian stage is manifested in his model for Bach's *St. Matthew Passion*, built 1912–14 (FIG.4). Its chief sources of inspiration – a twelfth-century Italian church, and mansions or 'boxes' from medieval staging – were architectural, like its method of construction. When work began on the model only sketches were on hand to go by: as his son Edward Craig records, 'there were no drawn plans or sections; the structure had to be worked out day by day, and Craig never stopped inventing'. Even with the help of several joiners, the nine-foot-high model took many months to build. Then it was rigged up with lights and dimmers for Craig to experiment with by 'painting' each section with coloured light to suit the dramatic mood. Lighting was also used to direct attention to different places in

FIG.1 Model by de Loutherbourg for 'Kensington Gardens'
scene in O'Keeffe's pantomime *Omai* (Covent Garden,
1785). V&A Theatre Museum.

FIG.5 Model by Barry Kay for Act I of *Anastasia* (Covent Garden, 1971). V&A Theatre Museum. (Photograph: Michael Werner). FIG.3 Working model of the stage of Normansfield Amusement Hall, probably used for scene designing. (Photograph: Courtesy of GLC Historic Buildings Division).

5

3

which mimed action illustrating the sung story of the Passion took place: in the boxes with grilles on the lower stage, on the platform, or on the grand steps ascending through the huge arch. Although never realized in performance, Craig's model was seminal to the design of modern theatres, inspiring the permanent architectural stage installed by Jacques Copeau in the Théâtre du Vieux-Colombier in 1919, according to Denis Bablet.

In recent decades the growing number of open and arena stages requiring an architectural or sculptural approach to design has caused models to play a more significant role in the early stages of designing than before. Even when designing for a proscenium stage Barry Kay usually commences by modelling with bits of wood and card to help visualize a space and how it can be used. This is particularly important in ballet where the dance space must acquire a definite sense of location and yet not be constricted. He tends 'to alternate between building things very roughly . . . and making drawings which further those ideas', developing both simultaneously. 'As I'm dealing with something three-dimensional, I find it confining just working it out on paper. It would all remain too flat when starting to build the actual model' (interview with A. Schouvaloff, 1980). For his model of Act I of MacMillan's ballet *Anastasia* (1971) in FIG.5, Kay made a finished design based on preliminary sketches of Russian timber churches whose domes and method of construction inspired the curved screens and birch wood with sawn-off stumps – the setting for an Imperial family picnic of 1914. The sense of vortex about to engulf the Tsar suggested by the screens emerged in the final act when photographs of pre-revolutionary figures were projected on to them as Anastasia recalls the events leading up to the massacre of the Tsar and his family.

How a model takes shape varies of course according to the designer and the work in hand. The pure white box Sally Jacobs designed for Peter Brook's production of *A Midsummer Night's Dream* (1970) (FIG.6) reflected a desire to eliminate traditions which had grown around and obscured the play. Drawing on experiences in California where she had been living for three years, Sally Jacobs had made Christmas cards with a grid of black lines containing fluorescent-coloured dots on a white ground which were inspired by a Los Angeles exhibition of Tantric designs from India. On the basis of one such card she and Brook fell to modelling a white space out of typing paper before knowing even what the coloured dots of the card represented, ending up with a group of fluorescent colours, a piece of wire suggesting trees, a Hopi Indian kachina doll she had brought with her, and the red feather Brook plucked from its head. After this first session she quickly built the model and this collage based on a photograph of it records her intended colours: the feather is now Titania's suspended bower, and downstage is Oberon dressed in red (later altered to purple). The exciting use of overhead space and trapezes solved the problem of limited space in the box. In this case, as in most modern productions, the model emerged out of the close collaboration of designer and director. After only a week of rehearsals a mock-up of the set was constructed in scaffolding, but this was exceptional. In normal circumstances the model remains the only available form for the cast to visualize the set before it is built.

Although some designers prefer to build the whole model themselves, many now employ an assistant for the purpose whom they supervise closely. Only very large institutions such as the National Theatre or the Royal Opera House Covent Garden have their own model-making departments which designers may call upon when designing for those theatres. At Covent Garden the model-shop with its staff of three comes under the control of the production manager, Jeffrey Phillips, and FIG.7 shows some of the design materials they have to work from. This may range in one extreme from a rough sketch of the set with explanatory notes from which they must build a model, to sketch models in white card not unlike the duplicate model made in place of a lost original (FIG.8), to a model finished by the designer down to the last detail, which merely requires checking. Designers will collaborate with the building of the models at Covent Garden to varying degrees. When finished, the measurements and sightlines are checked inside working models of the Covent Garden stage visible in the background of FIG.8, and working drawings are prepared for the technical departments to build from.

From the technical standpoint, the finished model is a vital point of reference for the lighting designer (FIG.9), for the carpenters and property makers who may borrow pieces of it to help visualize what to build, and for the stage technicians who will erect and work the set. As construction and rehearsals proceed, details of the model may be modified in response to practical and artistic demands. At the end of the production process models may become battered to an extent that the designer may make a replacement as a record of the production.

FIG.2 'Modelling a Scene' after a drawing by W. Telbin,
engraved by C. Carter, 1889. National Art Library, V&A.
FIG.4 Original model by Edward Gordon Craig for Bach's
St. Matthew Passion, built 1912–14.
(Photograph: Mr Brown).

2   4

FIG.7 Model-making department at Covent Garden, 1982.
(Photographs FIGS.7–9: J. Fowler).   FIG.9 Lighting
designer Mark Henderson consults the model at Covent
Garden designed by Richard Hudson for Corder's ballet
St. Anthony Variations (Sadler's Wells Royal Ballet, 1983).
FIG.8 Replica in white card of Terry Bartlett's original
model for Bintley's ballet *Night Moves* (Sadler's Wells
Royal Ballet, 1981).

7

9

8

European Works of Art

An oil painting of *The Angel Appearing to Abraham and Sarah* (circa 1760) by Giovanni Domenico Tiepolo hangs above a Louis XV black lacquer and ormolu commode by Bernard van Risenburgh. Two early eighteenth-century bronzes by Massimiliano Soldani-Benzi, *Athlete Holding a Vase* and *Flora,* flank an early eighteenth-century bronze saltcellar by Francesco Bertos on the top of the commode.

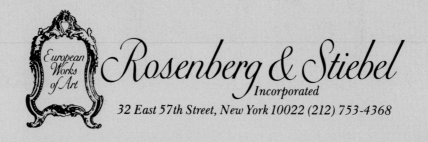

When in Basel visit its 26 Museums

Anatomische Sammlung / Antikenmuseum und Sammlung Ludwig / Feuerwehrmuseum / Museum Für Gegenwartskunst / Gewerbemuseum / Historisches Museum Barfüsserkirche / Jüdisches Museum der Schweiz / Haus zum Kirschgarten / Kunsthalle / Kunstmuseum / Kupferstichkabinett / Kutschen- und Schlittensammlung / Ausstellung der Basler Mission / Sammlung alter Musikinstrumente / Basler Papiermühle / Schweizer Pharmazie-historisches Museum / Schweizer Schiffahrtsmuseum "Unser Weg zum Meer" / Römerhaus und Museum Augst / Skulpturhalle / Spielzeug- und Dorfmuseum Riehen / Schweizerisches Sportmuseum / Stadt-und Münstermuseum / Museum für Völkerkunde / Schweizerisches Museum für Volkskunde / Ausstellungsraum Kaserne / Sammlung Karikaturen & Cartoons Basel

BASEL, SWITZERLAND

GUCCI

27 Old Bond Street, London W.1.

The Director at lunch

TRAVELS WITH THE V&A

A personal reminiscence by Professor Charles and Mrs Anne Foster

The journey to the Renaissance courts of Italy undertaken by a party of friends of the V&A in May 1982 was based on the ancient city of Bologna. Here we stayed in a most comfortable hotel, which had formerly been a convent and whose charming cloister garden remains, although to serve a somewhat different function!

If Tobias Smollett on *his* Italian journey in 1765 had had the good fortune to have had his travel organised by Jean Neilson and Julie Laird he could never have written: '. . . the accommodation is intolerable. We were almost poisoned at supper. I found the place where I was to lie so close and confined, that I could not breath in it, and therefore lay all night in an outward room upon four chairs, with a leathern portmanteau for my pillow.' We were equally fortunate in having the Director of the V&A, Sir Roy Strong, as our guest lecturer: his wit and erudition (and his straw hat) gave pleasure to us all.

The tour itself was inspired by the prestigious Gonzaga Exhibition mounted at the V&A in 1981. In the following there is only space to single out aspects of our journey which were particularly memorable for us.

From Bologna the party of thirty or so travelled out daily for a week by private coach in a series of radial directions. As we sped along the autostrada to our various destinations Sir Roy spoke of the attributes, conventions and customs of courtly life in the Renaissance. We heard about the device or *impresa* derived from the coins of Imperial Rome: the triumph (*trionfo*) again originating in ancient Rome, celebrating not so much military achievement, but more abstract ideas such as love and the virtues and brought to the fore by the poems of Petrarca. The explanation of these and other notions clarified many aspects of the art of this period.

As is well known the artistic and other achievements of the Renaissance courts depended greatly on the character and wealth of the princely families who governed them. The Gonzagas are a remarkable example of patronage extending over a long period.

Bologna, our base, we were able to explore *a piedi*. This splendid city is notable for its arcaded streets (greatly admired by Goethe), its ancient university famous throughout Europe and female professors as early as the thirteenth century. One such, remarkable for her beauty is said to have lectured in a veil ' . . . in order to keep the students' minds on jurisprudence . . .'.

Here is the huge unfinished brick gothic church of S. Petronio whose central portal has fine sculptures by Iacomo della Quercia and two of the oldest (fifteenth and sixteenth century) organs in Italy. An artistic highlight is to be seen in the sixteenth century Palazzo Magnani-Salem where the fine frieze in the salone d'onore was decorated by members of the Carracci family and tells the story of Romulus and Remus. Opposite in the church of S. Giacomo Maggiore is the fifteenth century Cappella Bentivoglio frescoed by Lorenzo Costa and commemorating a family who, in spite of not infrequent assassinations and other problems, governed the city for many years.

Ferrara lies north-east of Bologna and is today very different from when Dickens visited it in 1845 when '. . . the grass so grows up in the streets, that anyone might make hay there, literally, while the sun shines'. Now it is a busy place with the solemn, massive and moated Castello Estense at its centre, formerly the abode of the Este family whose court became one of the most famous of the Italian Renaissance encouraging not only artists but scholars and poets. Ariosto and Tasso lived here as did the sixteenth century musician Carlo Gesualdo who married Leonora

d'Este as his second wife having arranged the murder of his first. A bright spot in this rather sombre building is the Sala dei Giuocchi, whose ceiling was frescoed by members of the Filippi family and shows lively representations of naked men engaged in a variety of athletic activities. Unfortunately, brief mention can only be made of the Sala dei Mesi in the Schifanoia palace whose considerably damaged fresco cycle relates to the months of the year. Here are scenes of everyday life as well as Triumphs and astrological allusions, subjects which had been discoursed upon by Sir Roy.

Modena, Parma and Mantua all lie in the flat lands of the Po. Both Modena and Parma have impressive romanesque cathedrals, the latter having the famous Assumption of Correggio decorating its cupola. In very different vein the same artist, at the instigation of the abbess of the former Convent of S. Paolo decorated the vault of her refectory with mythological scenes: '. . . where the learned abbess entertained humanists at her table, not one understands, with too much regard for the rule'.

A short distance from Parma across the Po valley lies the sixteenth century fortified cittadina of Sabbioneta, founded by Vespasiano Gonzaga and a good example of town planning. It contains a ducal and a garden palace both richly frescoed. The fascinating Teatro Olympico is similar in design to Palladio's more famous example at Vicenza. Still in active use, it was littered with the paraphernalia of television.

Enea Piccolomini, Pope Pius II, was in Mantua in June 1459 presiding at a Congress of the Church. There was much delay and the delegates became impatient and in his words: '. . . they did not like the flat wine or any of the other things necessary to sustain life, very many were catching fever, nothing

The group

Culture — the a.m. start

Jean Neilson, tour organiser,
with Himself

It rains

It still rains

The Hat

The Chat

Charles Foster in a somewhat
disconsolate group

Our Leader speaks

was heard except frogs'. Mantua still has a watery aspect but is no longer malarial, has fewer frogs and excellent wine – as we discovered!

Most of the party had already been to Mantua mentally if not corporeally through seeing the Gonzaga Exhibition. Dott. Ilaria Bertelli who was to have escorted us through the massive Palazzo Ducale was unable, at the last minute to do so and some delay ensued. However, we were able to see many memorable and beautiful things, albeit at the trot. Foremost among them was the Camera degli Sposi whose walls and ceiling are covered with splendid frescoes by Mantegna illustrating episodes in the lives of the Gonzagas and it will be remembered that this was reproduced on a reduced scale at the exhibition. In the Hall of the Dukes there was recently discovered as the result of much detective work a fresco cycle by Pisanello, in which personages and emblems of the Gonzaga court are incorporated into episodes from Arthurian legend. In sharp contrast to the great galleries and rooms of the palace was the Paradiso of Isabella d'Este wife of Francesco Gonzaga consisting of three small rooms where this astute and cultivated lady would retire among her treasures to read or play the lute.

Just outside the city is the former summer residence of the Gonzagas – the Palazzo del Te. It is sumptuously decorated by Giulio Romano and others. Most impressive perhaps is the Sala dei Giganti described by Dickens as 'an apoplectic performance' where giants struck down by Jupiter bring everything else crashing down with them – an allegory of Power it is said.

Back in the city and in beautiful weather lunch was taken *al fresco* in the Piazza delle Erbe. The Bacchanalian scene is shown here and noteworthy features are our Leader in his *cappello di paglia* and the beautiful rinascimentesco centrepiece – the food and wine were noteworthy too!

The longest excursion was to the city of Urbino associated with the great Renaissance court of the Montefeltros and Della Roveres. Raphael was born here and some very celebrated artists of the quattrocento worked here, attracted to the court of the humanist duke, Federico de Montefeltro – among them Pisanello and Piero della Francesca. The ducal palace is considered one of the finest of the period. Now the National Gallery of the Marche it contains fine ornamental doorways, chimney-pieces and intarsia work by Botticelli as well as masterpieces of many artists.

Calls were also made to the Biblioteca Malatestiana at Cesena and the Tempio Malatestiano at Rimini. This, both a church and personal monument to the notorious Sigismondo Malatesta contains works by di Duccio and others. Sigismondo, a strange amalgam of ruffian and patron of the arts had the unique experience of being 'canonised to Hell' by Pius II – 'No mortal heretofore has descended into Hell with the ceremony of canonisation. Sigismondo shall be the first to be deemed worthy of this honour.'

At our last dinner together, a short speech of appreciation and thanks was given to Sir Roy, Julie Laird and Jean Neilson to whom we were so indebted for making our Italian journey such a success. Some praise should also go to the Friends themselves who by so assiduously following the straw hat never (or almost never) got lost, even during the marathon at Mantua!

It is also good to know that a handsome donation to the Friends of the V&A resulted from this happy visit.

THE ROYAL SCOTTISH MUSEUM

Roman Flask
containing a miniature vessel attached to the base.
4th century AD
1983.61

The Royal Scottish Museum in Edinburgh is a national institution.
It is the largest comprehensive museum in Europe with collections
in the Decorative Arts, Archaeology, Ethnography, Natural History,
Geology, Technology and Science.

Open: Monday to Saturday 10-5; Sunday 2-5
Closed Christmas and New Year
Admission Free

J. & M. Wolber

"ANTIQUAIRES A PARIS"

DIDIER AARON & CIE
32, av. Raymond-Poincaré - Paris 16e - Tél. (1) 727.17.79

AVELINE & CIE
20, rue du Cirque - Paris 8e - Tél. (1) 266.60.29

ETIENNE LEVY S.A.
178, Fg Saint-Honoré - Paris 8e - Tél. (1) 562.33.47

MICHEL MEYER
24, av. Matignon - Paris 8e - Tél. (1) 266.62.95

JACQUES PERRIN
3, quai Voltaire - Paris 7e - Tél. (1) 260.27.20

MAURICE SEGOURA
20, Fg Saint-Honoré - Paris 8e - Tél. (1) 265.11.03

BERNARD STEINITZ
4, rue Drouot - Paris 9e - Tél. (1) 246.98.98

Association of seven famous antique dealers who are top specialists in French 17th and 18th century Furniture, Works of Art and Old Master Paintings. Their skilled knowledge and professional reputation offer collectors a guarantee of QUALITY and AUTHENTICITY.

RAINER ZIETZ LIMITED

39 TITE STREET, LONDON S.W.3. 4.J.P.

TELEPHONE : 01-352 0848

A FLORENTINE OAKLEAF JAR MADE IN THE WORKSHOP OF GIUNTA DI TUGIO
IN ABOUT 1431 FOR THE PHARMACY OF THE HOSPITAL OF SANTA MARIA NUOVA IN FLORENCE.
THE SADDLE-BACK BOAR IS THE BADGE OF THE ANCIENT PISTOIAN FAMILY OF PANCIATICHI.
PROVENANCE: SIR THOMAS INGILBY, BT

FIG. 1 A musician with dancers on a terrace, from the Music Room of the Quinta Formosa, Portuguese (Lisbon), about 1720–30. C. 51–1973.

PICTURES BY POTTERS

Michael Archer

It is in Portugal, more than anywhere else in Europe, that one is most aware of the part which painted tiles can play in the decoration of buildings. Complete façades can often be seen shimmering in the sun and interiors, particularly of churches are frequently lined from floor to ceiling with elaborate geometric designs like huge oriental carpets covering the walls. Sometimes these patterned tiles form a background for pictorial panels, most commonly showing religious, mythological or genre subjects. The museum possesses a number of panels of about 1720 to 1730 which once formed the dado of a music room at the Quinta Formosa (FIG.1) They are painted with musicians on a terrace entertaining gallants and their ladies who are shown dancing or seated drinking wine. These agreeable scenes in shades of blue must have made a delightfully cool room in which to escape the summer heat. On a much larger scale are two other panels made somewhat later in 1741 (FIG.2). These show classical gods and godesses painted in brilliant colours and they once stood on either side of a stone fountain in the garden of the Quinta dos Azuleijos at Carnide.

The word *azuleijos*, meaning 'painted tiles', derives from Arabic, reminding us of the ancient origins of decorated tiles in the Middle East. As early as the sixth century B.C. the gates of Babylon had tile pictures built into them, as did the palace of Artaxerxes II at Susa two centuries later. These pictures were in relief and so perhaps relate more to sculpture than to painting. The earliest surviving example of tile pictures set vertically into the wall and painted as if they were frescoes were found in a 9th century palace at Samarra. Although during the Middle Ages tiles were used extensively on interior and exterior walls in the Arab world, pictures of any size showing animals or humans were unusual. This

was partly because of religious scruples about the representation of living creatures but also because of a predelection for and talent in designing vigorous and intricate ornament. These factors make the panel shown in FIG. 3 all the more remarkable. It is said to have been made for the Hall of the Forty Columns at Isfahan, one of the buildings ornamented by Shah Abbas I (1587–1629). A lady reclines on cushions in the open air, waited on by several attendants. Her languid posture and the androgenous nature of some of her companions contrasts oddly with their doll-like features and the graceful simplicity of the flowering trees and plants. Picnics are always at the mercy of the weather and this scene has a strong feeling of *carpe diem* in a short Persian springtime.

The panel owes much of its charm to the cheerful colours which remain quite distinct from and unmixed with one another. The effect depends on a technical discovery of the Islamic potters in the early Middle Ages. A line of greasy pigment which disappeared in the firing kept the colours apart. This process, known in Spain as *cuerda seca* (dry cord) spread throughout the Moslem world. Although admirable as far as it went, it was much more limited than the maiolica or faience technique which became the most commonly used in Europe and involved painting with bright enamel pigments on a brilliant white tin-glaze. These materials gave painters considerable scope for sensitive brushwork, as well as control over colour and tone. Tin glaze, like *cuerda seca*, was first used in the Middle East and seems to have come to Europe by way of Southern Italy. Italian potters became acknowledged masters in the use of tin-glaze and produced superb painted wares and tiled pavements but they did not make tile pictures until the seventeenth century and then only on a very limited scale. It is

difficult to explain this in view of the popularity of tile pictures in Spain and Portugal during the same period but it may perhaps have been due to a preference for using frescoes as wall decoration in Italy.

The earliest European tin-glazed tile picture seems to have been on a mysterious tomb erected in the cathedral of St. Mary at Hamburg in about 1320. It showed the recumbent figure of Pope Benedict V and was painted in a thoroughly Gothic manner. It vanished when the cathedral was destroyed in 1806 and is now known only from a few fragments and an engraving. It seems to have existed in a complete vacuum and it is not until the sixteenth century, when the tin-glaze technique spread from Italy to other countries, that tile pictures became at all common. Francesco Niculoso of Pisa went to Seville in about 1500 and produced a number of tiled altar fronts and other pictures but he made little impression on the local traditions of tile production. However the Italian potters who went to Flanders were more successful; from the early sixteenth century at Antwerp and particularly after about 1564, when the war with Spain led to many potters moving to the Northern Netherlands, the production of tin-glazed tiles became well-established.

Although tile pictures were a very small part of the total output, there was a modest but continuing demand for house-signs. The Museum has a particularly early example of one of these showing three pots filled with flowers (FIG.4). It illustrates the name of the house *In de 3 Blompotten*, as well as the arms of the Van Arkel family and those of the city of Gorinchem where they lived. It was probably painted in about 1620 by Antoni de Hoogh. With the exception of signs for shops, tile pictures were generally made for the interiors of buildings. One exception was the Rozendaal Castle near Arnhem

FIG.2 Apollo and Marsyas, the panel once flanked a garden
fountain at the Quinta dos Azuleijos at Carnide, Portuguese
(Lisbon), 1741. C. 55–1973.

which had tile pictures on external walls and another provides what is perhaps the most extraordinary picture in the collections. Made up of 357 tiles and standing eight feet high, it is painted in blue and a few touches of purple with vast figures of the Virtues, Love, Fidelity, Unity and Steadfastness. It came from a building in the Osterhaven in Gouda which once formed part of the pottery of Willem Verswaen and this provenance as well as its unfinished condition suggests that it was intended as an example of what his painters could do. The great majority of Dutch tile pictures derive from prints but in this case the original was a cartoon by Joachim Utewael produced in 1599 for a vast painted glass window still in the Groote Kerk in Gouda.

One of the best known painters of tile pictures was Cornelis Boumeester of Rotterdam (c. 1652–1733) to whom three panels in the collection can be attributed. One of these, a hunting scene, he signed in full and another

showing a whaling expedition carries his initials (FIG.5). The third, painted with ships and yachts tacking chaotically to and fro firing salutes, can be attributed to him on grounds of style. His initials have optimistically been added to one of two early nineteenth century panels of scenes on the Vecht near Utrecht (FIG.6). The banks of this river were lined with fine country houses which were illustrated in a set of views entitled *De Zegepraalende Vecht* published in Amsterdam in 1719 and a number of tile panels were made based on these prints.

But by far the most spectacular of the Dutch panels in the collections are three painted in polychrome with large urns abundantly filled with exotic flowers (FIG.7) Two of the urns stand on plinths while the third is supported on the back of a Kylin, a genial, uncomplaining mythical beast a little like a Pekinese dog. Pictures of this kind were understandably popular outside Holland and some of the best are at the Château of Rambouillet and in the

Amalienburg, the hunting lodge built in 1739 in the park at Nymphenburg outside Munich. The kitchen of the lodge, where Maria Amalia and her ladies could do a little light cooking to pass the time, is lined with a magnificent series of tile pictures showing urns of flowers and Chinese scenes of the greatest freshness and gaiety.

Tile pictures of this type were evidently very expensive and so it is not surprising that most Dutch panels exported to other countries were in blue or manganese purple. An example in the collection is the *Crucifixion* from a series of *Stations of the Cross*, signed by Jan Aalmis the younger and painted at the 'Flowerpot' factory in Rotterdam in about 1770. The inscription on it is in Spanish, showing that it was intended either for export to Spain or perhaps for a Spanish church elsewhere. So successful was the Dutch export trade that the majority of surviving tile pictures are now outside Holland. They are particularly numerous in Portugal where they inspired the

FIG.3 A picnic scene, said to have been painted for the Hall of
the Forty Columns in Isfahan, Persian, first half seventeenth
century. 139–1891.   FIG.4 A sign for a house named 'The
Three flower-pots' in Gorinchem, with the arms of the
Van Arkel family, probably painted by Antoni de Hoogh in
about 1620. C. 475–1923.

3

4

FIG.7 A vase of flowers, Dutch (Delft), second quarter of
eighteenth century. Mellor Bequest. C. 107 to II–1965.

FIG.5 A whaling scene signed by Cornelis Boumeester,
Dutch (Rotterdam), about 1700. Given by Henry Van der
Bergh. C. 744–1925.   FIG.6 A scene on the river Vecht,
Dutch (Delft, Blompot factory), early nineteenth century.
734–1864.   FIG.8 St. Mary Redcliff Church, Bristol, with
the arms of Joseph Butler, Bishop of Bristol (1738–50),
English (Bristol); mid-eighteenth century. Given by
Hugh Owen. 3144–1901.

5

6

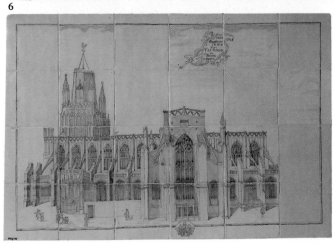

8

FIG.9 Rustic Lovers, Spanish, Valencia del Cid, (Valls pottery), mid-nineteenth century.

local potters, as can be seen, for example, in the Quinta Formosa music room panels (FIG.1).

Although England is so close to Holland geographically, we were largely indifferent to the fashion for tile pictures either as imports or by producing them in our own tin-glaze factories. Only just over a dozen English delftware examples survive and of these only three are in polychrome. The Museum possesses four, all painted in blue, three of which show strong Dutch influence and may perhaps have been painted by Dutch potters working in England. The fourth is a highly detailed view, based on a print, of the church of St. Mary Redcliff at Bristol (FIG.8). It came from a butcher's shop in the town, for which it was probably made by local potters, possibly the Taylor family of Redcliff Street.

Such wall tiles as the English used in the 18th century were on the whole limited to fireplaces, dairies and the very occasional bathing room but by the middle of the nineteenth century this situation completely changed. The Gothic Revival provoked a surge of interest in floor tiles and this in turn led to increased production of wall tiles and pictures. Other countries in Europe saw a comparable enthusiasm and tiles made in a variety of techniques, some of them newly invented, began to play an important architectural role. Unfortunately the Museum has few Continental tile pictures of this period. There are two vigorous panels by Eugène Rousseau, one of which shows the *Spies Returning from Canaan* and is particularly striking. The others are all Spanish from the pottery of Rafael Gonzalez Valls of Valencia del Cid. These are painted in a precise, somewhat naive manner of great charm (FIG.9). They show flowers, landscape views, rustic lovers, dancers and a bull-fighting scene as well as the shop sign of Valls himself.

The nineteenth century English tile pictures in the Museum vary enormously, as might be expected in a period of such wide eclecticism. There is a deliberately simple, picture-book interpretation of the *Sleeping Beauty* story painted by Edward Burne-Jones in the early years of William Morris's firm; a ploughing and sowing scene in red and gold lustre designed by Walter Crane for Maw and Co. in 1889 (FIG.10) and a large bright illustration of *Mary, Mary quite contrary* made by Doulton in about 1900 which came from a children's ward at University College Hospital. Finally there is the sequence of pictures made for the old Grill Room in the Museum (Cover and FIG.11). These were designed by Edward Poynter in 1866 and represent the *Seasons* and the *Months*. They were painted by ladies of the South Kensington Art School on blanks supplied by Minton who also fired them on completion. The fashion for tiled decoration reached its apogee in the years around 1900 and we need only walk as far as Harrods' food halls or the Michelin garage in the Fulham Road, to take two nearby examples, to see how lively, varied and attractive tile pictures of the period could be. Since then the tendency towards simplicity in decoration has led to a neglect of the tile panel although a fresh revival of interest is clearly on the way. This is apparent in such recent acts of public patronage as the tile decoration of the stations on the Victoria Line.

FIG.10 Ploughing and sowing, designed by Walter Crane for
Maw & Co. of Jackfield, about 1889. C. 310–1953.
FIG.11 The old Grill Room with tile decoration painted in
colours, designed by Edward Poynter in 1866 and painted on
Minton blanks by the ladies of the South Kensington School
of Art.

10

11

  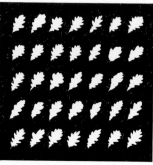 

Upton Lodge Galleries

**Avening House, Avening, Tetbury, Gloucestershire GL8 8NH
Telephone: Nailsworth (045 383) 4048**

The Drinking Trough
Signed and dated 1912

by Stanhope Alexander Forbes, R.A.
1857-1947

Oil on canvas
56 in by 46 in

Stanhope Forbes studied at the Royal Academy Schools and in Paris before settling in Cornwall, where he became leader of the Newlyn School and from about 1885 was a major influence in British art.

110

RCL GALLERY *Rudolf-Clemens Stinner*

Collection of 19th Century Barbizon and Pre-
and Post-Impressionists paintings
as well as British Watercolours 19th and 20th Century

Narcisse Virgile DIAZ DE LA PENA (1807–1876)

L'ECOLE DE LA NATURE

' Fleurs '
oil on panel
41,0 x 35,5 cm
signed lower right
Prov. Ancienne Collection B. du Chatenet

Viewing strictly by appointment.

Eselsweg 7a
4050 Mönchengladbach 1
West Germany
Tel. 02161 / 532666

Ashe Abbey
Campsea Ash, Woodbridge
Suffolk IP13 OPJ / GB
Tel. 0728 / 746292

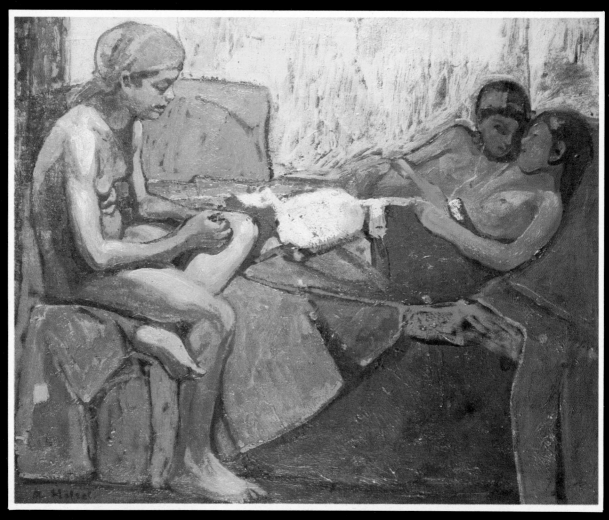

Adolf Hölzel 1853–1934, Composition with figures.
Oil on canvas, ca. 1908/10. 69 × 85 cm. Signed.
Venzmer IV 2.15.

BERND DÜRR GALLERY

20th Century Art

**Maximiliansplatz 20 · 8000 München 2 · Telefon 089/292626
Schellingstraße 13 · 8000 München 40 · Telefon 089/280873**

PAINTINGS · WATERCOLOURS · DRAWINGS
PRINTS · POSTERS · SCULPTURES
SECESSION · "JUGEND" · "SIMPLICISSIMUS"
EXPRESSIONISTS · CONTEMPORARY ART

"Local News" by James Hayllar, R.A. Exhibited at The Royal Academy 1890, 102 cm x 152 cm.

FIG.4 Governess – 'She sees no kind domestic visage near',
inscribed Richd Redgrave 1844, oil on canvas 90·7×60·3cm.
Sheepshanks Gift FA 168.

RICHARD REDGRAVE, RA
Artist and Administrator

Lionel Lambourne

On 26 May, 1861, in a rare moment of justifiable pride, Richard Redgrave wrote in his diary: 'Today the Ellison gift of watercolour paintings was opened to the public for the first time. I have taken much pains to secure the gift for the South Kensington Museum, and much trouble on the whole subject of watercolour art, of which there is now the beginning of a good collection, both in point of view of beauty and historically. I wonder whether I shall ever get the credit of having been the means of securing both the Sheepshanks and the Ellison Gift for the public?... Here is a bit of egoism!'

The Sheepshanks and Ellison gifts formed the foundation of the great collections of paintings at the Victoria and Albert Museum, and in 1983, a year which saw the opening of the Henry Cole Wing, named after Redgrave's longtime friend and collaborator, it is fitting that credit should be paid to the man chiefly responsible for forming the nucleus of the collections within the building. Curatorship was however only one of Redgrave's careers, for he also achieved eminence as artist, designer, teacher and art historian, and staunch and loyal friend to a whole generation of British artists. This brief account of his varied life will it is hoped reveal some aspects of the work of the twinkling, yet shrewd old gentleman who contemplates us quizzically, but hopefully with approval, in the vivacious sketch by his friend Sir Francis Grant in the National Portrait Gallery (FIG.1).

Richard Redgrave was born on 30 April, 1804 in Pimlico. Until the age of twenty he was employed in his father's wire-making factory, years which taught him, in his own words 'a real knowledge of several trades practised in the manufactury. Thus I became in time a pretty good carpenter, smith, wire worker, painter etc...' – skills which gave him invaluable practical experience utilised in his later roles as designer and administrator. But even more important as seminal influences on the young man who was to become one of the most compassionate artists of his time, were Redgrave's early experiences as debt collector for the business – 'the most painful period of my life', and his involvement with the domestic tragedies of his family circle.

Two incidents suffice from his autobiographical account of his early years to indicate Redgrave's gift for describing in words scenes which reveal his painter's eye for vivid pictorial detail. His mother suffered from consumption and 'knew she must soon leave her seven little ones... One evening the servant brought in the candles as I sat on a little stool by the invalid's side, and, hastily lighting them, left the room. The wicks were only just tipped with the slightest spark of flame, and I was about to move to try to make them burn, when my mother stopped me, saying "let them be, Dicky; if they

FIG.1 Richard Redgrave, aged 69, pen and wash sketch 15·3×11·6cm by Sir Francis Grant (1803–1878). Inscribed Richard Redgrave Esq RA., National Portrait Gallery NPG 1966–4486.

light I shall get better". How intently we both watched them! They had been cut too low, and first one, and then the other, choked with grease, died out into darkness.' Some years later in 1829 he writes of the death of his 'charming and beautiful sister, Jane; she pined over the duties of a governess away from home, caught typhoid fever, and was brought back only to die among us... in her twentieth year. An early winter had set in, but as we gathered round the narrow chasm into which her coffin was to be lowered, we perceived that it was not merely strewn with the rarest and choicest flowers, but that the floor of the grave was a perfect bed of blossoms. All we could learn was that a gentleman had driven to the churchyard early in the morning, and had carefully placed them in the grave'. How vividly both these prose descriptions anticipate the subjects of the artist's work in the 1840s, his most productive decade, when in a series of genre paintings he frequently depicted scenes of mourning and took pride 'in calling attention to the trials and struggles of the poor and oppressed'.

In 1826 at the age of twenty-two Redgrave entered the Royal Academy Schools, and for the next few years supported himself by an arduous routine of teaching, while exhibiting landscapes and the illustrative literary genre subjects so beloved by the early nineteenth century public. Even in these works his choice of subjects reveals his preference for themes in which woman's fortitude in unhappy circumstances was predominant, for he painted the story of Chaucer's patient *Griselda* on no less than three occasions, and scored early successes with a picture of George Crabbe's ill used heroine *Ellen Orford* in 1838, and *The Reduced Gentleman's Daughter* from Samuel Johnson's *The Rambler* in 1839. A fine example of a work of this

FIG.3 Cinderella about to try on the Glass Slipper, inscribed Richd Redgrave, oil on canvas 105·8×121cm. Sheepshanks Gift FA 167.   FIG.2 Ophelia weaving her Garlands, inscribed Richd Redgrave 1842, oil on canvas 75·6×63cm. Sheepshanks Gift FA 71.   Unless otherwise stated all works are by Richard Redgrave and in the Victoria and Albert Museum.

3

2

FIG.5 The Outcast, inscribed Richd Redgrave 1851, oil on
canvas 78·1×103·3cm. The Royal Academy of Arts.

FIG.11 Donatello. Signed with monogram, oil on canvas 262×86·9cm. Donatello is depicted holding the Martelli mirror (8717-1863), now catalogued as being Mantuan late fifthteenth century, but bought by J. Robinson, Redgrave's contemporary, in 1863, as being a Donatello. One of a series of paintings for the embrasures of the South Court of the Museum.

type is his *Ophelia weaving the Garlands* (FIG.2) exhibited in 1842, the same year in which he showed his *Cinderella about to try on the Glass Slipper* (FIG.3) a charming example of the early Victorian delight in pictures derived from fairy tales.

It was, however, in paintings implicit with contemporary social comment, that Redgrave found his most rewarding themes. They frequently dealt compassionately with the role of women, as in his other exhibit of 1842, *Bad News from the Sea*, and the extremely successful *The Sempstress* of 1844, inspired by Thomas Hood's poem *The Song of the Shirt*, a powerful comment on the 'sweated labour' which was the only available work for many women.

Another great success was the painting exhibited in 1843 as *The Poor Teacher*, which was so well received that he was commissioned to paint three additional versions of it, including one for John Sheepshanks, entitled *The Governess – 'She sees no kind domestic visage near'* (FIG.4). On receiving it, Sheepshanks objected to the terrible loneliness of the forlorn governess in the empty room, and at his request Redgrave added the playing children seen through the doorway. Every detail adds to the pathos of the scene – the words of the music on the piano 'Home, sweet Home', the tears in the governess's eye, her silk mourning dress, the well worn black edged letter, even the thin, dry toast on the plate. The success of such a work for its contemporary audience lay in its truth to their experience, and it is interesting in this respect to quote from an actual governess's letter, written in 1827 by Elizabeth Coxen (later the wife of John Gould, the ornithologist) the mood of which uncannily anticipates Redgrave's painting. She describes her pupil 'She is a perfect child in mind and manners, so that I cannot communicate a single thought or feeling in which she could share, and then for a little while I feel it miserably, wretchedly dull... The wind is howling a good deal tonight, & I think of my dear brother much & of the beloved lost one. I feel I shall be very miserable here... I was reading a few minutes since and met with some lines... which are certainly very appropriate to me just now:

'And I have not a common hope with any
... In uncommunicating solitude
Alone am I'.

Although it is significant that his choice for his Diploma picture, presented to the Royal Academy in 1851 when he became an Academician was *The Outcast* (FIG.5), depicting an unmarried mother, Redgrave was not, however, solely concerned with what would be described today as 'Feminist' themes. The cold statistical facts of emigration from Great Britain record that from a population of twenty-six millions over four millions emigrated during the two decades between 1840 and 1860. When interpreted in the terms of a family circle these statistics meant that one in six people left home for abroad in those years, rarely to return. The theme of emigration in literature and art was a topical one, immortalised by Dicken's Mr Micawber and Madox Brown's *The Last of England*. In 1858 Redgrave exhibited his own moving treatment of the subject *The Emigrant's Last Sight of Home* (FIG.6), now in the Tate Gallery. It is one of his most successful works, combining both his interest in the moving topic of those:

'Forced from their homes, a melancholy train
To traverse climes beyond the western main'

as described by the lines printed under the title in the Royal Academy catalogue, and one of his most attractive landscapes, the pictorial activity which was to preoccupy him increasingly during the latter part of his career as a painter. It was probably painted in Surrey near Abinger where in 1856 Redgrave had purchased a cottage for

FIG.6 The Emigrant's Last Sight of Home, inscribed Richd
Redgrave 1858, oil on canvas 67·9×98·4cm. The Tate
Gallery T 2100.

FIG.7 Wine Tray of papier mâché, inlaid with gold, mother of pearl ivory, and designed by Richard Redgrave, manufactured by Jennens and Bettridge. 132–1865.
FIG.8 Silver Christening Mug, with figures of guardian angels protecting children, inscribed on the base 'Hary Emanuel/ Manufacturer/ London 1865/ Chesnau/ chaser/ Designed by Richard Redgrave RA/ for Felix Summerly's Art Manufactures/ 1848'. 371–1865.   FIG.9 Water Carafe, clear glass enamelled and gilt with design of water plants, probably made by T. F. Christie & Co. 4503–1901.

7

8

9

FIG. 10 The Wedding Morning – The Departure, inscribed
Richd Redgrave 1845, pencil, heightened with white and
touched with colour 525×35cm. E2202–1932.

his summer vacations, only four miles from the holiday home of his friend Henry Cole.

It is not easy to summarise Redgrave's relationship with Henry Cole, but their friendship and working methods had some resemblance in comic terms to that of a 'straight man' – Cole, and his 'feed' – Redgrave. Together they certainly proved an unstoppable combination, for they shared a passionate belief that art education could improve society, which inspired their joint endeavours in founding the museum at South Kensington, and establishing Art Schools throughout the country.

They met in 1841, and Redgrave played a major part in all Cole's energetic schemes in the next decade to improve standards in the applied arts, editing *The Journal of Design*, founded in 1849, and designing some of the most attractive of Felix Summerly's Art Manufactures between 1846 and 1848. This venture was inspired by Cole's belief that it would 'promote public taste' if well known artists produced designs for manufactured articles in everyday use. Redgrave's contributions included a witty design for a shaving mug made by Wedgwood's; a wine tray of papier mâché made by Jennens and Bettridge (FIG. 7); a silver Christening mug produced by Hunt and Roskell (FIG. 8) and perhaps the most successful artifact a glass water carafe decorated with a naturalistic design of water plants (FIG. 9).

In 1846 Redgrave's letter to the Prime Minister, Lord John Russell, suggesting improvements in the Schools of Design, launched him on an intensely busy career as an administrator of the arts. He became successively Master, Head Master, Art Superintendent of the Department of Art, and Director of the Art Division, South Kensington Museum. When he retired in 1875 he could look with pride

at 120 flourishing Schools of Art where his elaborate curriculum of exercises and examinations enabled every child in the country to acquire a sound knowledge of 'elementary drawing'. But though he believed passionately in the value of drawing as a daily discipline, he himself was not one of Art's natural draughtsmen, like his friends Wilkie and Mulready, as a highly finished presentation drawing of 1845 *The Wedding Morning – The Departure* reveals (FIG. 10). For all its accomplishment, the drawing provides laboured evidence of a professionally acquired skill rather than a natural facility. It might almost have been produced to demonstrate that by taking pains it was possible to attain excellence as a draughtsman.

The official duties at South Kensington were only a part of the many activities which preoccupied Redgrave in the 1850s, and his daughter's *Memoirs* paint a lively picture of his crowded life – the design of the Duke of Wellington's funeral car, the organi-

sation of a large exhibition of British art in Paris, the hectic visits to Italy with Cole in search of exhibits for the for the Museum in South Kensington or ideas for the decorative schemes which to this day embellish its walls (FIG. 11). But it was his appointment, in 1857, on Cole's suggestion, to the post of Surveyor of the Queen's Pictures, which most occupied him, providing him with yet another career, that of Art Historian. He published an exemplary catalogue of the Royal Collection, and with his brother Samuel wrote *A Century of British Painters*, the first introduction to the history of the British School, which still today remains eminently readable, principally for the illuminating anecdotes on the artists Redgrave had either known personally or learned of by word of mouth from senior Academicans.

Such varied activities left far too little time for the active practice of painting, which became more and more restricted to the holiday months of summer at Abinger, and devoted solely to landscape. These late landscapes have been adversely criticised in recent years as being timid, dry and quasi-Pre-Raphaelite. But it would be hard to find more attractive examples of Victorian landscape painting than the watercolour of *Parkhurst Woods, Abinger* (FIG. 12), or the oil painting *The Sweet Summer Time*, (FIG. 13), both works rich in colour, and evocative of the heat and shade of high summer.

Although Redgrave was to live on until 1888, the last five years of his life were tragically marred by increasing blindness, and it is fitting to take our leave of him in the shared enjoyment of the fine sunshine of an English summer's day. It is hoped that in 1988 a centenary exhibition will be held in the Cole Wing which will fittingly commemorate the work of the man whose breadth of vision did so much to create the collections which we enjoy today.

FIG.12 Parkhurst Woods, Abinger, Surrey Inscribed. Richd
Redgrave 1865. Watercolour. 184–1889.   FIG.13 Sweet
Summer Time – Sheep in Wotton meadow near Dorking.
Inscribed Richd Redgrave 1869. Oil on panel
37·1×23cm. 232–1885.

12

13

GALERIE
BRUNO MEISSNER

Bahnhofstraße 14, CH-8001 Zürich   Telefon 01-211 90 00

Lucas Gassel
(1480–1555)

"Le Christ, Pierre et les disciples au lac de Tibériade"

Oil on wood
35 × 54 cm.

GALERIE
KURT MEISSNER

Florastraße 1, CH-8008 Zürich   Telefon 01-251 51 10

125

Galerie Römer

Rämistrasse 23, CH-8001 Zürich

Tel. 0041/1/476087

JEAN-ETIENNE LIOTARD

CHRIS BEETLES LIMITED

English Watercolours

104, Randolph Avenue
London W9 1PQ
Tel: 01-286 1404

A Watercolour dealer specialising in mainly 19th Century watercolours but with the largest stock in England of over 2000 watercolours from 1750 to contemporary works. The Gallery which is situated in Maida Vale (a mile from Marble Arch) can be viewed at any time including evenings and week-ends but by appointment only please.

ALBERT GOODWIN R.W.S. "Venice from Riva Schiavoni."
Signed, inscribed and dated 1896.

The above artist is one of those in which this gallery has specialised holdings. Other artists include: Alfred William Hunt, R.W.S., Myles Birket Foster, R.W.S., Helen Allingham, R.W.S., Hercules Brabazon Brabazon, John William North, A.R.A., William Henry Hunt, O.W.S., George Weatherill, William Fraser Garden, George Clausen, R.A., R.W.S. There is also a large stock of illustrators.

The art school huts, 1863, removed from Marlborough House to South Kensington, watercolour by A. Stannus, A.L.2817.

QUEEN MAB'S CHARIOT AMONG THE STEAM ENGINES

The V&A, the RCA and the Reform of Design

Christopher Frayling

The period immediately following the Great Exhibition of 1851 saw the transformation of the Government School of Design into the National Training School of Art, the transformation of the Government School's motley collection of visual aids into a Museum of Practical Art, and the building of a permanent home for them both on the estate of the Exhibition in 'South Kensington'. These great transformations were accompanied by a public debate about the proper role of art and design education, and the proper role of a Museum of design and decorative art (education and museum were usually treated by the participants as two sides of the same coin) – and the issues raised by this debate are not only of great relevance today, they are unresolved today. The Government School of Design begat the National Training School of Art, which in turn begat the Royal College of Art (in 1896). The visual aids begat the Museum of Manufactures, which begat the Museum of Ornamental Art, which begat the South Kensington Museum, which in turn begat the Victoria and Albert Museum (in 1899). College and Museum have tended to go their separate ways in the twentieth century – as the Royal College of Art has built on its world-wide reputation to become the only postgraduate university of art and design in Great Britain, and as the Victoria and Albert Museum has become the finest museum and archive of the decorative arts in the world – but it seems most timely, during the year in which the two institutions have formally re-established links with one another, to reconsider the circumstances and public debate to which they both owe their origins.

For the fifteen years between its foundation in 1837 and its transformation in 1852, the School of Design (together with its small assemblage of plaster casts and works of ornamental art) had been housed in three apartments at Somerset House which had been vacated by the Royal Academy: the School's exhibits had been specially purchased as aids for teaching in 'drawing from casts', 'modelling', 'outline drawing' and the 'History, Principles and Practice of Ornamental Design'. In summer 1852, these visual aids (which had been unceremoniously dumped in the cellars of Somerset House, because of 'want of accommodation' in the class rooms 'as well as in the house temporarily hired in the Strand for the female pupils') were moved to Marlborough House, where they formed the nucleus for a Museum of Manufactures: the School was moved there a year later to make room the General Registrar of Births, Deaths and Marriages at Somerset House. While the Museum was located in Marlborough House proper, the School was content with accommoda-

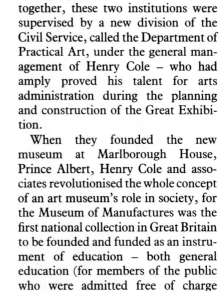

The School of Design at Somerset House, 1843 From the *Illustrated London News*.

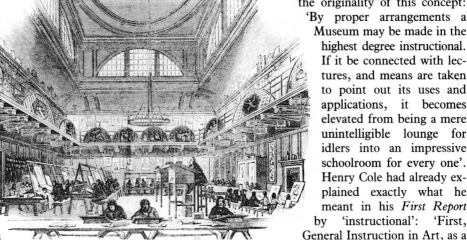

tion in some wooden huts which had been purpose-built in the courtyard: together, these two institutions were supervised by a new division of the Civil Service, called the Department of Practical Art, under the general management of Henry Cole – who had amply proved his talent for arts administration during the planning and construction of the Great Exhibition.

When they founded the new museum at Marlborough House, Prince Albert, Henry Cole and associates revolutionised the whole concept of an art museum's role in society, for the Museum of Manufactures was the first national collection in Great Britain to be founded and funded as an instrument of education – both general education (for members of the public who were admitted free of charge during the first half of the week, and on public holidays) and education for the students at the National Training School (who were granted privileged access to the collection during the second half of the week, for purposes of examining individual pieces and copying them, provided they washed their hands first). *The First Report of the Department of Practical Art*, released in January 1853, drew attention to the originality of this concept: 'By proper arrangements a Museum may be made in the highest degree instructional. If it be connected with lectures, and means are taken to point out its uses and applications, it becomes elevated from being a mere unintelligible lounge for idlers into an impressive schoolroom for every one'. Henry Cole had already explained exactly what he meant in his *First Report* by 'instructional': 'First, General Instruction in Art, as a

1 The Museum of Ornamental Art, Marlborough House,
1857, watercolour by W.L. Casey, A.L.7280. (Photograph:
Sir Geoffrey Shakerley). 2 The Duke of Wellington's
funeral car, 1852, detail of a lithograph by T. Picken after
L. Hague. (Photograph: Sir Geoffrey Shakerley).

1

2

The Science and Art Department's pillar box, 1857–9,
designed by the art students. (Photograph: Crown Copyright,
National Postal Museum).

branch of national education among all classes of the community, with the view of laying the foundation for correct judgement, both in the consumer and the producer of manufactures; second, Advanced Instruction in Art, with the view to its special cultivation; and lastly, the Application of the Principles of Technical Art to the improvement of manufactures, together with the establishment of Museums, by which all classes might be induced to investigate those common principles of taste, which may be traced in the works of excellence of all ages'. It was important for Cole and his associates in the Department to stress the 'instructional' aspect of the Museum's work, for the educational argument had helped parliament to vote the necessary funds. Equally, it was important for him to stress the commercial implications of the Art School's work – the National Training School would improve the quality of industrial design, which 'is so important in recommending the productions of industry to the tastes of the consumer' – for the commercial argument had persuaded a reluctant parliament to fund the Government School of Design in the first place. Nevertheless, these pragmatic considerations aside, Henry Cole fervently believed that a Museum of Manufactures could 'lay the foundation of correct judgement', and it could also play a crucial role in both the practical and the theoretical education of budding craftsmen and designers for industry. Not so very long before, members of the Select Committee on the Elgin Marbles had asked witnesses (in all seriousness) whether they had noticed a marked improvement 'in the state of the arts in this country, since the Collection has been open to the public': they asked this at a time when the Marbles had been 'open to the public' for just nine years.

The evangelising zeal of design re-

formers such as Henry Cole and Owen Jones was (and still is) easy enough to satirise. Charles Dickens was one of the first (and most famous) writers to make fun of their pretensions. In the second chapter of *Hard Times* – 'Murdering the Innocents' – a representative from the Department of Practical Art steps forward to take over Mr Gradgrind's lesson in elementary aesthetics. 'A Mighty man at cutting and drying, he was; a government officer; in his way (and in most other people's too), a professed pugilist;

always in training, always with a system to force down the general throat like a bolus, always to be heard of at the bar of his little Public Office, ready to fight all England . . . And he had it in charge from high authority to bring about the great public-office Millenium, when Commissioners should reign upon earth'. This formidable 'government officer' is visiting Coketown, perhaps to ensure that the teaching of Ornamental Art is in line with the principles laid down at Marlborough House rather than those laid down at Somerset House which have recently been superceded. When one of the students attending the lesson tells him that she would rather like to own 'a carpet bearing representations of flowers upon it' because she happens to be 'very fond of flowers', the man from the Ministry sternly informs her that in future she is '*never* to fancy', and then launches a fully-blown exposition of the Marlborough House theory of design and ornamental art:

'You are not to have, in any object of use or ornament, what would be a contradiction in fact. You don't walk upon flowers in fact; you cannot be allowed to walk upon flowers in carpets. You don't find that foreign birds and butterflies come and perch upon your crockery: you cannot be permitted to paint foreign birds and butterflies upon your crockery . . . You must use for all these purposes, combinations and modifications (in primary colours) or mathematical figures which are susceptible of proof and demonstration. This is the new discovery. This is fact. This is taste.'

At much the same time as the new system of art and design teaching was being 'forced down the general throat' in Coketown, a quiet City man by the name of Crumpet was visiting an exhibition of 'articles such as are of daily production' in the first room of the Museum of Manufactures at

1 Women art students painting tiles to decorate the Museum,
1870, from *The Graphic*. 2 Presentation of prizes to art
students by Prince Teck, in the Museum's new lecture
theatre, 1870, from *The Graphic*.

1

2

1 'Gentlemen's Mural Room'. (Photograph: RCA). 2 The sculpture school, 1905. (Photograph: RCA). 3 The sculpture school, 1932. (Photograph: RCA). 4 Students of 1905.

1

2

3

4

Marlborough House. This exhibition, which was linked to the course of instruction at the School of Art in the courtyard outside, showed a collection of objects 'which are only remarkable for their departure' from the principles of design which had been given the good housekeeping seal of approval by the Department of Practical Art and in particular by our friend 'the government officer'. Henry Morley wrote about Mr Crumpet, and his reactions to the exhibition, in an article for Charles Dickens' *Household Words* entitled *A House Full of Horrors*. It appears that after visiting Marlborough House, Mr Crumpet was shattered to discover that most of the fixtures and fittings in his own home were rather like the exhibits he had just seen in the Museum – and a consoling cup of tea only leads to further confusion in his mind: 'a Butterfly inside my cup! How horr horr horr i ble!'

That Dickens had Henry Cole in mind, when he introduced a 'government officer' to Mr Gradgrind's model school at the beginning of *Hard Times*, is revealed by the notes he took when preparing the novel (notes which are bound up with his manuscript draft of *Hard Times*, now in the Forster Collection, Victoria and Albert Museum) and by a letter he wrote to Henry Cole Esquire shortly after the novel's publication. In Dickens's notes for the second chapter, he lists 'Cole' among the cast of characters in Mr Gradgrind's classroom, and in his letter (dated 17 June 1854) he tells Henry Cole that he is passing the summer 'in the society of your friend Mr Gradgrind': 'I often say to Mr Gradgrind', he goes on, 'that there is reason and good intention in much that he does – in fact, in all that he does – but that he overdoes it. Perhaps by dint of his going his way and my going mine, we shall meet at last at some halfway house where there are flowers on the carpets,

and a little standing-room for Queen Mab's chariot among the Steam Engines'.

For Charles Dickens, it seems, the truth of the matter lay midway between the systems of Somerset House and Marlborough House – and the whole business could be shrugged aside as he got on with the work of promoting *Hard Times* (which makes no further reference to the 'government officer'). For others, who did not think that the 'government officer' and his system were quite so funny, the debate had a more urgent significance. Ralph Wornum, who was at that time a lecturer at the School of Design (and who was to become Keeper of the National Gallery) defended the School's mode of teaching – particularly its orientation towards the principles and practice of Fine Art – in a series of articles for the *Art-Journal* (January–February 1852). Wornum was concerned that Henry Cole's plans for a National Training School would result in too much *training* and not enough *education*: he was also convinced that it was wrong to base the School's curriculum exclusively on industrial and commercial applications. 'There is a distinct study of Design or Ornamental Art wholly independent of its application', he wrote, and the School's proper purpose should be 'to offer instruction of the highest description to all who desire to obtain a knowledge of Ornamental Art, and to supply a complete and systematic course of education in relation to *every kind* of decorative work'. Since industrial processes were changing all the time, the Training School could not hope to keep up with the latest developments or to teach designers to make best use of them: training of this kind could only take place in the industries concerned. There had undoubtedly been problems during the first fifteen years of the School of Design – resignations

of successive directors, student revolts, indecision about whether it was a trade school or an art school – but Henry Cole and his associates should never lose sight of the fact that the students needed (and wanted) 'cultivation of their taste' and 'aid in the principles and general capabilities of Ornamental Art'.

When he expressed the hope that teaching at a central School of Design would continue to be based on the principles and practice of Fine Art, Ralph Wornum was explicitly referring to the ideas of Sir Joshua Reynolds on the governance of 'an Academy of Arts'. For Reynolds had written in his *First Discourse* that 'an Academy founded upon considerations merely mercantile can never effect even its narrow purpose. If it has an origin no higher, no taste can ever be formed in manufactures: but if the higher Arts of Design flourish, these inferior ends will be answered of course'. Where the critics of the Somerset House system were concerned, there was no *of course* about it. The editors of the monthly *Journal of Design and Manufactures* – Henry Cole, Richard Redgrave and Owen Jones – were shocked to discover that 'although we have been studying drawing from the human figure, *it has not led us forward in ornamental design*'. On the contrary, the Government School had merely produced students with Fine Art aspirations who 'normally cover dog kennels with crochets and finials . . . and fall back on the dreary expedient of copying scroll and shell work or gothic panneling'. Since these students had been taught by 'dilettanti half-informed bunglers' (including Ralph Wornum, presumably) who had encouraged 'the sons of labouring men and such like to copy Ghiberti's gates, or the best of Giulio Romano's or of Mediaeval ornaments', the poor results were hardly surprising. 'No successful results can ever be

1 Industrial design workshop in the Royal College of Art.
(Photograph: RCA). 2 The Darwin Building of the Royal
College of Art, Kensington Gore. (Photograph: RCA).
3 Students of the History of Design and Decorative Art
course in their room in the Museum, 1983. (Photograph:
RCA).

QUEEN MAB'S CHARIOT AMONG THE STEAM ENGINES

Royal College of Art Charter Day, 1967. The Duke of
Edinburgh and Sir Colin Anderson; seated is Sir Robin
Darwin. (Photograph: RCA).

attained', the *Journal* concluded in February 1851, 'until the designer and the engineer know each other's business'.

In the event, Cole, Redgrave and Jones won the day. The National Training School opened in the courtyard of Marlborough House, and the *Journal of Design and Manufactures* immediately shut up shop, its mission achieved. The School's first major commission was the Duke of Wellington's funeral bier – designed by Richard Redgrave and Gottfried Semper and manufactured by the students. In the light of the *Journal's* comments about 'the designer and the engineer', it was ironic that this extraordinary construction – a showpiece for 'the government officer's' ideas – should turn into an engineering disaster: the wheels were far too small to carry the weight of the carriage, and the Iron Duke's last journey was interrupted as his transport sank into the ground in the middle of Horse Guards parade. History does not record how Ralph Wornum reacted to this unfortunate mishap.

The arguments used by the protagonists in the great debate about art and design education which occurred

in the years surrounding the Great Exhibition are still high on the agenda today. Should a School of Art and Design's prime objective be to *educate* or to *train* or *both*? If Fine Art is to be at the centre of a School's activity, is it necessarily the case that 'inferior ends will be answered *of course*'? Should a School of Art and Design aim to offer 'a complete and systematic course of education'? Is it such a bad thing to 'cover dog kennels with crochets and finials' (as it were)? The debate is as heated and as unresolved as ever. Only the elegance of expression has been lost.

The debate has even found its way in recent years into the new discipline known as the History of Design – a discipline which is even now in the process of maturing. Should this History of Design be a facsimile of the traditional History of Fine Art, with research into an apostolic succession of designer-heroes instead of artist-heroes, and with historians writing about the anglepoise lamp as if it had been designed by Leonardo da Vinci? Or should this History of Design take into account the sorts of considerations which designers and decorative artists must take into account in the real world – the principles, the processes,

the products, in short the many contexts for decisions about design? The joint Victoria and Albert Museum/ Royal College of Art Master of Arts course in *The History of Design and Decorative Art* aims to keep these important issues alive, and to contribute to the debate, by developing in its postgraduate students a historical, practical and aesthetic sense of design and design processes both in the past and in the present. One feature of the course will be to look back to the time when there was so much public interest in matters of 'Design' that novelists of the calibre of Charles Dickens felt impelled to write about them. A time when the histories of 'the Museum of Manufactures' and the 'National Training School of Art' were closely linked. The course has been founded in the belief that the Victoria and Albert Museum and the Royal College of Art still have much in common, in the 1980s. Henry Cole and Ralph Wornum may have disagreed about how best to establish a School of Art and Design, but on one thing they would surely have agreed. The two institutions belong together.

138

*crafts*council

12 Waterloo Place, London SW1

■ INFORMATION

*on makers, courses, materials,
shops, galleries, events*

■ SLIDE LIBRARY
■ INDEX

*over 20,000 slides for
reference or loan;
an index of selected makers,
and a register of craftspeople
all over England and Wales*

■ EXHIBITIONS

*a changing programme
of exhibitions in the
Crafts Council Gallery
at Waterloo Place.
The Crafts Council also
tours many of its
exhibitions nationally*

■ COLLECTION

*objects available for
loan to organisations*

■ PUBLICATIONS

*books, catalogues,
slidepacks, video, films,
Crafts magazine*

■ EDUCATION

*conferences, seminars,
school visits, school
newspaper*

■ GRANTS & LOANS

*schemes to assist makers at
various stages in their careers*

■ COFFEE BAR

*enjoy a visit to the
Crafts Council*

*The Crafts Council administers an
annual grant from the Office of Arts
and Libraries for the support of the
crafts in England and Wales and the
promotion of the work of artist
craftspeople.*

*Details of the Council's work in the
fields of grants and loans, education,
conservation, information, exhibitions and publications may be obtained
by visiting the Gallery and Information Centre, or by post or telephone.*

*12 Waterloo Place
Lower Regent Street
London SW1Y 4AU*

*For further information
telephone 01-930 4811*

*Tuesday – Saturday 10 – 5
Sunday 2 – 5
Closed Monday and public holidays*

M. DARLING
LIMITED
FINE ANTIQUES AND WORKS OF ART

250 MERCER STREET, MERCER SQUARE B 707, NEW YORK, NEW YORK 10012

TELEPHONE: 212-598 4166

CABLE: DARLINGART, NEW YORK

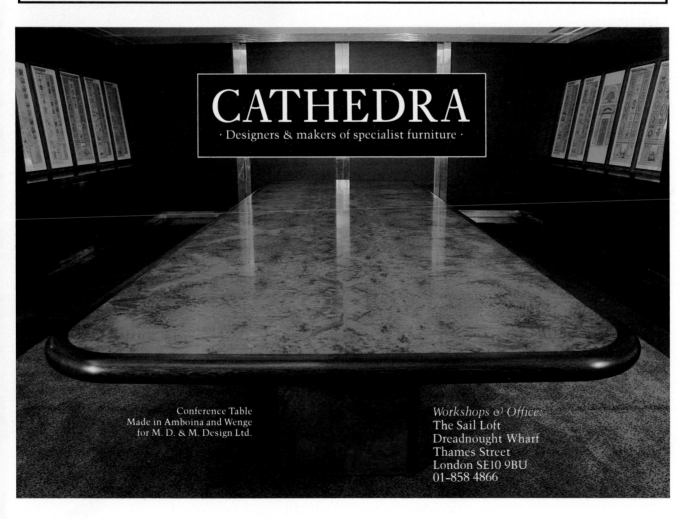

FIG. 1 The Kitchen. (Photograph: Sir Geoffrey Shakerley).

THE SEVENTEENTH-CENTURY KITCHEN AT HAM HOUSE

Caroline Davidson

Question: what is the most difficult room to restore in an old house? Answer: the kitchen.

Kitchens contain far more objects than any other room (a well stocked library is the only exception). Furthermore, a large proportion of kitchen objects, being humble and ephemeral in nature, are now obscure. Innovations in cooking technology, changes in eating habits and the introduction of new materials and manufacturing methods make this inevitable. And, of course, the further back one goes in time, the harder it becomes to find surviving examples in good condition. Providing one has the money, it is really much easier to restore a state bedchamber or a drawing-room than a kitchen. But not, I suspect, so interesting or as much fun.

When I first saw the kitchen at Ham House one cold winter's morning in January 1980, it was almost bare. There was an imposing Victorian-style iron range stamped 'Dobbie Forbes and Co, Lambeth 1947' in the fireplace, with a separate iron boiler jutting into the room. On the stone flags stood various domestic curiosities of the nineteenth century: a coal waggon, a fire extinguisher on wheels, a 'Kent' knife cleaner, and a hastener for warming plates and dishes before the fire. (These and several other interesting oddments are now on display outside the kitchen.) From the walls dangled unidentified rusty objects dug up by the gardeners. All that remained of the seventeenth century was the enormous table in the middle of the room which must have been built with the house in 1610, the thick dresser boards running along the wall opposite the fireplace, most likely of the same date, two shelves above on carved supports which could be dated to the 1670s, a marble mortar and a black hearth brush. Another dresser with built-in cupboards below was probably eighteenth century, as were some of the extra shelves.

Peter Thornton and his colleagues had long wanted to restore the kitchen to its appearance during the 1670s when Ham House was enjoying its greatest prosperity under Elizabeth, Countess of Dysart, and her second husband, the Duke of Lauderdale, Secretary of State for Scotland under Charles II. They had already restored the lavish state and family apartments on the two floors above, but now wanted to bring to life some of the main rooms below stairs. Fortunately, the three inventories compiled in 1677, 1679 and 1683 which had proved so useful upstairs also listed the contents of the kitchen and the other domestic offices. (These consisted of two larders, a scullery, dairy, bake-house and still-house, four cellars for beer and wine, the Usher of the Hall's office, the servants' hall and a laundry.) Since the Department did not feel competent to deal with them, they invited me to help, knowing that I had already done a certain amount of work on seventeenth-century domestic life and had a particular interest in kitchens.

After collating the three inventories, I came up with an 'official' list of contents for the kitchen which included approximately 180 objects (see below). The inventories showed that the kitchen at Ham House was at the forefront of technological progress in cooking methods. For example, entries for a coal basket (1677) and an iron range with a sliding cheek to alter the size of the fire (1683), prove that food was being cooked over a coal-burning 'open' range rather than a simple hearth burning wood or peat. This arrangement was about a century ahead of its time: Thomas Robinson is usually credited with having 'invented' the open range with his patent of 1780. The listing of a jack with three chains is another indication that the kitchen was avant-garde, since the turning of spits by mechanical means was still a novelty in seventeenth-century England. The six stewing pans listed in 1677 and seven stewing dishes listed in 1683 are also significant, since they suggest that there must have been a charcoal-burning brick stewing stove in the kitchen, a feature which was rarely found in country houses before the middle of the eighteenth century.

The inventories were also very helpful in providing a 'shopping list' of the most valuable items in the kitchen: the furniture, fittings, and substantial metal objects. But that was as far as they went. They did not mention any treen, ceramics, glass, or textiles, the less expensive but still indispensable things which create the 'clutter' found

FIG.5 Frontispiece from *The Queen-like Closet: or, Rich Cabinet*, stored with all manner of rare receipts for preserving, candying and cookery, by Hannah Woolley, first published in 1670.

FIG.6 One of several food-related illustrations from Johann Comenius's Latin primer for children, *Orbis sensualium pictus*. This invaluable book, which shows scenes from everyday life with explanatory keys, was first published in Nuremburg in 1658. The first English edition, published in London in 1689, made use of the same illustrations. This one is entitled 'cookery'. (Courtesy, Henry Francis du Pont Winthertur Museum Library: Collection of Printed Books).

in a working kitchen.

To identify these missing items, I started to read seventeenth-century cookery books in a new light. I was less interested in learning about the gastronomy of the period than in spotting references to kitchen equipment in the recipes and noting their context and frequency. The results were extremely interesting. For one thing I discovered the universality of the pipkin, a small pot or pan, with or without a lid, usually made of earthenware, which came in different shapes and sizes (pipkins were used interchangeably with earthenware dishes and pans). The pipkin was commonly used for boiling and stewing, but also as a temporary storage vessel ('let the broth stand in an earthenware pot or pipkin till it be cold') and as a bain-marie (one way of cooking salmon was to put it and some liquid into a large pipkin with a cover and immerse this in a brass water kettle of 'seething' water). For another, I found that seventeenth century cooks employed all sorts of things for strain-ing food: coarse or fine lawn cloths, hair sieves, jelly bags, strainers made out of tiffany or cushion canvas, as well as earthen and metal colanders. They beat egg whites with birch whisks, boiled puddings in napkins and wiped away crumbs with birds' wings. To see whether boiled pippins (apples) were tender they tried to prick a rush or a bodkin through them.

The more recipes I read, the more details I picked up. I hadn't grasped, for example, that seventeenth century cooks used so much paper. Pasties were often put on paper before baking and almond biscuits baked on 'paper plates'. By the time I had subjected five cook books to a complete textual analysis, I felt I was going mad: there were so many new categories of ephemeral culinary objects to worry about. How could I know exactly which ones would have been in the kitchen at Ham House in the 1670s?

Fortunately, it was just at this point that I had a stroke of luck. This was the discovery that among the seventeenth-century manuscript archives from Ham House, carefully catalogued and conserved in the strong room of the Buckminster Park estate office near Grantham in Lincolnshire, were numerous documents dealing with the kitchen. I had written to the descendants of Elizabeth, Countess of Dysart, by her first husband, Sir Lionel Tollemache, to see if they had any relevant family papers in their possession. A helpful letter soon came back from Major General Sir Humphrey Tollemache saying that his son, Mr Lyonel Tollemache, had consulted the index to the family archives and found 'a dozen or so references which would seem to be worth following up'. Mr and Mrs Tollemache then very kindly invited me to spend a couple of days looking at the archives at Buckminster Park. Little did I expect the treasure trove which awaited me. For the archives are so comprehensive in their scope that, if properly analysed (preferably with the help of a computer), they would present an almost complete

FIG.7 An important English source of visual and written information is Randle Holme's treatise on heraldry, *The Academy of Armory*, 1688. A typical page of useful illustrations is reproduced here. 1 Covered salt seller; 2 Salt seller with an open cover; 3 Jugge; 6 Viall, or viniger bottle, or a cruce; 7 Ewer; 8 Cup-ewer; 9 Square salt or dish stand; 11 Capsula, Chopping knife, Ladle skellet; 15 Silver dust, or peper pot; 16 Dish; 17 Ovall dish; 18 Potinger, Fire or Grate Rack; 19 Stand, or a stand for a dish; 23 Spoone; 24 Scummer, Cake Paddle or Back Spittle; 25 Ladle between a paire of Racks; 26 Fire shovell; 27 Paire of Tonges; 28 Paire of Tonges; 29 Paire of Bellowes; 30 Three square Trevett . . . also called Brandretts, Brand Irons, Iron crowes, with three feet; 31 Trevet or a Tripode; 33 Square Trevett; 34 Engine rack, Oval dripping pan; 35 Square dripping pan with handles; 36 Forke, or a Flesh forke; 37 Two table forkes, or two toasting Forks; 38 Flesh pott, or a Brasse pott; 39 Paire of hanging pot hookes; 40 Pott rack; 41 Grid-Iron; 43 Besom; 44 Possett pott; 46 Stew pan; 53 Cullander, Chaffeing dish; 54 Warming pan, Frying pan; 55 Ferris, or steel to strike fire jack broach; 56 Morter and Pestell; 57 Morter; 58 Tub, or Turnell with handles; 59 Basket, or round Twiggen Basket; 85 Fruite Baskett; 86 Round Twiggen Arme baskett; 87 Egge Baskett, or a Butter Baskett; 90 Kettle; 93 Tub; 94 Possnett.

FIGS.2,3 The Kitchen. (Photographs: Sir Geoffrey Shakerley).

2

3

FIG.4 The Larder. (Photograph: Sir Geoffrey Shakerley).

FIG.8 This illustration by Wenceslaus Hollar was taken as a model for restoring the larder adjacent to the kitchen at Ham House. It comes from an edition of Aesop's Fables published in London in 1665. (By permission of the Trustees of the British Museum). FIG.9 'Angling', detail of a print by Wenceslaus Hollar, mid-seventeenth-century. The fish basket was specially reproduced for the kitchen at Ham House. (By permission of the Trustees of the British Museum). FIG.10 Another of Wenceslaus Hollar's illustrations for Aesop's Fables. The cupboard in the background is strikingly similar to the dresser with built-in cupboards in the kitchen at Ham House. The rush-seated chair by the fireplace provided one of the prototypes for reproduction. (By permission of the Trustees of the British Museum). FIG.13 Print by Geertruyt Rogman showing numerous kitchen utensils, Dutch, mid-seventeenth-century. (By permission of the Trustees of the British Museum).

8

9

10

13

FIG. 11 Illustration from a Dutch emblem book, *Het Leerzaam Huisraad* by Jan Luyken (1649–1712). This sort of picture is helpful in showing the arrangement of objects on the shelves and on the floor. (Courtesy, Henry Francis du Pont Winthertur Museum Library: Collection of Printed Books). FIG. 12 Another of Jan Luyken's illustrations for *Het Leerzaam Huisraad*. The hearth brush in the middle of the picture is almost identical to the one found in the kitchen at Ham. (Courtesy, Henry Francis du Pont Winthertur Museum Library: Collection of Printed Books).

picture of life at Ham House during the seventeenth century.

For the purpose of restoring the kitchen, I made three important finds. The first consisted of five volumes of detailed weekly accounts of general domestic expenditure from 1661 to 1683. These books record all the everyday objects and materials that were bought to keep the house going, some of which are specifically recorded as being 'for ye cook'.

The second discovery consisted of 12 volumes of detailed weekly expenditure on food from 1661 to 1697 showing exactly what foodstuffs were being consumed at Ham, the quantities bought, and their cost. This meant that I could restore the kitchens to a particular time of year, with typical foods on display. (I plumped for late June/ early July, this being peak visiting time.)

Finally, I found a collection of bills which threw new light on the kitchen itself. For instance, a mason's bill of November 1674 for some new ironwork 'about ye stove in ye kitchen' confirmed my view that there must have been a stewing stove in the room. A bricklayer's bill for 1673 for making up a wall at the kitchen door, suggests that the passage from the kitchen to the courtyard was added to the house at this date. (This passage, incidentally, is included in the kitchen restoration, along with the larder next door.)

So much for establishing what fixtures, fitments and objects filled the kitchen three centuries ago. This was only part of the job. I also had to know what the objects looked like and how they were made. Fortunately, this was surprisingly easy. Had I been restoring a farm labourer's kitchen in some isolated part of England, I would have

been limited to English picture sources, surviving artifacts, and evidence from local archaeological digs. But not so with Ham House. Elizabeth, Countess of Dysart, and the Duke of Lauderdale were wealthy, sophisticated people. They had travelled in Europe and had no difficulty in ordering anything they fancied from the Continent, as the account books at Buckminster Park testify. I therefore felt justified in supplementing my English picture sources with Continental ones (particularly illustrated emblem books and Dutch genre paintings) and examining objects in Continental museums.

As the specifications file grew fatter, I began to spend more and more time combing antique shops and markets in search of acquisitions for the kitchen. As I expected, I didn't find much. It was necessary to widen the search. I

11

12

FIG.14 Print by Abraham Bosse (1602–1676) of bakers at work, French, c.1640. (By permission of the Trustees of the British Museum.)

began to scour the reserve collections of other museums for objects to borrow (many of my finds are now on display in the kitchen). I also launched a public appeal for information and donations. The response was most enthusiastic. People wrote in with useful suggestions and, in many cases, with specific offers. Some of these, of course, turned out to be unsuitable (one old lady presented a 1920s tin spoon, confident that it was pewter and 'very old'), but others were just what was wanted. Furthermore, an increasing number of antique dealers came to hear of the project and to take an interest in it. At the same time, I was commissioning, on behalf of the Museum, reproductions from some 20 craftspeople, a

fascinating but time-consuming operation because of the detailed preparation and discussion required.

By the end of June, when the kitchen was opened to the public, its restoration was by no means finished. But this 'work in progress' at Ham House already presented the most complete picture of a late seventeenth-century kitchen in England.

The official list of contents of the kitchen at Ham House, based on the inventories of 1677, 1679 and 1683:

1 tin APPLE ROASTER. 1 copper BASKET. 1 copper BASIN. 1 pair of BELLOWS. 2 iron CANDLE-STICKS. 3 CHAIRS. 1 leather CHAIR. 2 CLEAVERS. 2 COLANDERS (at least one being brass). 1 COPPER to boil meat. Iron serving DISHES. 7 stewing DISHES. 4 brass DISHES for servants' meat. 2 copper DISHES for meat. 2 tin DREDGING BOXES. 4 DRESSER-BOARDS. 1 FENDER. 1 FLOUR BOX. 1 fire FORK. 1 flesh or beef FORK. 1 FORM. 1 iron GRATE with sliding cheek. 1 tin GRATER. 2 GRIDIRONS. 1 JACK with three chains. 1 brass water KETTLE. 1 fish KETTLE and false bottom. 2 chopping KNIVES. 3 mincing KNIVES. 1 brass basting LADLE. 1 brass LADLE. 12 brass LARDING PINS. 1 brass MORTAR with an iron PESTLE. 2 marble MORTARS with PESTLES. 1 stone MORTAR with wooden PESTLE. 1 brass PAIL. 1 PAIRING SHOVEL. 1 large carp PAN and COVER, with false bottom. 2 iron dripping PANS. 3 frying PANS. 9 SAUCEPANS. 6 STEWING PANS. 4 PATTYPANS with 3 COVERS and 2 sets of PATTYPANS. 12 PATTEITS. PEWTER PLATES, DISHES and MAZARINES. 2 pastry PEELS. 2 POT HOOKS. 5 brass POTS and 4 COVERS. 1 pair iron RACKS. 2 iron RINGS. 1 ROLLING PIN. 2 SHELVES. 1 fire SHOVEL. 2 SKIMMERS. 1 SPICE BOX. 6 SPITS. 9 lark SPITS. 1 brass SPOON. 1 iron STAND. 1 TOASTING IRON. TONGS. 1 wooden TRAY. 9 iron TRIVETS. 3 TUBS (1 for rinsing, 1 for salt and 1 for flour).

Home Again

Mary Ellen Best, *The Kitchen at Elmswell Hall, York,* signed and dated May 1834, watercolour, 254 by 35.5 cm.
Sold at Sotheby's New York on 21st January 1983 for $4,125 (£2,567); purchased by the Victoria & Albert Museum.

This delightful little watercolour recently crossed the Atlantic to Sotheby's
saleroom in New York, before returning to its final home in
the Victorian & Albert Museum.
It is one of forty seven recently discovered paintings by a nineteenth century
amateur artist, Mary Ellen Best. She left a fascinating record of her family and
friends, painting them in the interiors of the Yorkshire homes in which she grew up
— Elmswell Hall, Langton Hall and Howsham Hall.
Painted in May 1834, the kitchen at Elmswell Hall is typical of the painstaking
attention to detail which makes her work a valuable record of nineteenth-century
domestic life.

Sotheby Parke Bernet & Co.,
34-35 New Bond Street, London W1A 2AA Telephone: (01) 493 8080 Telex: 24454 SPBLON G

Sotheby's

aren/ki REVISITED

by Tom Lee

Ensconced in the stalls at the Royal Opera House, in excited anticipation of the premiere of Nureyev's balletic treatment of 'The Tempest', Shakespeare's "terminal search for the divine secrets of his own art", I was jolted from my reverie by a dull thud (I guess from an over-anxious or clumsy scene-shifter) which recalled to mind something I'd read about Tsar Nicholas II. When one of his prime ministers was assassinated during an interval at the ballet, the undisturbed monarch at first thought the shot was the sound of an opera-glass falling from a box into the stalls below, a frequent occurence in the days when most well-heeled theatre-goers possessed their own.

Indeed, I remember handling an exquisite Fabergé opera-glass from the Tsar's collection, some months before, at the Arenski Gallery. In my mind's eye I could both feel and see it – a delicate cinnamon coloured enamel with twisted bands of leaves in yellow and red gold set with diamonds – a delight to look at as well as to look through.

Idly glancing through the programme I was pleasantly surprised to come across a reprint of an article I'd written about Arenski. It had been some time since my last visit, and as Tchaikovsky's concord of sweet sounds enveloped me, I determined to rectify the situation as soon as possible, as each previous visit had left me with further delightfully indelible memories.

Two days later, still buoyed-up with exhilaration at the sheer power of Anthony Dowell's Prospero, David Wall's forceful and dark Caliban, Wayne Eagling's soaring Ariel, and the touching love of Ashley Page and Lesley Collier as Ferdinand and Miranda; I arrived at the Arenski Gallery, a stone's-throw from the Wallace Collection in George Street W1, and after a lingering appraisal of the superb items displayed in the window, rang the bell and awaited admission.

It was mid-morning and a beaming Mr. Vaswani greeeted me, and at once asked me to join him and Mr. Arenski for a cup of coffee. Imagine my pleasure; not just a visit to a superb ever-changing collection, not only a guided tour, but the delight of good conversation. It is difficult not to be infected by the enthusiasm of such idealistic dealers and collectors.

Mr. Arenski delights in a sense of humour. When a recent prospective, but not very perspicacious, customer enquired, "Are these reproductions?" he replied, "Yes certainly – in the 19th century ideas were copied from the previous century." When a woman seeking a superb coffee table, but who had neglected to offer the courtesy of a good morning when she entered the Gallery, Mr. Arenski startled her by declaring, "I do hope you never find what you're looking for!" pausing for a well-timed second, and then qualified it with, "Just think, if you find it, the fun and excitement of your search will be over!" a fair summary of his own attitude to the finely crafted objects he sells. The dealer's urge to possess beautiful objects is complemented by buyers with like taste who by dispossessing the dealer drive him to seek replacements. Mr. Arenski would probably agree with Dostoevsky that: "Without art a man might find his life on earth unlivable."

David Arenski keeps away from customers because of his sardonic sense of humour, which he fears may on occasion quite unintentionally startle people. Sometimes mildly provocative and gently teasing, he is never malevolent. He informs, amuses and provokes yet with an assured uninhibitedness. One suspects that whoever is offended by his sense of fun deserves to be. He is more than often away searching and collecting for treasures and leaves the Gallery in the capable hands of Pritam Vaswani, an altogether gentler and far more patient character whose conversational manner gives one the impression that he is forever letting you into a confidence. He allows the customer to roam undisturbed, unless information is required, and such unobtrusive courtesy and friendliness so enhances the joy of looking.

While sale rooms have encouraged direct sales, the urgency engendered is often destructive of confidence. One doesn't have the time to choose carefully in a situation intent only on a quick turnover requiring immediate decision. But a dealer who encourages you to take your time, who offers you friendly advice, whose individual taste has dictated the content of his shop, a deliberate choice of quality objects which reflect his own enthusiasms; such a dealer inspires confidence and a like enthusiasm.

Fortified with excellent coffee drunk from fine bone china, and still chuckling at the anecdotes, I began a slow tour. A pattern and logic emerges as the eye is led from one resplendent object to another. The Gallery is filled with objects exposed to a good deal of indirect light from the large plate-glass windows and a few subtle spotlights. Light breaks and glows on the patina of fine furniture, the glass of cabinets, the bronze of statues themselves reflected in mirrors, each reflection like a note of music, building up to a whole run of chords that is both stimulating and soothing, and extraordinarily enjoyable. There is an element of unabashed theatricality.

Although there are pieces from other eras, the predominant period is the 19th century, and the bulk of it from the latter part, known as the Belle Epoque, those magical years before 1914 evoked by Proust in 'Remembrance of Things Past', and depicted superbly in a group portrait of four sisters by John Da Costa, 1867–1931, an unjustly neglected artist. The daughters of William Glen Walker are four nice young things, standing or sitting with winsome hauteur, immaculate and totally assured. Since Da Costa shortly after married one of them it was most likely a good natured sitting and the ladies certainly seem relaxed, even perhaps in jokey mood. By contrast, "The Spanish Hat" – a portrait of Mrs. Gerard Chowne, by Sir John Lavery, is of a very elegant and pensive lady. Not so 'Jane', one of the many superb and stunning portraits of his wife by Sir Gerald Kelly. Painted about 1924 it portrays a stylish and attractive woman, hand on hip, coolly examining us from eyes shadowed by her cloche hat, her chin hidden by an intimidating fur collar creating a feeling of mystery. Next to her is a beautiful portrait of a seated nude also by Kelly of a mulatto girl entitled 'Golly'. Her skin is palpably warm and in a deceptive light might well appear to breathe.

In a neo-Gothic cabinet resides fine English glass of 18th and 19th century. High up in another cabinet a magnificent pair of Minton polychrome Pâte-sur-Pâte vases, exhibited at the Paris International Exhibition in 1878, betray a Pompeian inspiration. They are superbly modelled pieces with gilt rope-twist handles, quite different from the many richly coloured glazed pieces of Minton majolica which Arenski also collects and which were among the most popular prized ceramics in the Victorian home. I must admit to having been bowled-over by a pair of majolica pots and stands replete with winged mermaids and exotic sea creatures.

Arenski is also an enthusiastic authority and collector of Georgian and Victorian papier mâché and japanned ware, and has gathered together an enviable collection ranging from armchairs and desks to beautiful trays, recently loaning a number of items to the Wolverhampton Art Gallery for an exhibition devoted to these wares. From the days when only the aristocracy could afford such fine things comes a most rare suite of early George III Mahogany Hall Seat Furniture, a pair of two-seater settees and four armchairs. From the same era an elegant pair of mahogany three-tier Dumb-Waiters with graduated revolving shelves on moulded scroll supports. The circular trays have little galleries made of turned spindles with a nice moulded top rail – the whole of a delicate design that required the luxury of some craftsman's long and costly labour.

I was attracted too by a couple of charming bronzes of children, apparently two of a quartet made of Queen Victoria's children, modelled as the Four Seasons by Mary Thornycroft; and an amazing Sheffield plated 'Teasmade' from 1810. Two feet high it probably graced an elegant sideboard in a drawing room, rather than a bedside cabinet, and dispensed both tea and coffee through separate spigots, the hot water descending from a revolving spherical upper container to the hemispherical base containing three separate compartments.

There is a small cabinet in the form of a sedan-chair housing some surprising bibelots by Fabergé, a couple of coronets (perhaps mislaid by absent-minded duchesses), a magnificent silver-gilt travelling picnic canteen made in the year that America declared its independence, and a truly lovely Minton Parian-Ware 'Boy on a Dolphin'. The modelling is so exquisite that what we see is not imaginary motion represented, but real motion momentarily arrested.

More sporting is a cabinet full of beakers, jugs and tumblers made by Doulton in the days of W. G. Grace, embellished with cricketing motifs. One Antipodean enthusiast for cricketing memorabilia phones Arenski from his home in Australia to arrange purchases of new pieces; ringing back several times to haggle over the price before settling for the original price. One suspects that he has come to enjoy the pleasure of good conversation even at such great a distance.

Current favourite exhibit is an Italian mahogany armchair that could have been made for Firbank's Cardinal Pirelli. Topped with a coronet between threatening eagle heads, the back and seat in scarlet upholstery, framed by twist-turned uprights and armrests in the form of amiable lions, on foliate carved legs with paw feet; it dates from 1870, that year when Pope Pius IX had the temerity to declare himself infallible, and almost immediately lost the Papal States to a newly united Italy. A small book resides on the seat as if the Cardinal has just stepped out for a moment. Maybe he's gone for a coffee?

The art of the 19th century measured itself against an ideal past, the craftsmanship of the Renaissance, and it had similar patrons. It was a new, or maybe continued, Renaissance among carpenters and blacksmiths, stone masons, and weavers, when they took creative pride in their work, and each generation found some new thing to do. It was a custom-built era. One's swelling admiration at the sight of an achievement must be for the man or woman from whom it came, for the power and the radiant vision within them. In an era without subsidies and hand-outs, men traded achievements and, like Prospero, conjured marvels from their imaginations.

Few of us can resist the temptation of looking through a window as we pass by. A peep into Arenski gives a fascinating insight into past decor, design and taste, when people decorated their household interiors to reflect the finest talent of their days, and when craftsmen passionately looted earlier historical styles, elaborating or simplifying them according to their taste and skill. The student of this period need not be afraid of rapidly exhausting its possibilities for surprise.

The Arenski Gallery is ever eager to indulge our nostalgia for a past of conspicuous consumers who taunted utility with indistrious ardour, at a time when luxury was still an art. The Gallery is a wealth of selection, not of accumulation. It justifies Andre Malraux's contention that, "Art seems the rectification of the world, a means of escaping from man's estate."

29-31 george /treet london wih 5pf   tel. 01 - 486 0678

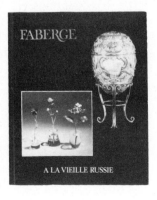

FIG. 1 Nautilus shell cup with enamelled gold mounts, Dutch, about 1630–40, perhaps by Jean Bellequin (c.1597–1636) of Amsterdam. Inv. no. M179–1978. H. 20.4 cm. (Photograph: Jeremy Whitaker).

NATURE, THE ONLY TEACHER
A Nautilus Cup from a Noble Polish Collection

Anna Somers Cocks

In 1978 the Metalwork department was lucky enough to buy an exquisite seventeenth century *Wunderkammer* piece with an ancient provenance (FIG.1). It is a nautilus shell, the outer striped layer partly etched away to leave a cage of C-scrolls on the surface, and with insects minutely engraved on the mother-of-pearl beneath. The mounts are of gold, enamelled white and then painted in black enamel with raggedy, fleshy leaves, insects and stylised flowers. The original case, of tooled red leather, survives, and on its side is a much rubbed coat-of-arms which is just legible as being that of the Mniszech family: *gules, three ostrich feathers sable*. According to family tradition among the Potockis, from whom the cup was bought, it was part of the dowry brought by Josephine Amelia Mniszech to her marriage with Stanislas Felix Potocki (d.1805). The most likely ancestor of hers to have acquired it is her great-great-great-grandfather, Francis Bernard Mniszech (d.1661), a brother of the famous Marina, best known in England for her part in the opera *Boris Goudonov;* she was married to first one, then the other pseudo-Dmitri, both pretenders to the Russian throne after the death of Boris.

The shell was originally inhabited by an inkfish called *Nautilus pompilius* L., a species found in the Persian Gulf and the seas around Ceylon, Malacca, the Moluccan Isles and Macassar. Such shells were imported in ever larger numbers by the Dutch East Indies Company during the sixteenth and seventeenth centuries. The accretions on the outside were cleaned off, and the outer striped layer either totally removed to reveal the mother-of-pearl surface beneath, or partly etched away, as here, to give contrasting texture or colour. The first four or five chambers of the 'coil' were nearly always cut through to resemble a helm with the mantelling and crest behind it. FIG.2

shows all that remains of this feature on the V&A's shell. Its mother-of-pearl has been meticulously engraved with insects of various sorts: in FIG.1, for example, three moths can be seen to the right of the strap mount, a may-fly is disappearing beneath the mount, while to the left of it are a garden cross spider, a bee and a fly; on the other side are another fly, three moths, a ground beetle, and one imaginative invention. The insects enamelled on the foot (FIG.3) repeat in a slightly simplified form, because of the relative clumsiness of the technique, some of the insects on the shell – for example, the imaginary one with six dots. This confirms that the mounts were made for this shell, and they can be dated around 1630–40 because of the style of the foliage. Such fleshy ivy-type leaves, combined with 'commas' and 'dots' is

FIG.2 The helm carved in the shell, traces of the engraved mantelling remain. (Photograph: Jeremy Whitaker).

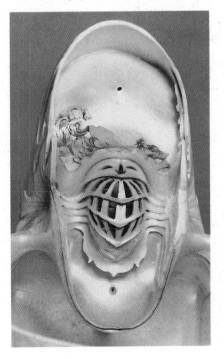

called the 'pea-pod' style and was used by goldsmiths, particularly enamellers, from the 1620s until about 1640 when it was replaced by a realistic naturalism. It seems to have been a French invention, as the published designs show: for example, Balthasar Lemersier's set dated 1626 and Pierre Boucquet's *Livre de toutes sortes de feuilles* of 1634. But the style spread quickly throughout Northern Europe, and can be found on goldsmiths' work from England to Prague, therefore one must return to the engraving on the shell to find out where this object was made.

There are four surviving shells which are clearly by the same hand. All have the outer surface etched away, leaving long sweeping C-scrolls which at certain points 'run through' each other; all have the helms engraved in the same way; two are engraved with insects just like ones on the V&A example, and two have insects combined with figures from Jaques Callot's (1597–1635) *Balli di Sfessania* and *Les Caprices et Les Fantaisies* published between 1621 and 1628.

Of the two with insects alone, one (Sted. Museum 'Het Prinsenhof', Delft) has a tall embossed silver foot and stem in the auricular style made by Willem Claesz Brugman in Delft in 1651; the other, a very broken example, (National Museum, Prague) is unmounted. The first shell (in the art trade, 1968) with engravings after Callot has a very plain silver foot made in the Hague in 1700, and it still has its complete coat of arms showing that it belonged to a certain Johannes Gansneb Tengnagel (d.1676) who was mayor of Kampen; the other Callot shell (Poldi Pezzoli Museum, Milan) is unmounted apart from a silver strengthening rim where the chambers have been cut away, through which a cord can be threaded so that the shell may be hung up. Its helm is also com-

FIG.3 Detail of the enamelled gold foot. (Photograph: Jeremy Whitaker). FIG.4 Detail of the incorrectly observed may-fly engraved on the shell.

plete and bears the arms and coronet of a Hapsburg Archduke. All the shells, the V&A one included, have a hole drilled through by the coil and it is probable that they left the engraver's workshop in this state, so that, like the Milanese one, they could be hung up in a collector's cabinet. If desired, a goldsmith could mount them up later. This explains why the two silver mounts just mentioned are later in date than the shells themselves, the V&A one being unique in having a more or less contemporary mount.

Now, the two Dutch mounts and the Dutch coat-of-arms begin to suggest an origin in the Netherlands, and indeed, the most famous engravers of shells were an Amsterdam based family, the Bellequin. The founder of the dynasty was Jérémie who moved from Metz to Utrecht, and then to Amsterdam in 1608, where he was described as a

'master mounter and engraver of muskets'. This would have involved him in engraving ivory and mother-of-pearl for inlay into the wooden stocks. His son, Jean (c.1597–1636), was described simply as an engraver of mother-of-pearl and he is the one to whom this shell may perhaps be attributed, as the other two Bellequins, his posthumous son Jan, born in 1636, and the famous Cornelis (worked c.1622–after 1696) are both too late to be possible candidates. Cornelis also engraved insects on some of his pieces, but combined them with the kind of baroque foliage which is quite distinct from the pea-pod decoration on the mounts of the V&A piece.

What makes the shell so interesting from the point of view of the history of entomology is that it seems to be one of the earliest attempts to depict insects accurately. At the National History

Museum the opinion was that the engraver of the insects was working from life, or perhaps from drawings from life, and only once or twice allowed himself to become fanciful. He was not, however, someone who had analysed the structure of the insects because he makes a number of mistakes: for example, with the may-fly (FIG.4) he has assumed that it has two wings of equal size, while in reality it has only one big triangular one, and a very small hind wing. The insects are not rare or exotic ones but common European species so that it is unlikely that it records a connoisseur's collection.

The first scientifically grounded book on insects was published in Bologna in 1602, Ulisse Aldrovandi's *De animalibus insectis libriseptem*, and their depiction in art became a well-established tradition before 1650.

3

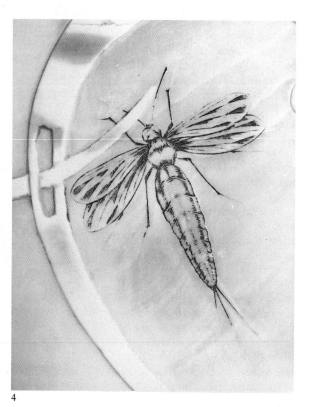

4

FIG.5 Jan van Kessel, study of insects and flowers, dated 1654.
(Reproduced by courtesy of the Richard Green Gallery,
Dover Street).

FIG.6 Jan van Kessel, Europe, from the set of the Four Continents, dated 1664. (Alte Pinakothek, Munich).

Paintings of animals, plants, fish and insects satisfied the Mannerist and seventeenth century collectors' desire for completeness, their attempt to represent in a microcosm the entirety of the universe, every natural creation as well as man's artistry and craftsmanship. Rudolph II (1552–1612), the collector of this type *par excellence*, commissioned Georg Hoefnagel (1542–1600) to paint a series of two hundred different animals (series, whether of towns, plants, ancestors or emperors were very popular everywhere), and at the Medici court, Jacopo Ligozzi (1547–1626) was drawing plants and flowers.

Jan van Kessel (1626–1679), famous for his miniature-like paintings and flower and insects (FIG.5), executed paintings of the Four Continents which sum up this aesthetic. Each continent is depicted in a larger central image (FIG.6) surrounded by sixteen smaller pictures of the appropriate fauna and topography. Europe is a political allegory with the continent personified as a woman with the imperial crown on her head, papal power next to her in the shape of the view of Rome, the tiara, the keys, a papal bull, and the portrait of Alexander VII. The statues in the niches represent the various monarchies subordinate to the Holy Roman Emperor.

Within this political framework is the whole of life: man's pastimes – a tennis racket and backgammon board – feats of valour – the arms and armour – and the wonder of nature – a volume of Pliny, doubtless his *Natural History*, shells, a still life of flowers, sea creatures on the frieze, and insects and butterflies of every sort: on the book to the right, on the central panel (with van Kessel's name signed in worms) and on the painting to the left, keeping company with mandrake roots. The artist delights in the precise and meticulous enumeration in painting of every item, realism is his aim and he might well have signed himself, as did Georg Hoefnagel, 'Nature sola Magistra', Nature, the only teacher.

The V&A's nautilus cup is therefore a quintessential collector's cabinet piece: the shell is a work of art made by Nature herself; man has added his artistry to it by the mounts enamelled on precious gold, and by the carving and engraving of it. Finally, the insects depicted with such care are a token of the variety and intricacy of the natural world, and mirabilia in their own right.

I am most grateful to Count Constantine Potocki who gave me the provenance of the cup, and to Dr Peter Whitehead and Mr Schaffer of the Natural History Museum, who told me about the history of entomology and identified the insects.

PAO & MOLTKE Limited
Oriental Art

118 Yorkville Avenue
Toronto, Ontario, M5R 1C2
Canada Telephone: (416) 925-6197

EARLY FURNITURE
ORIENTAL AND EUROPEAN
WORKS OF ART

Barling
OF MOUNT STREET LTD.

TELEPHONE: 01-499 2858
CABLES: BARGRO, LONDON W1

112 MOUNT STREET, LONDON W1Y 5HE

Important oak-framed settee, with adjustable wings, covered in late 17th century Italian needlework.
English, Charles II (1660–85).
Length: 5' 6".   Depth: 1' 11".   Height: 2' 11½".

The settee was supplied for the Crompton family of High Crompton, near Oldham, Lancashire, in the 17th century.

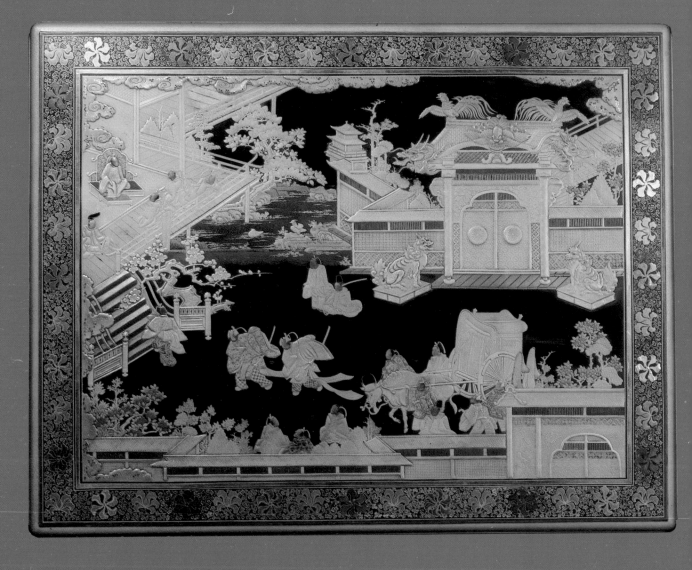

The van Diemen box, wood, decorated with black, red, gold
and silver lacquer and gold and silver foil, 16×48×36.7 cm.
Japanese, 1636–9. Lid, with scenes based on chapters 1 and 7
of the *Genji monogatari*.

TALES OF THE UNEXPECTED
The Decoration of Japanese Export Lacquer

Joe Earle

Among the many masterpieces of Chinese and Japanese decorative art produced for the European market which have come to rest in the V&A, the van Diemen box is outstanding for the quality of its workmanship, the detailed evidence concerning its manufacture and its illustrious subsequent history. The reverse of the lid is inscribed with the name of Maria van Diemen, whose husband was from 1635 to 1645 one of the most successful of all the Governors-General of the Dutch East Indies; the inscription gives us, as well as a romantic association, a firm date which has been pinpointed still more precisely, to the years 1636–9, following the discovery of a second box, of identical size and shape, made for the wife of van Diemen's second-in-command. After her husband's death in 1645 Maria's box presumably returned, with the rest of her large collection of things East Indian, to Holland – then it disappears for over a century. The first European document to mention it is the posthumous *Inventaire* of Madame de Pompadour, drawn up in 1765. Louis XV's favourite had probably acquired it in 1753, when she ordered a special glazed display stand to be made for a lacquer box, and at her death it remained the only piece to be honoured in this way.

After passing through two more distinguished French collections (at one time changing hands for the then record price of 6,901 livres) the box came to William Beckford, who was, aside from his other accomplishments, the most discerning connoisseur of Japanese lacquer at any time before the late nineteenth century. Its subsequent history parallels that of much else in Beckford's vast collections: it appears in both the Fonthill sale catalogues of 1822 and 1823 and then in the great Hamilton Palace sale of 1882, when it was bought by Sir Trevor Lawrence,

whose children gave it to the Museum in 1916.

Even in Paris, where from the 1740s there was such a fashion for fine 'anciens lacques du Japon', the box was admired for its outstanding quality. This is apparent not only from the special care which it received, the high prices paid for it and the ecstatic descriptions in the sale catalogues but also from the very fact that it has survived intact unlike the vast majority of pieces which ended their days cut into panels and set into furniture by French cabinetmakers. Beckford, too, regarded it with special admiration, mentioning it several times in his correspondence, and was even aware of something of its history, although he believed Maria to have been the daughter rather than wife of Anton. He also had a smattering of Japanese culture, gleaned from the writings of, among others, François Caron, a Frenchman who was in the Dutch service in Japan at the time of van Diemen, and Engelbert Kaempfer, a German doctor whose account of the country was first published, in English, in 1727. But his knowledge was far short of the task of identifying the significance of the scenes adorning the box, which to him consisted, according to the Fonthill catalogues, of no more than 'the Arrival of Ambassadors at a Palace, and various Landscapes'.

It is intriguing to trace the steps by which English and Japanese scholars have groped their way to a fuller understanding of the decoration. In 1894 it was shown at an exhibition of the Burlington Fine Arts Club and the scene on the lid is identified as '. . . in the grounds of the palace (Gosho) at Kiōto. The Court carriage in the foreground, noblemen (kugé) in Court dress dancing before the Emperor'. The catalogue also notes 'a strange mixture of Chinese and Japanese *motifs* . . . the Emperor, in the Court scene, is

seated on a throne and the style in places resembles the Chinese lacquer exported to Europe in the last century'. The V&A's own *Catalogue of Japanese Lacquer*, published in 1924, gives no further information on the subject-matter and takes the retrograde step of disbelieving the inscription and assigning the box to the middle of the eighteenth century on the 'expert' advice of a Mr G. Koizumi. It is only, in fact, in the last twenty years or so that a true appreciation has become possible as Japanese scholars have acknowledged the box as a product of their country and studied it from a Japanese viewpoint. Not until 1976, a year before the box returned briefly to Japan for the first time in over three centuries, did Professor Motoo Yoshimura describe the scenes as *Genji-e* ('Genji pictures') and identify the design on the lid as an episode from the first chapter of the *Genji monogatari* (Tale of Genji).

The *Genji monogatari* was written by a court lady, Murasaki Shikibu, who probably lived from about 975 to 1025, and has been generally regarded as the greatest work of Japanese prose literature. It enjoyed a great revival of popularity in the sixteenth century and had by the 1630s re-established itself as a source of subject-matter for painting by all the major schools, especially for pairs of sixfold screens which depicted all fifty-four chapters in fifty-four scenes separated from each other by bands of gold cloud. The recent publication of many of these screens has now made it possible to take up Yoshimura's original hint and pursue the Genji theme in greater detail.

The first chapter relates the love of the Emperor for a lady called Kiritsubo, not of the first rank, and the birth of a son remarkable in looks and accomplishments, Prince Genji Hikaru, 'the shining Genji'. When Genji is three years old his mother dies and at

Long sides, with scenes based on chapters 46 and 47 of the
Genji monogatari.

Short sides, one with a scene based on chapter 15 of the
Genji monogatari.

Reverse of the lid, inscribed with the name of Maria van Diemen.

six he comes to live with his father at court. The lid of the box shows the arrival of the twelve-year-old Genji at the coming-of-age ceremony: Genji's ox-drawn cart, the normal conveyance of the Kyoto nobility, approaches from the right and he is perhaps depicted a second time ascending the steps towards the throne on which the Emperor sits. But although the scene in many respects closely follows the conventional treatment found in contemporary painting, there is an anomaly. Two peculiar figures perform a dance, quite uncalled for by the text of the *Genji*, in front of the steps. These, it turns out, are intruders from chapter 7, where Genji and his companion Tō no Chūjō perform a dance called *The Blue Sea Waves* on the occasion of an autumn maple-gathering excursion.

There is confusion, too, on the long sides of the box, but of a different kind. Of the several boating expeditions contained in the narrative only two recommend themselves as having been in the decorator's mind. Both come from the

last ten chapters of the Tale, which take place after the death of Genji and principally relate the amorous adventures of Kaoru, who is believed by the world to be Genji's son but is in fact the grandson of one of his friends. In chapter 46, Kaoru and some companions cross the Uji river near Kyoto to call upon an old gentleman called the Eighth Prince as a prelude to the courtship by Kaoru and another prince, Niou, of his two daughters. In the following chapter the two princes go on a boating expedition on the Uji river and are secretly admired by the two princesses. Both episodes were chosen by the painters of Genji screens when they came to the two chapters, and elements from both are combined in the lacquer decoration. There is, however, a certain lack of consistency in the treatment. In particular, the text does not seem to justify the presence of ladies in the boats, but as we shall see the lacquerer's chief concern was more with overall effect than with individual detail. He was well aware that the future owners of the box were ignorant

of the very existence of the *Genji monogatari*.

On the short sides of the box, the figural decoration is with one exception too unspecific to admit of interpretation in Genji terms, but the group consisting of one courtier holding an umbrella over another refers to one of the more melancholy results of Genji's love affairs. Chapter 15 relates the sadly reduced circumstances of the Safflower Princess, whom Genji has loved in chapter 6, following the latter's period of exile away from the capital at Suma. She lives virtually alone in a tumbledown mansion and is eventually abandoned by her only companion, the daughter of her old nurse. At length Genji returns to his old life and one day while on a visit to another lady is struck by the desolate appearance of a ruined building which he passes. Assured by his friend Koremitsu that this is indeed the former residence of Prince Hitachi, the Safflower's father, Genji sends him to investigate and, after a long wait, is led in to a final meeting. On their way

through the garden, Koremitsu holds an umbrella over Genji's head to protect him from the rainwater dripping from the overgrown groves. The chapter has a relatively happy ending: Genji arranges for maintenance work to be carried out and sends the Princess presents, moving her two years later to a lodge near his own principal mansion.

Here, as elsewhere on the box, the episode is only fainted alluded to and is set out of context, evidence in itself that the decoration was conceived for ignorant foreigners. But there are several reasons for believing that in spite of the very specific nature of the commission, it was Chinese rather than Dutch foreigners whe were uppermost in the lacquer artist's mind. For one thing the whole conception of the design, narrative scenes involving figures and buildings contained within formal borders, is alien to the native Japanese tradition but is standard for Chinese lacquers of the Ming dynasty (1368–1644), many of which were exported to Japan. Secondly, there are some specifically Chinese features, of

which the most striking are the deliberately exotic-looking procession on one of the short sides and the very elaborately conceived architecture of the building on the right of the lid, which reflects the same conception of Chinese design as influenced the creators of the great Momoyama period (1568–1615) castles. The lid exemplifies, in fact, the schizophrenic character of all the decoration, the very Japanese building on the left, viewed from a high angle, clashing somewhat uneasily with the Chinese structures on the right and in the foreground which are disposed in a way which occurs time and time again in lacquers made in fifteenth and sixteenth century China. Thirdly, even some of the Genji-esque concoctions seem to have been put together in conscious imitation of Chinese designs, which would have been known to the lacquerer either through Chinese lacquer, or Chinese painting, or Japanese imitations of Chinese paintings. For example, the intrusive figures in the depiction of the coming-of-age ceremony were probably introduced to

make the whole composition resemble an illustration from a sixteenth-century Chinese work entitled *The Mirror of Emperors*, extolling the merits of virtuous rulers, which was reprinted in Japan in 1606 and also copied in screen format by Japanese painters.

Recent research at the Museum has established the motive behind the puzzlingly Chinese atmosphere of the decoration. Works by two Chinese scholars of the late Ming dynasty reveal that there is a whole class, as yet unidentified, of Japanese lacquers decorated with Chinese motifs and exported to China. The makers of the van Diemen box, with no idea of the artistic tastes of a Dutch Governor-General's wife (and probably, indeed, no idea who the box was meant for), had very likely made such pieces themselves and were forced to assume, in the absence of evidence to the contrary, that what had suited foreigners before would suit them again, whoever they were. A far cry indeed from the meticulous market research of their late twentieth century descendants!

Four case lacquer inro showing brocade
bags used in the Tea Ceremony
Signed: Nobuyuki saku
Japan, 18th century
Wood netsuke en suite depicting a basket
with charcoal
Provenance: Kelsch collection

 ESKENAZI

Oriental Art

Foxglove House
(opposite Old Bond Street)
166 Piccadilly
London W1V 9DE
Telephone : 01-493 5464
Cables : Eskenazi London W1

CHINESE UNDERGLAZE COPPER-RED DISH   DIAMETER: 7¾ inches 14th CENTURY

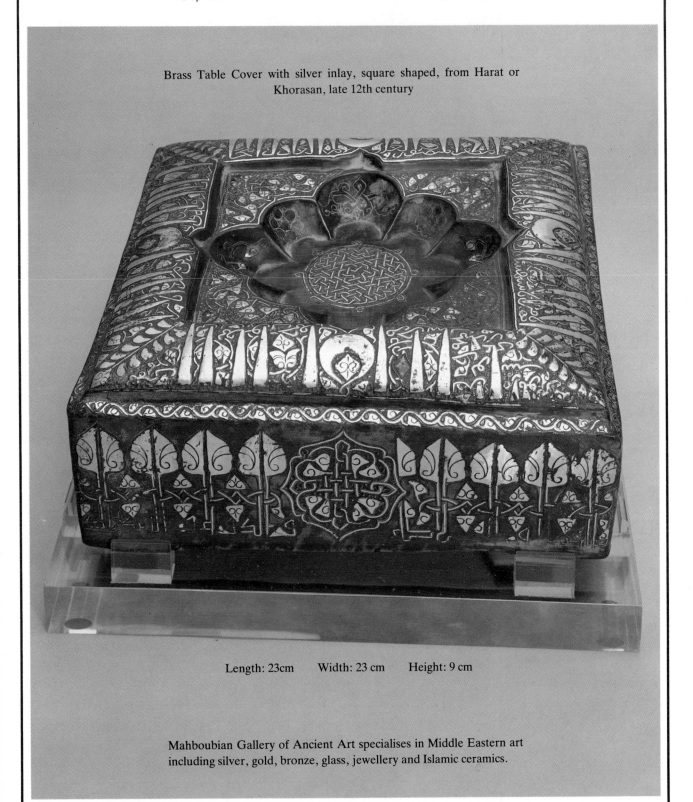

SOMEONE'S BEHIND US

Simon Tait

Somehow this has been Sir Henry Cole's year. So much has been achieved, for which the present Director and the staff deserve the accolades they have had, but somehow that arch-achiever Cole (FIG.1) has been at our elbows during this last twelve months – perhaps with the odd growl of irritation, but mostly, I fancy, with a grunt of approval.

Our founder and first Director was in our thoughts to start with because last year, 1982, was the centenary of his death. Then out came Elizabeth Bonython's delightful picture portrait book about Cole. That was closely followed by John Physick's highly praised *The Victoria and Albert Museum: The history of its building*, which is not only scholarly and a good read, but, for us, has become an indispensable reference. This book is dedicated to Cole, and is as much about him as a biography in that it shows us how much his inspiration filled this quaint and enormous pile, and still does.

In the summer our branches, the Bethnal Green Museum of Childhood and the Theatre Museum, were in the news after a Rayner Report had said that the only way to spend less money on the V&A would be to lop off these two limbs. A highly theatrical character and a great lover of children – he had eight of his own – Cole could almost have organised the public outcry that ensued. He was very successful at organising outcries. This one, however, was quite spontaneous, and in response to it the Minister for the Arts decided that both the Theatre Museum and the Museum of Childhood would continue.

The executioner's eye had glanced towards the two great houses administered by the V&A, though they are owned by the National Trust: Osterley

Park House and Ham House. These, too, the Minister has decided will stay in the family. And they are even more grand these days, with the Bed of Flowers – Osterley's State Bed (FIG.2) – wonderfully restored, and the seventeenth century kitchens at Ham House now to be seen as they would have been in their heyday.

In October we opened a new entrance to the museum in Exhibition Road, designed by Property Services Agency architects, and sprinkled it with our matchless collection of Rodin bronze sculptures. St. John the Baptist is seen by all who pass by, silently beseeching them to enter with his beckoning hand (FIG.3). The entrance is also a gallery, in the Cole sense of economy combined with showmanship, and it has now become as busy as the entrance at Cromwell Road, for it is the one to use to get to the new wing, the Boilerhouse Project, the south-western galleries of the Museum and the new press and information office. Few can resist St. John . . .

Cole had twin projects in the same ethic. The projects were the Schools of Design, now the Royal College of Art, and the South Kensington Museum, now the V&A. The ethic was education and instruction in design excellence. That is why something which happened in October would have pleased the merry old soul as much as anything – the start of the first RCA/V&A Master of Arts course called Design and the Decorative Arts: History and Technique. Nine scholars started a two-year course, which aims to combine the historical expertise of the V&A with the academic and technical skills of the RCA.

There were no primary galleries in his day, but Cole would have got round to them. They are the galleries which tell the story of design in a particular age or style, with objects brought from all departments of the Museum to illus-

trate it, so that visitors can relate to them in a fitting context. There is a programme to up-date the display of all the existing primary galleries, and eventually to introduce some new ones, and in December we reopened the first of our new-look primaries. All the major criticisms of the old galleries have been taken note of, and there is a feeling of space and air – in spite of there being as many or more objects than before – with the new labelling, lighting and specially devised explanatory panels (FIGS.4 & 5).

At Christmas we looked towards our little sister, the Bethnal Green Museum of Childhood, housed in what Henry knew as the Brompton Boilers when they were on the V&A's present site and contained his South Kensington Museum before being moved to Bethnal Green in 1872, a year before he retired. Here the Keeper, Anthony Burton, had put on his own particular hobby of an exhibition, *Spirit of Christmas* (FIG.6), which was a luscious look, through paintings, models, tableaux and objects, at Victorian Christmases of plum pudding, mulled wine, wooden toys and snow. Cole would have been in a state of glee there – after all, he did publish the first-ever Christmas card back in 1843.

And the Bethnal Green Museum did not have long to wait after Christmas to learn that its critics of the previous summer had been confounded by its fans. There was an increase of more than 30 per cent in the number of visitors for 1982, which, with 288,000, meant the highest total since records began to be kept. The old V&A itself did not do so badly, either; there was a modest increase of 22 per cent over the year before. I am sure H.C. would have approved of that: it was he who had the name of dreary old Brompton Village changed to posher-sounding South Kensington simply to attract more people.

FIG.2 The restored State Bed at Osterley Park House.
FIG.3 Rodin's St. John the Baptist in the new Exhibition Road
entrance hall.

The new year brought something that would change 130 years of the V&A's career; very much a time for reflection on what Cole had started with that Great Exhibition of his, the profits from which paid for the beginnings of the V&A under the administration of the Department of Science and Art. Introduced in the House of Lords in January this year was the National Heritage Bill, designed, in part, to bring the V&A and Science Museums out of the modern Department of Education and Science and under the administration of Boards of Trustees: a time of hope, uncertainty and challenge, in which he would have thrived.

But with the spring came another rebirth, one for which the whole Museum had been working for months, but which the Department of Prints, Drawings & Photographs, and Paintings has had close to its heart for five years. In March the Queen was to come and open the V&A's first expansion since her great-grandfather had opened the Museum as we know it in 1909 – the Henry Cole wing.

The great collections which Cole had wheedled and persuaded and then cajoled for are to be seen among the grand galleries converted from the tutorial rooms, laboratories, studios and lecture theatres of the building's former life, when Cole founded it, too, as the Schools of Science. Cole was also the first to introduce photography to a museum, and the V&A now became the first to have a gallery dedicated to the art of photography.

So, on March 17 the Sovereign opened the building by touring it, watched by a thousand applauding loyal subjects, all staff members and their families. She saw the Constable collection, now arrayed on the top floor where real light gives to the paintings and sketches the vitality of the artist's eye. In the futuristic conservation studio she saw the x-ray machinery, the computers and those priceless precision instruments of which the V&A has a matchless collection – the conservators, themselves.

In the Print Room she met the individuals of the Department whose home the Henry Cole Wing now is and in whose tender care the objects in it rest. Into this room the staff pride themselves on being able to bring any of the one million or more objects in store within ten minutes at the request of visitors.

After the National Collection of Portrait Miniatures, the exquisite little paintings which, in their new gallery, spring out of the dark fastness at the touch of a switch, and the great paintings of the Ionides Collection, Her Majesty came upon the extraordinary Panorama of Rome, painted in 1824, 44 feet long and the only 360-degree

2   3

FIGS.4,5 The newly installed English Renaissance primary
gallery.

4

5

FIG.6 The Spirit of Christmas Exhibition at the Bethnal
Green Museum of Childhood.

painting on show in the country. Coming from the Great North Staircase and through the photographic displays, she entered the first main exhibition to be held in the wing, *Pattern and Design*, which traced the development of dozens of pieces from the V&A's collections from their first appearances as designs on paper to their eventual creation.

Cole was a great friend of the Royal Family, and would have been as deeply honoured as we all were, but as to his new wing – from the inscription made in the terracotta by a stonecarver to the robotic light-sensitive blinds – I fancy he would have examined it inch by inch with critical eye, and that after several anxious moments for those around him, a loud grunt would have signalled total approval.

But as Cole strove relentlessly to develop ideas and projects, so does his creature. In June the Dress Collection opened in its rebuilt and redesigned court – Sir Aston Webb's huge Octagon Court, adapted to the needs and display techniques of today. Here is the story of dress design told as it has never been told before, for the benefit of those seeking knowledge, as well as the enjoyment of those after sheer enjoyment.

In July, just as our first Director had his triumphs, the V&A was able to share another with its present Director, a very personal one for Sir Roy Strong. On July 7 there was another Royal occasion in the Museum when Her Majesty Queen Elizabeth the Queen Mother opened *Artists of the Tudor Court. The Portrait Miniature Rediscovered 1520–1620*. This exhibition – controversial, revealing, colourful – represented the culmination of ten years of research for Sir Roy, and fittingly came in his tenth year as head of the Museum. And it rounds off a year unsurpassed for achievement for him, the V&A – and Old King Cole.

On 17 May 1983 Her Majesty The Queen
opened the Museum's extension, the
Henry Cole Wing.

Sir Roy Strong introduces Her Majesty to Mr Paul Channon,
the Minister for the Arts, Mrs Channon, Sir Alexander Glen,
Chairman of the Advisory Council, and Lady Glen.

1 Mr Adrian Pasotti, the Museum's bookbinder, presents Her Majesty with a specially bound volume of the book *The Victoria and Albert Museum: The history of its building* by Deputy Director John Physick, who can be seen over Sir Roy's left shoulder.   2 Dr Michael Kauffmann, Keeper of Prints, Drawings, Photographs and Paintings, explains a point in the John Constable Collection on the top floor.   3 Conservator Malcolm Green is gilding a frame as The Queen arrives in the new paintings conservation studio.   4 Her Majesty has a point about lettering and mounting clarified for her by Graham Holden in the new studio.

1

2

3

4

1 Sir Roy introduces Ray Smith, who retired in January after master-minding the transfer and restoring of over one million objects in the new wing.   2 In the Print Room, Miss Stella Ruff, the Department's typist, and Miss Lilian Vincent, paper keeper in the Print Room, are presented.   3 Mr Harold Barkley, Assistant Keeper of Prints and Drawings, and Mr Jim Murrell, Deputy Keeper of Conservation, show Her Majesty the National Collection of Portrait Miniatures. Sir Oliver Millar, Surveyor of The Queen's Pictures, is in the background.   4 Dr Kauffmann, the Queen and Sir Roy in the Ionides Collection. Chief Warder Tony George together with his wife and daughter are on the right.

1

2

3

4

1 The exhibition *Pattern and Design* gets royal approval,
with Deputy Keeper of Prints and Drawings Sue Lambert,
who organised the display, as guide.   2 It's farewell to
Sir Roy and Lady Strong, as Principal Photographer at the
Museum Peter Macdonald makes sure the record is up
to date.

1

2

THE GLC HISTORIC HOUSES

KENWOOD The Iveagh Bequest, Hampstead Lane,
An outstanding neo-classical house re-modelled by Robert Adam, 1764-73, for the 1st Earl of Mansfield, the famous Lord Chief Justice. The Library is one of the finest of Adam's creations, and has been restored in the original colours. The house contains the Iveagh Collection (bequeathed 1927) of Old Master and English paintings, including works by Rembrandt, Vermeer, Hals, Gainsborough, Reynolds and Turner. Exhibitions are held on the first floor, usually devoted to some aspect of eighteenth century painting or the decorative arts. Chamber music concerts are held in the Orangery and symphony concerts by the Lake in summer.

MARBLE HILL HOUSE
Richmond Road, Twickenham,
A complete example, both inside and out, of an English Palladian villa, built between 1724 and 1729, for Henrietta Howard, the mistress of George II, and later Countess of Suffolk. The design is based on a drawing by Colen Campbell, while the Great Room was inspired by Inigo Jones' Cube Room at Wilton. The grounds, going down to the Thames, were laid out with the advice of Alexander Pope. The house contains an important collection of early Georgian paintings and furniture.

RANGER'S HOUSE
Chesterfield Walk, Blackheath,
The house of the 4th Earl of Chesterfield, statesman and author of the famous 'Letters' to his natural son. The bow-fronted Gallery he added to the house in 1749, with "the finest prospects in the world," now houses the remarkable series of Jacobean portraits by William Larkin from the collection of the Earls of Suffolk. Concerts are held in the house and there is a collection of musical instruments.

GLC
Working for London.

Open daily all the year, including Sundays, from 10-5. Marble Hill is closed on Fridays, but Kenwood is open until 7 in the summer. Details opposite.

National Museum of Wales   **Amgueddfa Genedlaethol Cymru**

A wide selection of books have been published by the National Museum of Wales to mark the 75th anniversary of its founding

French Art from the Davies Bequest

By Peter Hughes. 84pp., 56 monochrome illus., 39 colour pls.
All the French paintings and sculpture from the important Davies Bequest are illustrated in this picture book. Translations in Welsh, French and German are also published. Price: soft cover £3.25 (£3.80 by post); hard cover £6.50 (£7.50 by post)

Celf Ffrengig o Gymynrodd Davies

Translated by Hywel Gealy Rees

L'art francais du legs Davies

Translated by Lise Perreault Jones

Französische Kunst aus dem Davies Vermächtnis

Translated by P. Stempel

Morels of Cardiff: the History of a Family Shipping Firm

By John Morel Gibbs. 184pp., 34 monochrome illus.
The story of a remarkable family enterprise founded by two Jersey brothers in 1861. Price £4.00 (£4.70 by post)

Evan Thomas Radcliffe, a Cardiff Shipowning Company

By J. Geraint Jenkins. 92pp., 29 monochrome illus.
The story of a prosperous Cardiff company, established in 1882 by two South Walians. Price £2.50 (£2.95 by post)

Coalface

By Richard Keen. 52pp., 59 monochrome illus.
A picture book recreating the flavour of life in a coalmining valley in Gwent at the turn of the century. Price £1.50 (£1.85 by post)

Classification of Objects in the Welsh Folk Museum Collections

Edited by Christine Stevens.
The basic format was settled in 1938 but since the establishment of the Welsh Folk Museum in 1946 and a more rapid expansion of the collections, new types of objects have been collected resulting in additional entries. Price £1.50 (£2.43 by post)

Llyfryddiaeth i Gerddoriaeth Draddodiadol yng Nghymru/ Bibliography of Welsh Traditional Music

By Wyn Thomas. 160pp.
The volume is divided into two main sections: the main printed collections of Welsh traditional music, together with details of their contents are chronologically listed and are followed by references in both Welsh and English to research publications related to the field of traditional Welsh music. Price £4.95. (£5.82 by post)

'Formed Stones', Folklore and Fossils

By M.G. Bassett. 32pp., 72 monochrome illus.
An account of the role of fossils in man's culture throughout the ages. Price 95p (£1.20 by post)

Lluniau Bywyd Gwerin/ Photographs of Folk Life

By Llew Morgan. 51pp., 70 monochrome illus.
A selection of photographs on various aspects of rural life in South Wales from the 1920s onwards. Price £2.00 (£2.33 by post)

The Cambrian-Ordovician Boundary: sections, fossil distribution and correlations

Edited by M.G. Bassett and W.T. Dean. 227pp., 315 figures, 5 tables.
The volume includes 15 papers by a team of experts from throughout the world. Price £17.00 (£18.70 by post)

Fossil Plants from Wales

By M.G. Bassett and Dianne Edwards. 42pp., 86 monochrome illus.
A study of the evolution of plants in the rocks of Wales. Price 95p (£1.30 by post)

Welsh Woods and Forests: History and Utilization

By William Linnard. 203pp., 36 plates, figs. and maps
The first comprehensive account of the history of Welsh woods from the earliest times to the present day. Price £7.00 (£8.30 by post)

The Flowering Plants and Ferns of Anglesey

By R.H. Roberts. 110pp.
A comprehensive list of the Island's flowering plants and ferns. Price £3.50 (£4.00 by post)

Welsh History through Seals

By David H. Williams. 48pp., 20 colour pls., 91 monochrome illus.
A selection of seals used to authenticate a wide range of deeds and documents from the age of the native Welsh Princes to the present time. Price £2.25 (£2.55 by post)

The Ewenny Potteries

By J.M. Lewis. x + 126pp., 4 colour pls., 61 monochrome illus., 51 figs.
An account of a group of country potteries and their history from the 18th century to their decline in the 1880s. Price £7.75 (£8.75 by post)

Allan Gwynne-Jones

72pp., 44 monochrome illus., 16 colour pls.
A bilingual catalogue to a large exhibition of paintings, drawings and etchings by the late artist. Price £4.50 (£5.00 by post)

Cooking on the Open Hearth

By S. Minwel Tibbott. 42pp., 31 monochrome illus.
The traditional utensils and their historical usage are described in relation to the preparation of dishes from readily available raw materials. Price £1.00 (£1.30 by post)

Agricultural Co-operation in Welsh Medieval Law

By Dafydd Jenkins. 18pp.
A revised version of a paper given at the British Agricultural History Society conference at Weymouth in 1974. Price 60p (85p by post)

Meddyginiaethau Llafar Gwlad

By Anne Elizabeth Williams.
Folk remedies used in Wales at the turn of the century

Agricultural Transport in Wales

By J. Geraint Jenkins.
A revised edition of a volume first published in 1962

Famous Fiddlers by the Reverend W. Meredith Morris

Edited with introduction and notes by D. Roy Saer.
An edition of a rare manuscript concerning the once widespread folk traditions of fiddle playing in Wales

Garlandstone

By Basil Greenhill, Director of the National Maritime Museum, London. 23pp., 12 monochrome illus.
A bilingual history of a sailing ship, now on display at Porthmadog. Price £1.40 (£1.65 by post)

The Willoughby Gardner Library

By J.R. Kenyon. 54pp., 10 monochrome illus.
A catalogue of Willoughby Gardner's collection in the Museum's Library. Price £4.50 (£4.80 by post)

Welsh Minerals

By R.E. Bevins and T. Sharpe. 28pp., 30 colour pls.
This picture book illustrates the typical form of the more common and interesting minerals found in Wales. It outlines the methods of mineral identification and the diagnostic characteristics of the specimens. Price £1.80 (£2.05 by post)

Mineralau Cymru

By R.E. Bevins and T. Sharpe.
A Welsh language version of *Welsh Minerals* translated by Trosol. Price £1.80 (£2.05 by post)

Nature in Wales

Edited by D.A. Bassett. Volume 1, part 1, 79pp
The first journal in a new natural history series for Wales and the Borderland. Price 75p (£1.35 by post)

Efengyliaeth yng Nghymru c. 1840-1875

By A.H. Williams. 32pp.
A lecture delivered at Yr Hen Gapel, Tre'r-ddôl on 11 September, 1982. Price 75p (£1.00 by post)

Traditional Farm Buildings in north-east Wales 1550-1900

By Eurwyn Wiliam. 334pp., 35 monochrome illus., 61 tables, 45 figs.
The geographical and historical background of the development of farm buildings and farmsteads is followed by an examination of their siting and lay-out, as well as the building materials used. Price £12.50 (£14.72 by post)

The Strange Genius of William Burges, 'Art-Architect', 1827-1881

Edited by J. Mordaunt Crook. 160pp., 198 monochrome illus.
A catalogue to a major exhibition on the brilliant architect-designer who rebuilt Castell Coch and Cardiff Castle. Price: soft cover £3.50 (£4.40 by post); hard cover £6.00 (£7.30 by post)

Coginio Traddodiadol: bara ceirch a rhai bwydydd eraill

By S. Minwel Tibbott. 15pp., 7 monochrome illus.
A description of traditional Welsh cooking utensils and the way in which they were used. Price 50p (70p by post)

Catalog o Gyhoeddiadau Amgueddfa Genedlaethol Cymru / National Museum of Wales Catalogue of Publications

Compiled by Hywel Gealy Rees. 59pp.
A bilingual catalogue of all Museum titles in print in April 1982. Available free of charge on request

Geological Excursions in Dyfed, south-west Wales

Edited by M.G. Bassett. 327pp., 121 line drawings
Excursion itineraries that give a wide geological and geographical coverage throughout the county. Price £6.50 (£7.55 by post)

The Maritime Heritage of Dyfed

59pp., 48 monochrome illus.
Published on the occasion of a large exhibition at the Welsh Industrial and Maritime Museum, the book traces, in words and pictures, the long-established seafaring traditions of West Wales. Price £1.95 (£2.30 by post)

Alan Sorrell: Das Alte Wales Wiedergeschaffen

By D.W. Dykes. 80pp., 10 colour pls., 74 monochrome illus.
A German version of *Alan Sorrell: Early Wales Re-created*, translated by Penny Stempel. Price £1.50 (£1.95 by post)

Anniversary Lectures

The public Anniversary Lectures on each of the major aspects of the Museum's work are published, together with separate translations in Welsh.

Wales and the Past: a Consort of Voices
By Glanmor Williams. The formal Anniversary Lecture.

Cymru a'r Gorffennol: Côr o Leisiau
Translated by Allan James

The National Museum as a Mirror of Ancient Wales
By Glyn Daniel

Yr Amgueddfa Genedlaethol fel Drych o Hen Hen Gymru
Translated by Trosol

Folklife Research: between History and Anthropology
By Bjarne Stoklund

Bywyd Gwerin: rhwng Hanes ac Anthropoleg
Translated by Mary Wiliam

Some Observations on the ethics of Conservation
By Sir Ralph Verney

Rhai Sylwadau ar Foeseg Cadwraeth
Translated by Trosol

For further information contact
Hywel Gealy Rees, Publications & Information Officer, National Museum of Wales, Cathays Park, Cardiff CF1 3NP

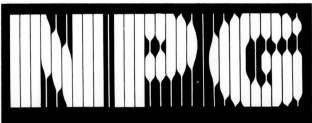

Inside the North Court, May 1863, from the
Illustrated London News.

AN ILL-ARRANGED AFFAIR

John Physick

The Museum has been organising private views, receptions and similar functions since it was opened at Marlborough House in 1852. Many of these have resulted in favourable comment from guests. On the other hand, there have been others which have remained memorable, not for their smooth-running, but for their horror, or for unexpected occurrences as, when at the private view of the Treasures from Althorp, an unfortunate visitor tripped in front of Earl Spencer, the host and Chairman of the Advisory Council, and flung his glass of red wine over an embroidered chair-back. Lord Spencer exploded in a fire-ball of incandescent fury.

A great deal of planning in the Department of Museum Services (in particular, by the Press and Information Office) precedes each event nowadays, with the reins firmly in the hands of the Director, but broadly following the pattern established between 1946 and 1970 by Charles Gibbs-Smith. If H.M. The Queen or another member of the Royal Family is to be present, then the Mayor and Mayoress of Kensington and Chelsea, as the first citizens of the Royal Borough, must be informed, the timetable has to be worked out in detail, various 'line-ups' have to be arranged with, perhaps, the Minister for the Arts, the Chairman of the Advisory Council, Keepers, organisers of exhibitions and so on.

Once the invitations have been sent out, the guessing-game begins. How many guests will turn up (as usually, not everyone replies)? On the accuracy of the guess will depend the success of the occasion. In addition, to this uncertainty, a frequent cliff-hanger is whether the catalogues will arrive from the printers in time.

One exhibition opening which caused near-chaos, was when, during the afternoon, Mr Khruschev came for the Russian Exhibition in 1966. For days before the Museum had been overrun by security men who inspected the Raphael Cartoon Court, where the opening ceremony was to be held, the route to the exhibition, and the exhibition itself. On the day, so many people came that the whole of the main ground-floor galleries seized up and no-one could move. To make matters worse, Mr Khruschev, while processing to the exhibition, wished to attend to a call of nature. His route had instantly to be revised, not an easy or popular change, in view of both the congestion and security.

It was assumed that when the Prince and Princess of Wales opened the recent Gonzaga exhibition, everyone invited would attend with a guest, and this assumption was correct. All would probably have been well if there had not been the unexpected and last-minute news that an entertainment was to be given by the Italians. Plans had to be revised at the eleventh hour, creating a state of apprehension, not helped by the knowledge that both the orchestra and dancers would not be arriving from Italy until a few hours before they were due on the stage. This had been hurriedly constructed in the Cartoon Court, where guests had unfortunately to be penned, to wait for a considerable time.

Such international or royal occasions frequently result in much behind-the-scenes diplomacy for, naturally, everyone wishes to be presented, but relatively few can be. Equally, the Press Office is bombarded with phone calls from people who cannot believe that they have not been invited. They are said to be great personal friends of the Director, or they are sure that the Trustees (which as yet we do not have), all of whom they know, must have omitted their names from the invitation list by mistake, or, more frequently, 'So many of my friends have received their invitations, that mine has obviously been lost in the post; please send another to me immediately'.

Should numbers be underestimated, then refreshment will be insufficient and be a cause of dissatisfaction. But, even so, the unexpected can happen. One remembers the Danish Art Treasures exhibition in the autumn of 1948. This was opened in Room 42 (now the Islamic gallery, but then empty and awaiting post-war reinstallation), by the King and Queen of Denmark, together with King George VI and Queen Elizabeth, Queen Mary, and most other members of the Royal Family, and was broadcast live by the BBC. The Danes had laid on a buffet lunch in the central hall (Room 43), but so many of the Museum's staff happened to wander down to look, and gave way to temptation and sampled the food, that the tables were noticeably and seriously depleted.

But in spite of plans sometimes going awry, nothing today appears to have been quite so bad as at least two events of the nineteenth century, which caused not inconsiderable unfavourable comment in the press. These were the private view in the North Court of the wedding presents of Alexandra, Princess of Wales, in 1863, and a reception organised by (Sir) Henry Cole for the Society of Arts in 1870, attended by both the Prince and Princess of Wales. Although the Museum was then occupying only a small section of today's huge building, nearly 5,000 people squeezed into the private view of the wedding presents, and over six thousand were estimated to have come to the soirée. Few found either occasion a success.

The wedding presents View was considered 'an ill-arranged affair' by the *Illustrated News*, with about six times as many people attending as could be accommodated reasonably. 'I was in the crowd for an hour and a half, during which I progressed at most about five-and-twenty yards.' Dresses were torn, and an irate correspondent to the *Standard* wrote:

'First came a densely packed *queue*, five or six abreast for some eighty or a hundred yards, in patient attendance at the entrance to the court adjoining that occupied by the gems and precious property. This throng was gradually narrowed and rendered more impact, resolute, and unyielding, as it wedged its length by *finesse*, or brute force, slowly into a stoutly-built lane of barricades, protected at either end with a bar, opened or closed by the customary unbending policeman. Thence the press of people was directed into a labyrinth or maze of passages, almost within sight of the sacred precincts, where the princely gift lay enshrined. But woe to the unhappy visitor who once passed into these barricades; such a stern, inexorable discipline is not often ensured to a London sightseer, especially when asked to a "private view". In varieties of stern intonation the loud-voiced constables bade the visitors to "pass on, as quickly as possible" . . .'

But worse was to come during the Society of Arts *conversazione*, when the *Daily News* recorded that 'loss of temper and derangement of toilettes were inevitable in a closely-packd crowd of thousands of persons, when every fourth lady required accommodation for a train a yard and a half long. We saw several members of Parliament, a bishop, and two eminent deans, buffeted to and fro . . . The last person we saw on leaving the Museum was . . . the American Minister, with a lady on each arm, making difficult headway towards the door, and enquiring here and there – for a long time to no purpose – how he could reach his carriage. The conversazione – as a conversazione – was therefore pre-eminently a success'.

But the last word should be left to the gentleman who wrote to the same newspaper, as a 'Survivor':

'On last evening the Society of Arts had a conversazione at the South Kensington Museum, which I venture to think will be remembered for some time by those who had the honour of being present. I do not know upon what plan of selection the tickets are sent out, but it seemed to me that every one in London who could get or borrow a dress coat, a pair of shoes, and an opera cloak was present on this agreeable occasion. Going in at the door, the first sight that presented itself was a crowd round an office similar to that at the entrance of a theatre on the opening of a pantomime. Some two or three hundred gentlemen trying to take off their overcoats at once and being at the same moment pressed and hustled by a constant stream of ladies made considerable confusion, and those who were not provided with crush hats had to continue the struggle for existence during the ensuing hours burdened with our national tile, which they dare not put out of the way, upon their heads. From the first, stopping to look at an object of art was simply impossible. The objects of art which we had, if you please, all come to see were the Prince and Princess of Wales, and for that purpose we ranged ourselves in lines through the central avenues of the Museum. I was drifted into the cartoon gallery, and endeavoured to anchor there with more or less success, but this I only achieved by clinging as close to the wall as I could. You may be aware that in the chamber there is as fine a collection of wooden chests as were ever got together in Europe, and many of us, wearied of pushing and being pushed, thought we might turn these gems of carpentry to account by sitting on them, but stewards with wands sternly warned us off. Sir, they spared neither age nor sex. My weight – taken by a chair in the Crystal Palace – is under nine stone, but it was supposed to injure a "cassone" on which an elephant might dance a hornpipe. Ladies, both fragile and the reverse – after suffering the rigours of the passages to the place – were not for an instant permitted to revive their jaded frames on the "Italian marriage chests", and so standing, ill at ease, they waited for the great event. Half an hour before it came off a steward, with an anxious face, as though he had a sense of "fire" on his mind, ran through the lanes of men and women, crying in a loud voice "ladies to the front – ladies to the front", this gallant consideration being intended to confer on them the advantages of a good view at Royalty. When the ladies had been to the front for twenty minutes a helmeted policeman (I didn't see his truncheon) rushed sternly through the gallery for all the world as though he had been acting in his repressive capacity and wished, after the fashion of his corps, to be late for a riot. He didn't arrest anyone, however, and I believe was only brought in to frighten us. At last the band strikes up "God Save the Queen", there is a hush and rustle quite religious and church-like in its effect, and the illustrious guests march in in twos, while a bigger snob than ordinary, with his mouth open, gapes at them from under the breast of the Apostle in the picture of the Beautiful Gate. I assure you, sir, the awe on that man's face was more deep and afflicting than the gaze of the stunted beggar at the countenance of St. Paul.

'A few minutes afterwards I formed a unit in the throng that was swept down a flight into the floor range where, as you know, we keep the trophies of the Abyssinian War, and that lovely painted statue of the dog and the constrictor. Fearing a tumult later on, I prepared to fight for the recovery of my top-coat. I met a bruised young lady and her mamma who promised me supper if I could join them outside. The scene at the coat office baffles my weak powers of description. Only for a good humour and the comparatively good manners of the applicants or petitioners for their clothing, ribs would assuredly have been broken. Certainly, the arrangements for compound fractures made on Wednesday evening by the Society of Arts left nothing to be desired. Sir, you had to shout, to bellow, to kick, to beg for your coat, and I shouldn't have got mine at all but for a big man who took compassion on me and to whom I surrendered my voucher. When I succeeded in gaining the street I ran a gauntlet through a thousand ragamuffins in search for the brougham which literally contained my supper. I remembered, however, that I had spent

Queue for the Wedding Presents exhibition May 1863,
photograph by Charles Thurston Thompson.

three-quarters of an hour battling for my coat, and so I was not surprised that my friends had disappeared. I need scarce say I know nothing of the hospitality of the Society of Arts. I am not now aware if they had anything to eat or drink for people under the rank of Dukes.

And now, sir, why should this bad example of overcrowding be set by a learned association. We have enough of it during the season, and some were in hopes thast things would mend this year. Surely Mr Cole, CB, might inform the society that the Museum is of certain dimensions, and is not composed of india rubber that it may stretch on the visit of Royal personages. And as for the starers, why, the Princess is in the Row day after day, and to see the Prince one has only to take a stall some night during a new bur-lesque; perhaps, however, the starers think that there is a sort of private air about these *conversazioni*, and that they are on the same footing, as it were, for the nonce with the princes of the blood. "God save the Queen", the policeman courant, and the procession of Fellows, ought to disabuse them of the idea, and suggest that they have only been asked to partake in a worship of rank as the humble congre-gation, while the savans of our country perform the functions of a priesthood during the instructive service.'

HERBERT ART GALLERY & MUSEUM, THE LUNT ROMAN FORT MUSEUM

COVENTRY'S MUSEUMS

MUSEUM OF BRITISH ROAD TRANSPORT, WHITEFRIARS MUSEUM CITY OF COVENTRY LEISURE SERVICES

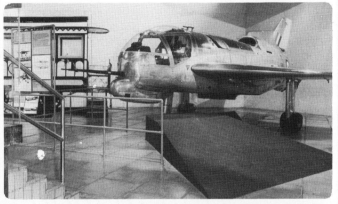

Silber – Keller
Tafelsilber

Antik, Jugendstil, Art Deco.

Lothar u. Veena Duncker, Stieve Str. 9 8000 München 19

West Germany

Telephone: 1781956, Privat 163468

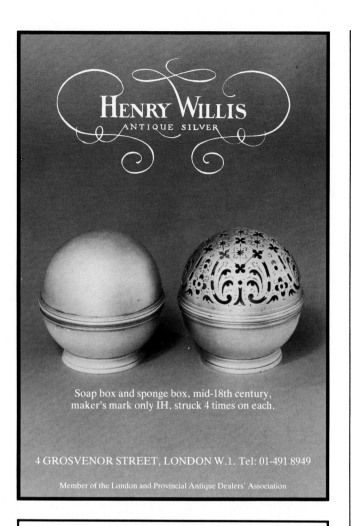

Get Carried Away...By The Extraordinary

Vermeil crab candleholders from our large collection of sterling silver candlesticks.
Eleven thousand two hundred dollars the pair.

TIFFANY & CO.

NEW YORK FIFTH AVE. & 57th ST. · ATLANTA · CHICAGO · DALLAS · HOUSTON · SAN FRANCISCO · BEVERLY HILLS

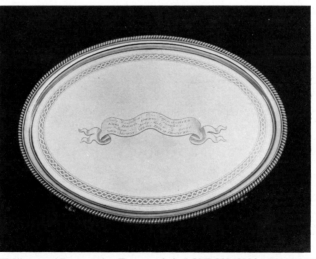

Brand Inglis Ltd

A VERY FINE GEORGE II
SILVER CAKE BASKET
By Peter Archambo,
London 1742
Length: 12 in. (30.5 cm.)
Weight: 52 oz. 10 dwt.

The arms are those of Shawe impaling
Cunliffe for William Shawe, Esq. of Preston,
co. Lancaster who married Anne, elder
daughter of Foster Cunliffe, Esq. and sister
of Sir Ellis Cunliffe, the 1st Baronet of that
family, who was twice Member of
Parliament for Liverpool.

**9 Halkin Arcade,
Motcomb Street, London SW1**
Telephone: 01-235 6604

Paul Bennett

SPECIALISTS IN ANTIQUE ENGLISH AND CONTINENTAL SILVER AND SHEFFIELD PLATE

75 George Street, Portman Square, Baker Street, London W1H 5PL   Telephone: 01-935 1555

A. D. C. Heritage

FINE ANTIQUE SILVER AND OLD SHEFFIELD PLATE

...arge pair of Victorian
...entation candelabra by
...nes Charles Edington,
...don 1837/1838.
...ght - 106cm (42 inches)
...ght - 31.5 kilos. (1015ozs.)
... Arms are those of the
...bient, Peter Howe,
...nd Marquess of Sligo,
...38 - 1845).

The one dated 1837 was presented to the 2nd
Marquess by the slaves of Jamaica and the one dated
1838 was presented to him by the inhabitants of
Westport, both in recognition of his role as one of the
leading abolitionists.

Valuations for Insurance, Probate & Division

2 Old Bond Street, London W.1   Tel: 01-493 5088

LAPADA

FIG.3 Chalice, silver, parcel-gilt, decorated with amethysts, garnets and *champlevé* enamels, Birmingham hallmarks for 1849; maker's mark of John Hardman & Company. Executed from the design of A.W.N. Pugin and shown first at the Birmingham exhibition of 1849 and then at the Great Exhibition of 1851. Acquired for the founding collection of the Museum of Manufactures, 1851–52, h. 23.2 cm. (1328–1851).

TROPHIES FROM THE GREAT EXHIBITION OF 1851

Shirley Bury

All researchers have their occasional moments of illumination when a single additional fact begins to make sense of a body of information patiently amassed over a long period. Museum people receive a further bonus when objects, long familiar from descriptions or illustrations, manifest themselves in palpable form, as happened to the Department of Metalwork last year on the arrival of a magnificent tea and coffee service (FIG.1) hitherto known only from an engraving in the *Art Journal Illustrated Catalogue* of the 1851 exhibition (FIG.2). Bearing the London hallmarks for 1850–51 and the maker's mark of Joseph Angell, the service had come into the possession of a private collector after the Second World War and was shown to us on behalf of his widow, who was anxious to dispose of it. Through the intercession of a silversmith who acted as intermediary, the V&A was able to purchase the service last April.

The wood-engraving in the *Art Journal*, barely two inches high, captures efficiently enough the concave angularity of the pieces in the service, which was designed with a mixture of neo-Tudor and rococo motifs, but utterly fails to convey their striking attractiveness. Form, decoration and colour are combined with great verve; the colour being furnished by gilding but, above all, by areas of lead-based green and purple translucent enamel fired over a gilt ground. The enamelled decoration was the *raison d'être* of the service. Hitherto the technique of enamelling had been practised in early Victorian England almost exclusively by the goldsmiths associated with the architects and designers of the Medieval Movement. A.W.N. Pugin, a Roman Catholic convert who upheld the automatic superiority of the gothic over all other styles as the only one fit for a Christian country, claimed to have revived the art of *champlevé*

enamelling so that his church plate might be appropriately decorated. There was a kernel of truth in Pugin's assertion, though his manufacturer, John Hardman of Birmingham, employed the services of enamellers in the jewellery trade, where the technique had never entirely died out. The enamels were usually fired in designs hollowed out in small silver or copper plaques which were then applied to the plate, as in the chalice in FIG.3, one of two of Pugin's design to be acquired from the 1851 exhibition for the founding collection of the new Museum of Manufactures, the ancestor of the V&A.

The Medieval Movement, flourishing internationally under the wing of antiquarianism, promoted research into obsolete and obsolescent techniques. The French seem to have anticipated the English interest in enamelling; an attempt to classify the various types of enamel was made by A. de Longpérier in 1842. The following year saw the appearance of the Comte de l'Escalopier's translation into French of one of the key medieval manuals on painting, book-illumination, glass-making, goldsmithing and metalworking in general. The author was a monk thought to have been working in about 1100 who certainly had experience of enamelling. Robert Hendrie produced a version in 1847 which was published under the English title of *An Essay upon Various Arts, in three books, by Theophilus, also called Rugerus, Priest and Monk*. The French lead was consolidated by the establishment in 1845 of a department devoted to enamelling on metal in the government porcelain manufactory of Sèvres.

French goldsmiths used enamel on religious and secular plate, while their English counterparts, since making a few experiments in the enamelling of domestic articles during the reign of

George IV (1820–1830), had concentrated mainly on ecclesiastical vessels. The Parisian firm of Jean-Valentin Morel did much to revive English interest in enamelled secular pieces after moving to London in 1849. An illustrated article on Morel's work appearing in the *Art Journal* in 1850 praised his enamelled jewellery, which expertly reflected the current taste and, more significantly, the gold vessels embellished with enamels and precious stones in which his firm specialised. The writer of the article exhorted English makers to turn their hands to similar work, a large request involving not only a high degree of skill but a large outlay in materials. Morel did well with his enamelled and jewelled articles at the Great Exhibition, attracting much publicity and gaining from the Jury a Council Medal, the highest award. English competition was negligible at the time, but a few London firms were inspired to emulate him at the International Exhibition held in 1862.

In 1851 Henry Cole's *Journal of Design*, never slow to recognize a promising trend, used the news that some English goldsmiths had been sending to Paris for their enamels to call for an English translation of Cellini's treatises on painting and sculpture, another source of information about enamelling techniques, in order to encourage a little enterprise at home. Cole, who was to be appointed in 1852 General Superintendent of the new Museum of Manufactures, was active on the Council of the Society of Arts, of which Prince Albert became President in 1843. As it was widely known in the late 1840s that the Society was planning a major exhibition of manufactures (which eventually developed into the Great Exhibition), it attracted to its ranks numbers of would-be exhibitors. Among the silversmiths in the Society were

FIG.2 Wood-engraving taken from a selection of illustrations of works by J. Angell, from *The Industry of All Nations, 1851. The Art Journal Illustrated Catalogue*, p.163.

Sebastian Garrard, a member of Garrard's, the Crown Jewellers, who joined in 1849, and Joseph Angell, who followed him in 1850. Both took care to let it be known in the right quarters that they were producing suitable pieces for the exhibition. Cole noted in his diary on 12 April 1850 that Garrard 'was preparing a Salver with enamels'. This proved to be 'The Great Railway Salver, or Brassey Testimonial', which was decorated with painted enamel portraits of English heroes of the Railway Age, with representations of their principal achievements. The salver was possibly a disappointment in artistic terms, for painted enamels had been popular since the late eighteenth century. The *champlevé* technique was regarded as far more important, as Joseph Angell, a third generation member of a family of London silversmiths, was acute enough to appreciate.

It was recorded in the *Transactions* of the Society that in early spring 1851 'Mr Angell . . . exhibited some pieces of plate of his manufacture, which he was about to place in the Exhibition of Industry of all Nations. He stated that his chief reason for thus submitting them to the inspection of the Society was, that in one of them (a large jug ornamented with medallions on the sides) he had succeeded in making some enamels on silver of a larger size than had been before executed'. The *Transactions* omitted the subsequent discussion, but it appears that the Chairman cast doubt on the validity of Angell's achievement but was then convinced by the silversmith's explanations. A subsequent editorial comment admitted that in the Middle Ages craftsmen had indeed enamelled on silver, but said that modern workmen had found difficulty in coping with the high rate of expansion of the metal under heat and of its consequent contraction on cooling, which frequently caused the enamel to crack and fly off. Angell, as we now know, fired his enamels on to a silver-gilt surface rather than direct on to the silver, and the high lead content of the vitreous material enabled it to fuse at a comparatively low temperature.

Angell bought space in the *Official Illustrated Catalogue* for an engraving of some of his wares, which included the flagon shown at the Society of Arts and a smaller silver-gilt claret jug encased in vines and cherubs, a popular design subsequently reproduced on several occasions. An 1851 claret jug now belongs to the Goldsmiths' Company. It is not enamelled; nor is another 1851 design, a splendid frosted and burnished silver tea and coffee service illustrating Aesop's fables which turned up in an auction sale in 1973 and was also acquired by the Goldsmiths' Company (FIG.4). However, Angell exhibited two enamelled services, both of which are illustrated in the *Art Journal* catalogue and again (using the same woodblocks) in his own catalogue which was published under the title of *Descriptive Particulars*. The new V&A acquisition appears as no. 2 in the *Particulars*, where it is described as 'AN ENAMELLED TEA AND COFFEE EQUIPAGE, comprising Coffee Pot, Tea Pot, Cream Ewer, and Sugar Basin, silver-gilt, and displaying in contrast the bright silver in line engraving, ornamented with medallions of purple and green ENAMEL sixteen in number upon each article. (The only specimen of the kind in the Exhibition,

and the last TEA AND COFFEE SERVICE is of silver, set with enamels. While adverting to the taste which has produced the whole of the objects we have engraved, we are bound to notice especially the beauty of the enamelling, which we scarcely remember to have seen equalled. The difficulty of enamelling upon silver is, we are assured, not easily surmounted.

FIG.1 Tea and Coffee Service, silver, parcel-gilt and
enamelled, London hallmarks for 1850–51; maker's marks of
Joseph Angell, h. of coffee pot: 32.5 cm. (M. 27-c –1983).

FIG.4 Tea and Coffee Service, silver, frosted and burnished;
scenes from Aesop's Fables, London hallmarks for 1851–52;
maker's mark of Joseph Angell, h. of teapot: 26 cm.
Collection: the Worshipful Company of Goldsmiths.

and the first ever manufactured.) Price £120'.

There are several points here requiring comment. Firstly, only four pieces are listed in the *Particulars* and only four are in the V&A set, though the illustrations depicts five. Perhaps the engraving was made from the original design and the fifth piece (presumably a slop bowl) was never executed. Secondly, though the statement about the service being the first to be manufactured does not absolutely rule out the existence of a contemporary duplicate, the chances are that the V&A service was the one actually exhibited in 1851. It is hallmarked for 1850–51; the exhibition opened on 1 May, and the date-letter for 1851–52 was not introduced until 29 May. As Angell boasted in the *Particulars* that his entire contribution to the Exhibition was executed in a mere five months, the strongest argument against the set having been duplicated is afforded by the complexity of its construction. Each of the sixteen separate enamelled parts in every article cited by Angell forms a spandrel between the flat lobes of the body above and below a wide girdle. Each of these components is individually hallmarked, showing that the service was submitted for assay before being decorated and assembled, a difficult task, even without the enamelling, which is reflected in Angell's price for the service, three times that of the average tea and coffee set.

Joseph Angell reaped his reward for ingenuity and industry. He was awarded a Prize Medal by the Jury for his enamelled wares. The purchasing committee for the Museum of Manufactures nevertheless saw no reason to acquire any of his works, and the service is thus the first example of Angell's 1851 plate to be purchased for the V&A collection. Several examples of *champlevé* enamel on silver were however acquired by the Museum in 1852. One was the Pugin chalice in FIG.3, and another, also a chalice, was made by a firm of watchmakers turned church metalworkers, Skidmore & Son of Coventry (FIG.5), whose work, ironically, had gone unremarked by the Jury and, indeed, by the Society of Arts. In terms purely of the size of the areas enamelled, the honours go to Skidmore. But the Skidmore enamels are an opaque and uniform blue, whereas Angell's, two-coloured and translucent, are far more in line with the work of the leading Parisian goldsmiths of the time, whose achievements were greatly admired and envied in England.

FIG.5 Chalice, silver, parcel-gilt, decorated with *champlevé* enamels. Birmingham hallmarks for 1850–51; maker's mark of Francis Skidmore. Acquired for the founding collection of the Museum of Manufactures, 1851–52, h. 20.3 cm. (1329–1852).

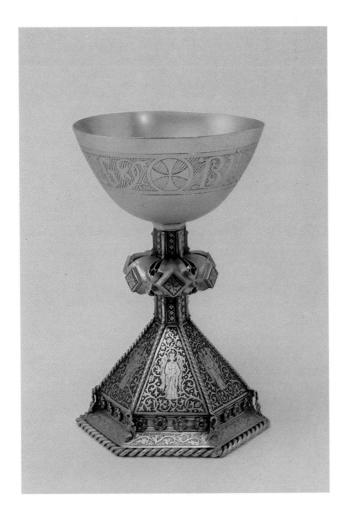

George II Silver

A fine pair of cast tablesticks made in London in 1734
by Thomas Tearle (Grimwade #2938)
with contemporary ciphers.
6⅜″ tall, weighing 11 oz. 5 dwt. and 12 oz. 2 dwt.
Fully marked.

A superb 20¼″ diameter
four-footed salver
by William Peaston
(Grimwade #3254)
London, 1754.
A solid 104 troy ounces in weight,
it bears the contemporary arms of
Popham, Littlecott, Wiltshire
impaling
Browning, Cowley,
Gloucestershire.
Magnificent silver.

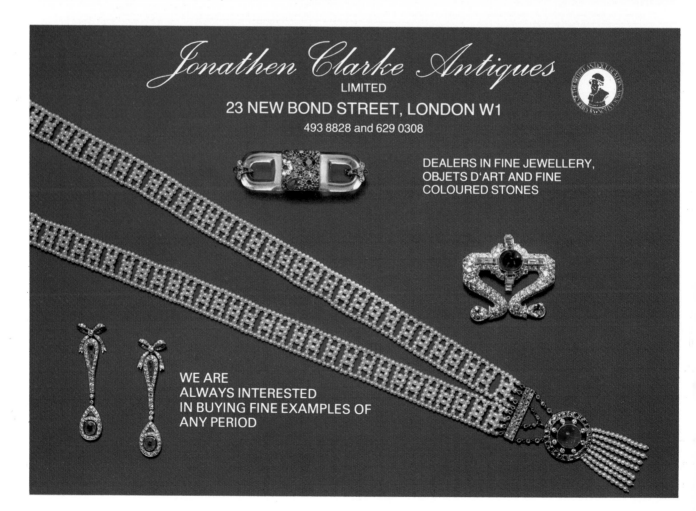

ANTONIO P. DA SILVA, LDA

A 17th Century Portuguese brooch pendant in gold and rose cut diamonds.

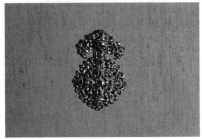

An antique cross-pendant set with six emeralds and a cushion cut diamond border mounted in gold and silver.

A pair of antique diamond ear-pendants in silver and gold.

An unusual antique monkey brooch with rose cut diamonds mounted in gold and silver

PRAÇA LUIS DE CAMÕES, 40–41
TEL. 32 27 28 – 32 63 20 – 32 63 69
END. TELEG. SILVAKAMOES
1200 LISBOA/PORTUGAL

DIRECTOR
F. MARQUES DA SILVA

FABERGÉ
Red gold frame with a carved green leaves gold border enamelled translucent pink and half pearls. Signed H.W.

SILVA'S

AUCTIONEERS, LTD

DIRECTORS
NAIR MARQUES DA SILVA
F. MARQUES DA SILVA

A famille rose tureen and cover modelled as a cock. Chien-lung

OFFICE
RUA EDUARDO-COELHO, 25-1° DTO.
Tel. 34 25 58
1200 LISBOA - Portugal

SALE ROOMS
RUA DO SACRAMENTO À LAPA, 24
Tel. 66 19 31 - 32 27 44
1200 LISBOA - Portugal

Maria Lalaounis wearing a diadem, necklace and
earrings in Gold, created by her father.

Ilias Lalaounis, new collection

"HELEN OF TROY"

was inspired by the fabulous Treasure of Troy, which disappeared
mysteriously at the end of World War II

ilias LALAoUNIS

219

PATRICK ALDRIDGE FGA

FINE JEWELS, GEMS AND OBJETS D'ART

GEMCUT S.A.
29 RUE DE LA RÔTISSERIE
GENEVA 1204
Telephone 22/217311

PATRICK ALDRIDGE LTD.
88/90 HATTON GARDEN
LONDON EC1
Telephone 01-242 3209

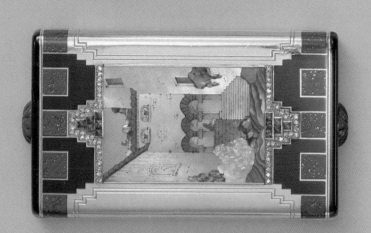

WE BUY AND SELL FINE PRECIOUS STONES, ANTIQUE AND MODERN JEWELS AND SMALL
WORKS OF ART.
PLEASE CONTACT OUR LONDON OR GENEVA OFFICES IN COMPLETE CONFIDENCE.

FELLOW OF THE GEMMOLOGICAL ASSOCIATION
MEMBER OF THE BRITISH ANTIQUE DEALERS ASSOCIATION
MEMBER OF THE CHAMBER OF COMMERCE
MEMBER OF THE LONDON DIAMOND BOURSE

HW
HARRY WINSTON
of New York

NEW YORK
718 Fifth Avenue

GENEVE
24 Quai du Général Guisan

PARIS
29 Avenue Montaigne

MONTE CARLO
Hôtel de Paris

ROYAL JEWELS IN THE V&A

Shirley Bury and Anna Somers Cocks

The term royal jewellery is capable of wide interpretation. It may refer to inalienable articles, often of great value, ranking as Crown Jewellery, such as the diamond circlet formed of the emblems of England, Scotland and Ireland alternating with crosses patée which was made in 1820 for George IV and subsequently dedicated to female use. All the subsequent queens regnant and consort of Great Britain have worn it; indeed, the present Queen is portrayed wearing it on current postage stamps. A great deal of lesser jewellery worn by royalty is of family or personal significance. This is complemented by articles commissioned or acquired solely for presentation to ladies and gentlemen in waiting, servants and other attendants; finally, jewellery and objects of vertu have traditionally been given and received by way of diplomatic exchange.

The jewellery in the V&A, though remarkably – indeed uniquely – comprehensive in its range, differs from several great collections on the Continent in that it is not based on the possessions of a royal family such as those of the Wittelsbach dynasty in the treasury in Munich, but has been accumulated by means of gifts, bequests and purchases. The pieces illustrated here exemplify all three types of acquisition, incidentally demonstrating that while the Museum has pulled off some striking coups by way of purchases, the quality of the collection is primarily due to the munificence of benefactors. To cite only three examples, the dress ornaments from the Russian Crown Jewels in FIG.1 come from a large (and unexpected)

bequest of Lady Cory in 1951, the bracelet clasps bearing the cipher of Marie Antoinette (FIG.2) were given by the late Dame Joan Evans, a distinguished scholar and collector whose generosity to the Museum was boundless, while the magnificent emerald and diamond necklace in FIG.3, forming part of a suite of jewellery presented by the Emperor Napoleon I to his adopted daughter Stéphanie Beauharnais in 1806 were first lent, then given in memory of her son, by Countess Margharita Tagliavia in 1978.

These three items are documented in different ways. Some of the dress ornaments have royal inventory numbers struck on their settings, the bracelet clasps are decorated with devices associated with Marie Antoinette at the time of her marriage in 1770, and a painting of Stéphanie Beauharnais, executed in 1806, shows her wearing the complete set of jewellery in which the necklace and earrings are clearly recognisable. It must however be confessed that the royal associations of several other pieces acquired by the V&A are more hazily grounded on tradition or hearsay, often enthusiastically accepted as a firm identification by former owners. The enamelled book cover of about 1570 in FIG.4 was purchased in 1862 with not one, but two, alleged associations. It was believed not only to have belonged to Charles I's queen, Henrietta Maria, but to have been executed by Benvenuto Cellini, whose virtuosity was so revered by the Victorians that they automatically attributed everything of exceptional quality to his hand. If

Henrietta Maria indeed owned the book cover, she almost certainly used it herself, perhaps to hold a book of devotions. Gifts from royalty to lesser mortals are represented by such pieces as the three *Gnadenpfennigs* in FIG.5, a favourite gift of German rulers, or the enamelled gold medallion in FIG.6, which bears the crowned cipher of George III and the date 1789, the year in which the British nation celebrated with his family and Court the king's recovery from a bout of insanity so distressing that while in its grip he sometimes failed to recognise his own children.

In 1899 Queen Victoria herself laid the foundation stone of the new frontage designed by Aston Webb for the Museum, an act commemorated by a change in its title. Known before, unofficially but universally, as the South Kensington Museum, the Queen re-named it the Victoria and Albert Museum, stylishly shortened to the V&A in recent years. For an institution bearing so august a name, the representation of jewellery associated with the Queen and her consort is disappointingly slight. With this in mind, the Museum successfully bid for the First Class badge of the Royal Order of Victoria and Albert in FIG.7 at a sale in Geneva a few years ago. The Order was instituted by the Queen on the first anniversary of her marriage following the unexpected and devastating death of the Prince Consort in December 1861, and it is thought that one of Victoria's daughters was the original owner of the badge which is now so appropriately in the V&A.

FIG.9 Detail.

FIG. 1 Four dress ornaments of diamonds set in silver from the Russian Crown Jewels, 1764. Cory Bequest. M.95–1–45–1951.

FIG.2 Pair of gold bracelet clasps with the cipher and marriage emblems of Marie Antoinette in diamonds on blue paste grounds, probably French, 1770. Given by Dame Joan Evans, P.P.S.A. M.51 & a–1962.

Lady Cory's bequest of 1951 included a set of three diamond bows and forty-six dress ornaments, from which come the four illustrated here. The bows and dress ornaments were among the Russian Crown Jewels sold off in Western Europe by the Bolshevik government after the First World War. Some of the ornaments are inscribed with Russian royal inventory numbers for 1764. The bows are roughly contemporary, and it has been suggested that they are the work of the royal jeweller, Duval.

The ornaments were designed to be sewn on to a costume to form a background for larger and more important jewels such as stomachers; such articles were already widespread in Europe by the sixteenth century and their use persisted well into the nineteenth century. Very few dress ornaments survive in their original form, though some are probably unrecognisable, having been converted by the addition of fastenings into other types of jewellery.

The decorative scheme of these clasps indicates that they were produced as royal souvenirs of the marriage in 1770 between Marie Antoinette (1755–1793), the fourteen-year-old daughter of Maria Theresa and Francis I of Austria, and the French Dauphin, who succeeded to the throne as Louis XVI in 1774.

On one clasp, Marie Antoinette's initials are surmounted by the wreath of Trianon, representing the splendours of the French Crown; on the other, below a similar wreath, are the turtle doves and hymeneal torches referring to her marriage.

The charm and lightness of the treatment accentuates the celebratory theme of a dynastic marriage which ended tragically in death by the guillotine for both Louis and Marie Antoinette.

FIG.3 Necklace and earrings of emeralds and diamonds, from a suite of jewellery given by the Emperor Napoleon I to Stéphanie Beauharnais, 1806. Given by Countess Magharita Tagliavia. M.3–b–1979.

In 1806, in order to consolidate the Confederation of the Rhine, Napoleon adopted Stéphanie Beauharnais (1789–1860), a sixteen-year-old relative of his Empress, Josephine, and immediately afterwards married her off to the Kurprinz of Baden, whose father was raised to the status of Grand Duke a few months later.

Napoleon's wedding gifts included a magnificent emerald and diamond suite such as seems to have been owned by all the female members of the Emperor's family, comprising a tiara (and possibly a comb), pair of bracelets, necklace and earrings. The set was reputedly made by Nitot, one of Napoleon's favourite Court jewellers. Stéphanie was painted in 1806 wearing the complete set; the portrait, attributed to Gerard, still survives in the possession of her descendants at Baden.

Stéphanie, still 'that most lively, fascinating little creature', gained the admiration of the Duke of Kent when he visited Baden in 1816, and a quarter of a century afterwards his daughter, Queen Victoria, was impressed alike by her liveliness and her bejewelled elegance. Stéphanie was a frequent visitor to England and Scotland in the 1840s and 50s; her daughter, Princess Marie, having been married in 1843 to Lord Douglas, later the fifth Duke of Hamilton. Though the Grand Duchess of Baden is known to have given her daughter a great many jewels on the occasion of the marriage, the emerald and diamond suite stayed in Baden. Items from the set were sold off at the end of the Second World War when the necklace and earrings were purchased by Count Tagliavia for his wife.

FIG.4 Book cover of enamelled gold, Munich, probably by Hans Reimer, about 1570. 736–1864.

This was bought in 1862 from Lady Dunsany as having once belonged to Henrietta Maria, wife of Charles I. It was also thought to be by the most famous of all Renaissance goldsmiths, Benvenuto Cellini.

Its iconography is rather complicated and still a little obscure; the front cover depicts the Creation of Eve, a religious subject, but the back cover shows the Garden of Love with Cupid crowning a fountain. There may, however, be a parallel between the two earthly Paradises, one before the fall and the other after. It is significant that in the Garden of Love a woman is being pursued by a serpent.

It remains unproven whether this exquisite little book cover ever did belong to Henrietta Maria but it is clear that, far from being by Cellini, it is not even Italian. It almost certainly comes from the workshop of the Munich goldsmith, Hans Reimer, who worked almost exclusively for the Bavarian Court.

Two signed and dated enamelled gold cups by him survive in the Wittelsbach treasury in Munich, along with other pieces which can be attributed to him. His enamel-work is outstanding and uses an exceptionally wide range of colours: an opaque turquoise and apple green, a translucent green and vivid red, all of which appears on the bookbinding. His decorative motifs are very similar as well: bold, three-dimensional C-scrolls, small rosettes, clusters of vegetables and, paralleled, on the sides of the book, champlevé enamelled rosettes linked by green stems, black-hatched C-scrolls, and lambrequins.

Thus, whatever its late history may have been, this book cover probably started life in a Bavarian Court goldsmith's workshop.

FIG.5 Three Gnadenpfennigs of enamelled gold, German, late sixteenth and early seventeenth century. 69–1867; M548–1910; M547–1910.

FIG.6 Pendent medallion of enamelled gold, commemorating George III's recovery from an attack of insanity, English, 1789. Bequeathed by Mr W.J.W. Kerr. M.34–1757.

A *Gnadenpfennig* (literally, a 'grace coin') is a peculiarly German phenomenon. It is a medal of a ruler or dignitary, which has been made into a pendant. The splendour of the setting depends largely on the rank of the recipient: for example, in 1612 the painter Rubens, was given a gold *Gnadenpfennig* set with two rubies and with the Bavarian coat-of-arms in enamel, by Duke Maximilian I. By comparison, these are relatively humble examples. They would have been handed out as part of the diplomats' merry-go-round of gift exchanges, and to reward some loyal retainer or notability. On the left is a medal by Alessandro Abondio dated 1612, of Archduke Maximilian II (1557–1618), son of Emperor Maximilian II. The coats-of-arms allude to his title and functions. In the middle is Wilhelm the Pious (1548–1626) son of Duke Albrecht V of Bavaria; and on the right is his son, Albrecht VI of Bavaria (1584–1666).

George III (1738–1820) succeeded his grandfather George II to the thrones of England and Hanover in 1760. His last years were clouded by madness, giving rise to the Regency of his son, later George IV. It has been argued in recent years that George III's insanity was caused by porphyria, a condition undiagnosed during his lifetime. The King's first major attack of insanity started in October 1788 and lasted until the spring of 1789. The diarist Fanny Burney, then serving his Queen, Charlotte of Mecklenburg-Strelitz, as her junior keeper of the robes, wrote a poignant account of the months in which the King talked incessantly and slept little, his seemingly delirious state terrifying his wife, children and gentlemen-in-waiting. But he was much-loved, and relief at his recovery was widespread. It would have been in keeping with the generous and considerate nature of the King when in health to commission and distribute medallions celebrating his recovery to those who had served him in his illness.

FIG.7 First class badge of the Royal Order of Victoria and Albert, English, about 1864. M.180–1976.

FIG.8 Watch, enamelled gold, probably English, about 1630–40. 446–1884.

Among the most evocative images of the widowhood of Queen Victoria (1819–1901), appearing in several state portraits, sculptures and photographs of the Queen, is her First Class badge of the Royal Order of Victoria and Albert. The badge in the V&A is not the Queen's own, but once belonged to a royal princess: membership of the First Class was confined to ladies of Royal birth. Sold anonymously in Switzerland in 1976, the badge was acquired by the Museum in the knowledge that the diamonds on the outer frame had been replaced by pastes. The design, however, is unimpaired, and the fine double portrait cameo of Victoria & Albert, engraved in Rome by Tommaso Saulini, who died in 1864, indicates that the original owner came from the English Royal family. The Queen instituted the Order on 10 February 1862, and her own elder daughters were the first to be admitted to the Order. Saulini, who signed the cameo, used as his model the obverse of the medals of the Great Exhibition of 1851, engraved by William Wyon. The cameo was set in London by R&S Garrard, the Crown Jewellers, with a design inspired (at some distance), by the projecting strapwork of such Elizabethan miniature cases as the Heneage or Armada jewel in the V&A.

The Queen never came out of mourning for the remaining forty years of her life, and the importance she attached the Order is demonstrated by her giving a badge to Alexandra of Denmark on the eve of her marriage in March 1863 to Victoria's eldest son Edward, Prince of Wales, the future Edward VII. Alexandra wore the badge on her wedding day.

This watch, whose movement and dial are a later replacement, has a plain outer case of silver engraved with the Stuart Royal Arms in the Garter and the monogram C R, and with an inscription which reads 'This watch was a present from ye King to The Earl of Menteith'. Which earl, and which king is revealed in the notes made between 1789 and 1808 by Elizabeth Hastings, daughter of the 9th Earl of Huntingdon, who records that when Charles II was ill, he gave this watch, which had belonged to his father, to William Graham, the last Earl of Monteith (1661–1694). Both parts of this story are supported by the evidence of the watch and case themselves. The enamelled gold work, with its 'pea-pod' design and swirling foliage on the lid must date from around 1630–40, while the style of the armorial engraving on the silver case, is of the late seventeenth century, added perhaps, by the proud new owner.

FIG.9 Chain and pendant of enamelled gold, set with pearls, and with diamonds, about 1600. The chain marked RV. 696–1898.

These were bought in 1898 as having come from Schloss Ambras. This castle near Innsbruck was famous as being the love nest of Archduke Ferdinand II and his morganatic wife, Philippine Welser. While his court remained at Innsbruck, his private life unfolded at the castle and it was there that he assembled one of the finest of sixteenth century collections of works-of-art, antiquities, curiosities and armour. Unfortunately the chain and pendant cannot have belonged to him or Philippine as they died in 1595 and 1580 respectively and the pendant (probably also the chain) must date from 1600 at the earliest because of the leaf-shaped settings of the stones. But there is no doubt that the filigree-enamelled chain comes from the same, as yet unknown, workshop which made some of the little dress jewels given by Ferdinand's two nieces, Maria Christierna and Eleonora to the neighbouring convent at Hall when they took the veil there, and which also made the mounts on a small horn cup still in the Imperial collections. On the other hand the pendant, which is a much grander, more substantial piece, is related to work produced by the Imperial workshop in Prague around this time, so while there is no proof that this piece came from Ambras, circumstantial evidence does suggest that the legend is true.

FIG.10 Presentation Box of enamelled gold, set with diamonds, made for Tsar Nicholas II by Fabergé of Moscow and St. Petersburg between 1897 and 1903. M.1–1974

Peter Carl Fabergé, Court Jeweller to Tsar Nicholas II (1868–1918) and his father Alexander III, was responsible for a remarkable variety of works, all exquisitely executed. Some of his firm's finest productions were created for the Russian royal family; they ranged from intricate jewelled eggs which opened to reveal a 'surprise', most of which were gifts between the Tsar and Tsarina, to a series of gold boxes bearing the portrait or monogram of the sovereign which were made for presentation to distinguished personages. The box in the V&A, struck with the mark of Michael Perchin, one of Fabergé's workmasters, carries the Tsar's cipher in brilliant-cut diamonds in a crowned oval frame set with the same stones which are mounted over a lozenge of translucent enamel, with a black-enamelled Imperial eagle set over translucent yellow enamel on each corner. The name of the original recipient is unknown; the box was bequeathed to the V&A by Sir William Seeds, K.C.M.G., H.M. Ambassador in Moscow, 1939–40.

A carat or more.
When a man's achievement becomes a woman's good fortune.

A carat or more - one in a million.

Every diamond is rare. But of all diamonds found, only one in a million is a gem diamond of a carat or more.

And, like love, becomes more precious with time.

A miracle among miracles. Born from the earth. Reborn on a woman.

The extraordinary diamond solitaire of a carat or more. Show the world you couldn't have made it without her.

A diamond is forever. De Beers.

Jewellery from Hennell ⚜
—— SINCE 1736 ——
12 NEW BOND STREET, LONDON W1
TELEPHONE: 01-629 6888

To help you survive the slings and arrows of outrageous fortune, it's comforting to reflect on the fact that you have one or two rather nice things from Hennell.

OUTFIT BY SONIA RYKIEL AT BROWNS

ANTIQUE AND
ESTATE JEWELLERY

Harry Hofmann

BAHNHOFSTRASSE 87 & 79
8001 ZURICH
SWITZERLAND

VDW

Snake evening bag in gold,
rubies, diamonds, amethysts,
black and white mother of pearl.
Real dimensions.
Each model is deposited, signed and catalogued.

Marina B

Geneva, 9 Place du Molard – 1st floor – Telephone 21 53 53 – Telex 427 077

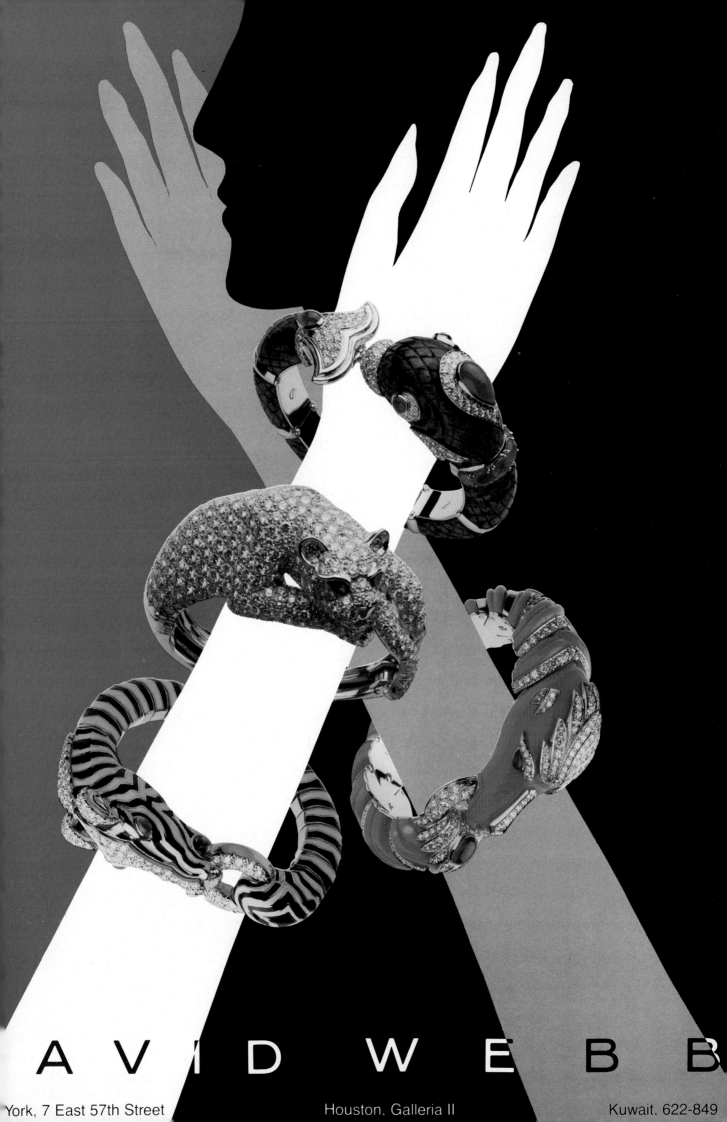

·CHARLES DE TEMPLE·
52 JERMYN STREET · LONDON SW1 · TELEPHONE 01-499 3639

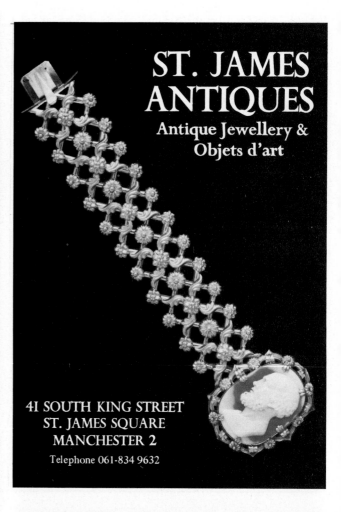

Window 20, the translation of Elijah in a fiery chariot,
King's College Chapel. (By permission of the Provost and the
Scholars of King's College, Cambridge.)

SAVING STAINED GLASS

June Lennox

I happened recently to visit the Chapel of King's College, Cambridge, and the notion came to my mind, as I looked at the stained glass, that I was, as it were, within what might fairly be described as the biggest painting ever made.

Leaving aside the West window of 1879, the work of Clayton and Bell, the remaining 25 windows, amounting to something over 6,000 square feet of glass, are essentially the work of one directing intelligence operating upon a unified theme over a period of thirty years or so, 1515 to 1547. It is true that that directing intelligence operated through the medium of a number of partners, pupils or assistants. It is true, too, that these assistants necessarily had a good deal of discretion allowed them in their own interpretation of the Master's broad conception: given the scale of the works, both in regard to space as well as to time, it could hardly be otherwise. Nevertheless the Master's spirit was strong to control; strong enough indeed to carry his influence over three hundred years, for essentially Clayton and Bell fulfilled merely the Master's original intention, which the death of his patron had left him without the means of completing.

This struck me as a remarkable circumstance, and even more remarkable the fact of the Master's comparative obscurity: an obscurity which cannot be said to have been fully penetrated even today, and which it is not my intention to attempt to penetrate here. Of course, the obscurity of Medieval master craftsmen is a commonplace, not confined solely to the stained glass business: but stained glass is a business very likely to augment any such tendency to obscurity. I have spoken already to the sheer scale of the project, 6,000 square feet is a lot of glass, as a problem bearing upon the designer's capacity to control the work of his subsidiary designers and other craftsmen, but the actual process of making stained glass windows compounds the problem by the number of subsidiary processes which go to the completion of any work – designing, cartooning, cutting, painting, staining, firing, glazing, cementing and fixing – largely to be carried out upon a material whose conventional attribute, brittleness, is proverbial. It is not remarkable that some more amenable matrix should have been looked for, and found, for the continuing of that long-continued human preoccupation with painting.

There are a number of reasons adduced for the rise to pre-eminence of oil painting on canvas as the matrix of European painting, ranging from the sentimental – that the texture and spring of the canvas is sympathetic to the brush – to the cynical – that their comparative portability made them a convenient medium of exchange, particularly fine wrought Treasury Bills as it were. Certainly nothing has less elasticity than glass, if that is the reason; nor might the ceiling of the Sistine Chapel, say, very conveniently be exchanged in the normal way of business. The true reason, I fancy, is a good deal more mundane: no matrix permits the painter so great a freedom to change his mind; '. . . this my hand will rather The multitudinous seas incarnadine, Making the green one red'. A change of mind is not lightly to be undertaken at any stage in the course of making a stained glass window. Whatever the reason, financial or otherwise, the pre-eminence of canvas painting has certainly the effect of devaluing all other matrices to a more or less significant degree. And this, perhaps, is what is most remarkable in the relationship between King's College Chapel and North European painting in general, that it can hardly be said that any such relationship is ever perceived. Or at any rate the relationship never is alluded to in any significant way.

Hindsight operates to distort our view of painting, and particularly North European painting, prior to 1500. We know that easel painting in oil on canvas rose to a pre-eminence which it still holds and naturally enough there is a tendency to look at the art of former times with a view to categorising the precursors of this particular mode which was not then pre-eminent. I will not beg the question as to quality but it must be plain that there is a gross imbalance here in regard, at the very least, to quantity.

No doubt it will be thought crass to be seeming to compare King's College Chapel with, let us say, the Ghent Altarpiece upon no other criterion than their respective gross area, but it seems a circumstance no less crass when I consider the index of a book which I have before me. This is a conventional enough general history of art published in 1957. It is perhaps convenient that the place of origin should be the United State of America since thereby any European chauvinist bias may be presumed to be obviated.

Under 'Stained Glass' the index gives six references, three to the text and three to illustrations. Two of the textual references are passing comments only, the third is a body of text amounting to slightly less than a page. Turning now to 'Jan van Eyck' I find thirteen textural references and four illustrations, not to mention two further textual references to the van Eyck family in general. Slightly less than a page is devoted to the Ghent Altarpiece alone as well as an equal space given to each of the Arnolfini Marriage and the Madonna of Chancellor Rolin respectively, and this is connected directly to two of the illustrations, a whole view of the Altarpiece itself and a detail of the Adoration section. There is no mention whatsoever of King's College Chapel. To put this simply, we have here what purports to

Window 8, left: Elisha raising the Shunamite's son; right:
the triumphs of David, King's College Chapel. (By permission
of the Provost and Scholars of King's College, Cambridge.)

1 Christ on the Cross, King's College Chapel.
2 The Virgin at the foot of the Cross, King's College Chapel.
3 The unrepentant thief, King's College Chapel. 4 Window
11, Christ before Annas, the High Priest, King's College
Chapel. 5 Window 16, Jonah and the whale, King's College
Chapel. (By permission of the Provost and Scholars of King's
College, Cambridge.)

be a general history of art running to some 757 pages which dismisses the whole vast corpus of nearly 1,000 years of painting on glass in the space considered requisite to the discussion of a single oil painting. It does not seem to me to be disparaging the Ghent Altarpiece to suggest that there is something disproportionate in this allocation of resources. It may be thought curious, too, given the thesis being developed, that the Ghent Altarpiece is not, no more than are the windows of King's College Chapel, the actual workmanship of a single man.

Now there is no intention here of developing romantical notions as to some presumptive superiority inherent in glass. Even if there were theoretical superiority, and indeed there is that capacity of glass to gain its effect by the transmission, as opposed to the reflection, of light, this would be of null effect in the face of the general acceptance of canvas painting as the criterion of artistic excellence now.

Nor am I much concerned, not, at any rate, in my professional capacity as a conservator, with the art historical ramifications of the matter here developed: although I feel bound to say that it seems to me remarkable that so little attention should be given to the artistic history of the period between,

say, the year 1000 and, the year 1432, as it bears upon the subsequent development of canvas painting: the period that is during which the concept encapsulated in the phrase 'North European Painting' may not unreasonably be taken as synonymous with the concept encapsulated in the phrase 'Stained Glass'.

What does concern me is the cast which this insensible depreciation of alternative modes of painting gives to the mind which comes to consider any particular example of such an alternative mode in regard to its conservation. There is a very thorough guide to the glass in King's College Chapel, by Hilary Wayment, published by the College itself which, after an historical and technical preamble, comes to consider each of the windows in detail, congruent to the unifying theme. Most of these conclude with an account of the extent to which the glass has been damaged. In regard to nine of the windows specific percentages of 'restored' area are given, amounting in some cases to as much as 16 or 17 per cent. Over and above the percentages given, or in those cases where no percentage is given, there is usually more specific detail given of loss or alteration. Specified heads, as well as other detail, are noted as defective in some way, or

as being of eighteenth or nineteenth century make. Disordering of fragments in releading, and the commonplace circumstances of the intrusion of wholly alien fragments to make good losses, is also mentioned here and there. These are all, indeed, fairly obvious to the casual glance, without the aid of the guide, as is another commonplace circumstance not mentioned in the guide – that is, the extensive intrusion of arbitrary leads, not only through heads and other significant detail, but generally throughout the architectural and landscape (or seascape) background, which conduces to the conventional acceptation of stained glass as a minor branch of the art and craft of patchwork. Broadly speaking this is a Museum of the decorative arts, a disingenuous phrase which seems to have come to connote anything which is not oil painting, so that we are not much given, at any rate, in the Conservation Department, to attaching judgments of value to the objects in our care, as between one object and another, or as between one mode and another. But it is difficult to escape the conclusion that, outside the Museum, the pre-eminence of canvas painting has tended to a depreciation of the notional value of alternative modes of painting.

1 The cutline, laid over the cartoon prior to cutting the glass.
2 Applying the glass paint. 3 The firing in of the glass paint.
4 The leading of a window prior to soldering.

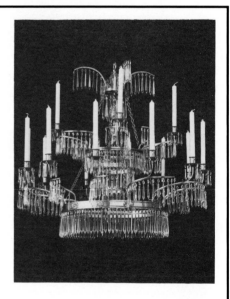

249

TWENTY YEARS OF CERAMIC AND GLASS DESIGN
The Collections of the British Institute of Industrial Art and Industry

Jennifer Hawkins Opie

On 6 July Harold Stabler, the noted enameller, jeweller, silversmith, ceramic sculptor and designer, wrote to the Board of Trade. His letter was sent to Sir Hubert Llewellyn Smith and suggested the setting up of an alternative scheme to replace the financially foundering Arts and Crafts Exhibition Society. His particular concern was to form a new association of the producing members of the Society and to run a showroom in the West End 'as near to the shopping centre as they could afford'. He hoped to bring to public attention the work being done by craftsmen of all types and wondered what would be the chances of government recognition.

As it happened his approach was unusually timely. Moves had begun following the British contributions to the international exhibitions held in Ghent (1913) and Paris (1914) and Llewellyn Smith himself suggested a 'permanent National Exhibition of works of Modern British Artists in the Capital of the Empire'. He also recommended that a sales agency be attached to the Exhibition. These proposals were referred to in correspondence with Sir Cecil Harcourt Smith, then Director of the Victoria and Albert Museum (1909–1924) as 'our scheme' and the Museum's records make it quite clear that for some time discussions had been underway with the Board of Trade. Harcourt Smith's own version was issued on 30 April 1914 and was entitled *Proposals for a Museum and Institute of Modern Industrial Art*. As a postscript he suggested, since the Institute should in his view have such a close connection with the Museum, that this should override the commercial preference for somewhere more central and instead it should be based in the South Kensington neighbourhood. 'As a matter of fact' he noted 'there is at this moment a piece of ground immediately opposite the Vic-

toria and Albert Museum which is for sale and which looks as if it might be adaptable for the purpose'. His main suggestions were that an annual exhibition should be held with categories corresponding to the main Museum Departments (Ceramics, Metalwork, Textiles etc.) and judged by a committee especially appointed for each Department. From each annual exhibition the best pieces would, he hoped, be acquired for a permanent Museum collection of modern industrial art and in time, the cream of this group would transfer to the V&A's historic holdings.

Correspondence continued throughout May but by August it was recognised that the international political situation was likely to affect any official moves and by March 1915 all practical developments had ceased. Nevertheless discussion continued, not least because individual craftsmen, quite independently, wrote in to the various Museum and Ministerial Departments suggesting similar schemes. Also, the Arts and Crafts Exhibition Society's future looked increasingly black and, curiously, an extremely successful exhibition of German design was held at the Goldsmiths' Hall in 1915 – both these factors contributing to the general concern felt by craftsmen, designers and some manufacturers.

One result of the German exhibition quite suddenly deflated the official plans somewhat. The committee responsible for its organisation set up a new group, the Design and Industries Association whose founder members included Harold Stabler and also Ambrose Heal. In April 1915 it was noted by the V&A's Director, with mingled envy and alarm that they were 'urging forward their project with great energy and success'.

Meanwhile the necessity for official support and finances kept real progress to a minimum, but although nothing could be achieved while the war lasted

or during the immediate aftermath, both Sir Hubert and Sir Cecil continued lobbying for opinions and information stepping up their activity in late 1917. By May 1918 a new outline for the British Institute of Industrial Art had been drawn up. The Institute was finally set up in February 1920 and the first exhibition was held at 217 Knightsbridge from June to September in the same year. The introductory section to the catalogue summarised the BIIA's aims as 'raising and maintaining the standard of excellence in works of industrial art produced by British designers, craftsmen and manufacturers and of stimulating the demand for such works as attain to a high standard of excellence'.

The Ceramics Department's representative was its Keeper, Bernard Rackham, who selected from this very first exhibition three pieces by Bernard Moore including a 'long necked bottle with crimson streaky flambé glaze' and a 'small vase and cover, brilliant turquoise & purple glaze', (both illustrated FIG. 1). Rackham also chose, after meticulous consideration, two pieces by Pilkington, two by Doulton, one by Carter of Poole and one by Minton, all to join the proposed collection of modern industrial art. The catalogue to this exhibition shows a mouthwatering list of ceramics and glass such as a 'collection of Painted, Powder Blue, Powder Ruby and Lustre China, Earthenware, Basalt and Jasper. Manufactured by Josiah Wedgwood and Sons'; a case of 'Royal Brierley Crystal manufactured by Stevens & Williams', including coloured and clear glass, cased, cut and engraved; a case of Pilkington's Royal Lancastrian pottery in ruby and silver lustre decorated by Gordon Forsyth, Richard Joyce, W.J. Mycock and Gwladys M. Rodgers and wares by various other manufacturers. The Doulton stand, from which Rackham also made

FIG.5 Two mugs, earthenware, cream glazed. Designed by Keith Murray (1892–1981), made by J. Wedgwood & Sons, Etruria, c.1934, ht. 23 and 10.5cm. Both acquired with the CAI for the exhibition English Pottery Old and New, V&A, 1935, the second also shown in the international exhibition in Paris, 1937, Cat. no. 275. C.138–1935. Circ. 21–1938. Bowl, earthenware, 'Moonstone' glaze. Designed by Keith Murray (1892–1981), made by Josiah Wedgwood & Sons, Etruria. 1933–5, diam. 30.5cm. Given by the CAI. Circ. 310–1954. Axis deer, earthenware, cream glazed. Designed by John Skeaping (b. 1901), made by J. Wedgwood and Sons, Etruria, 1927, ht. 37.5cm. Given by John Skeaping to the BIIA Permanent Collections in 1927. C.426–1934.
FIG.9 Part of a coffee set, 'Studland', cream earthenware, with 'Apple Green' glaze. Designed by Harold Stabler (1872–1945), made by Carter, Stabler & Adams, Poole, c.1933 ht. of coffee pot 17.5cm. Shown at the international exhibition Paris 1937, cat. no. 206. Lent to the Museum by the CAI from about 1938, given in 1954.
Circ. 306+A – 309+A-1954.

5

9

FIG.6 Two vases, colourless glass with cut decoration. Designed by Clyne Farquharson (dates unknown), made by John Walsh Walsh, Soho & Vesta Glassworks, Lodge Road, Birmingham, 1937, ht. 19.5 and 20cm. Lent to the Museum by the CAI from about 1938, given in 1954. Circ. 402 and 405–1954. FIG.7 Vase, green glass, with wheelcut decoration. Designed by Keith Murray (1892–1981) made by Stevens & Williams, Brierley Hill Glassworks, Stourbridge, c.1937, ht. 28cm. Shown at the international exhibition Paris, 1937, cat. no. 386B. Given to the Museum by the makers following negotiations with the CAI. Circ. 16–1938. FIG.8 Bowl, colourless glass with opaque white lines. James Powell & Sons, Whitefriars Glassworks, Wealdstone, c.1937, diam. 13cm. Shown at the international exhibition Paris 1937, cat. no. 350. Given to the Museum by the makers following negotiations with the CAI. Circ. 13–1938. Decanter and stopper and two wine glasses, colourless glass, with cut decoration. Designed by Keith Murray (1892–1981), made by Stevens & Williams, Brierley Hill Glassworks, Stourbridge, c.1937, ht. of decanter 27.5cm. Probably shown at the international exhibition Paris 1937. Given to the Museum by the makers following negotiations with the CAI. Circ. 295+A, 296 & 297–1939.

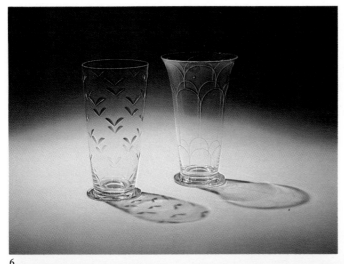

6

7

8

FIG.2 Panel of nine tiles, stoneware, painted in sepia. Bernard Leach (1887–1979), St. Ives c.1926/7, each tile 9.5cm. sq. Given by Bernard Leach to the BIIA Permanent Collections in 1927. C.403–1934. Vase, stoneware decorated after Chinese 'Cizhou ware' of the Song dynasty. Hamada Shoji (1894–1978), St. Ives, 1926, ht. 20cm. Given by Bernard Leach to the BIIA Permanent Collections in 1927. C.411–1934.

a small selection, was described as showing a 'collection of Old Sung Glaze, Crystalline, Grand Feu and Flambés'. The Doulton Titanian vase, here illustrated (FIG.1), was probably part of this display since it was presented to the BIIA in 1920.

Soon after this exhibition the question arose of premises for the BIIA's Permanent Collection. The hopes for a separate building (on the 'piece of ground immediately opposite') were never fulfilled and far from this, by August 1921 the North Court of the Museum had been offered to the Institute. This plan was put into effect and for thirteen years both the BIIA Permanent Collection and the temporary exhibitions were housed there under the charge of Miss A.P. Carter. The Permanent Collection was open to the public daily and the travelling versions of many of the exhibitions were launched from the North Court under the Keepership of H.A. Kennedy. Price lists accompanied these exhibitions for the use of local art schools and colleges who might wish to purchase similar work from the various craftsmen, designers or manufacturers.

In its time the BIIA was closely involved in a number of prestigious events such as the British Empire Exhibition of 1924 and the annual British Industries Fair; it arranged special exhibitions at centres around

the country and also contributed British sections to several overseas exhibitions. Another important aspect of its work was the production of various reports on the state of contemporary design and industry.

Throughout its existence the BIIA was bedevilled by lack of adequate financial support. This problem was already having its effect when the Board of Trade grant had not been renewed after the first two years and the Institute was supported by private subscription only. The resulting uncertainty about its future drew a prompt response from the Museum regarding the accommodation loaned to the Institute and by this early date the sharing of the Permanent Collection among the Museum's departments was already under discussion. In answer to this possibility Bernard Rackham was able to recommend for the Ceramics Department, the acceptance of two vases by Bernard Leach and three vessels and a panel of tiles with sport scenes (by Edward Bawden) all made by Carter, Stabler & Adams and also Carter & Co. at Poole.

Despite all these difficulties, the Institute maintained an impressive reputation. The catalogues to the exhibitions held in 1922 and 1923, and in subsequent years, show a range of wares that now would be welcome additions to any collection. They include ceramics and glass by the major manufacturers such as Wedgwood, Worcester, Minton and Doulton, James Powell, Webb and Stevens & Williams. Also included were displays by smaller potteries like Bernard Moore's, the Ruskin Pottery and the Moorcroft Pottery, as well as a vast number of individual pieces such as figures by potters who were enormously popular in their day – Charles Vyse, and less well known now, Reginald Wells, Stella Crofts, Irene Brown, Gwendoline Parnell – and

flambé ware by E.R. Wilkes, domestic wares by the Walberswick Pottery Co and Upchurch Pottery. Not all of these joined the Permanent Collection, but a small selection was made after each exhibition.

In 1929 Mrs Armitage (neé Bulley) offered to lend her impressive private collection of modern decorative art to the BIIA. It was to be shown at Bethnal Green Museum, a branch of the V&A where, it was agreed, the collection might be housed. The Margaret Bulley Collection (as it became known) includes work by Duncan Grant, Vanessa Bell, the Omega Workshops, E. McKnight Kauffer and others, as well as Raoul Dufy and a number of Continental artists. This 'very generous' offer was accepted. It was subsequently left as a bequest to the Museum and constitutes a major section of the twentieth century collections.

1929 was also notable for the successful exhibition quaintly titled *British Industrial Art for the Slender Purse*. This exhibition, like the others, was held in the Museum's North Court despite the Institute's own slender purse. Finally, in 1933, the Institute was partly responsible for the arrangement of *British Industrial Art in Relation to the Home*, held at Dorland Hall. This was one of the major exhibitions of the 1930s, a decade in which several were mounted, each acting as a milestone in the history of design in Britain and each raising a storm of criticism and comment.

However, in this same year, the BIIA's finances were in serious trouble and the question of dissolution was being raised. By April 1933 the decision had been taken and the BIIA was to be wound up. On its final closure in 1934 it was agreed that the Museum should take on the Permanent Collection and this was done, with special arrangements for the different

categories of gifts, purchases and loans to the BIIA and for the Collection's maintenance and display at Bethnal Green where, with the Margaret Bulley Collection, it was to form the basis of the Museum's modern section under the officer-in-charge, A.K. Sabin.

In this way a large number of highly regarded productions of the 1920s, including particularly ceramics and glass, made their way into the Museum's collection by means of gift, or purchase with the aid of the Spielmann Memorial Fund. These pieces now form the mainstay of the earlier twentieth century collection and many of them will be on show in the twentieth century primary gallery.

In papers relating to the closure of the BIIA it was stated that the 'existing British Institute of Industrial Art had decided to dissolve itself so as to leave the field open for the new Council proposed to be established under the Board of Trade – as a result of the Gorell Report – to foster closer relations between industry and art'. In 1931, the Board of Trade with fresh finances, re-entered the fray surrounding the improvement of industrial art and appointed a Committee on Art and Industry under Lord Gorell, to inquire into the production and exhibition of articles of good design in everyday use. Recommendations were made regarding the V&A Museum, many of them very similar to the principles laid down on the founding of the BIIA – principles such as a permanent exhibition of industrial art in London and travelling exhibitions to the provinces. The committee members included various personalities eminent in the design and art world. As well as Sir Hubert Llewellyn Smith of the BIIA and Sir Eric Maclagan, then Director of the Museum (1924–1944), pottery manufacturers were represented by A.E. Gray and by Harry Trethowan, designer and the buyer for Heals.

The Report resulted in the appointment of a Council for Art and Industry under the Chairmanship of Frank Pick, so influential as Vice-Chairman and Chief Executive of London Passenger Transport Board and also President of the Design and Industries association.

Under Pick, the Council plunged into a round of activities and reports on a scale which quickly equalled the BIIA achievement. An exhibition of silverware was arranged at the Museum in 1934, the Council's first year of existence and the success of this show was repeated on a larger scale the following year with *English Pottery Old and New*. In the preliminary plans it was agreed that Bernard Rackham and Mr Ronald Copeland (of the pottery manufactory) would start the selection and first visits were made to Waring's, Goode's, Harrod's, Heal's, Maple's and Fortnum and Mason's. Later it was agreed that Harry Trethowan, with the potter W.B. Dalton, should be co-opted onto the committee. Harry Trethowan had an added advantage in that working for Heal's he was able to supply covering materials for the exhibition case fittings and screens and he sent a selection of hessians, linens and twills in buffs, beiges and greys to the Museum. The exhibition was opened on 15 April 1935 and a leaflet was distributed explaining its purpose. 'It has been planned to show some of the best work done in English pottery, old and new, and at the same time to illustrate the living tradition maintained in the art from medieval times to the present day'. Congratulatory letters were received from many people including the Josiah Wedgwood of the day and the exhibition proved such a success that its run was extended. At the end of the year it was proposed to celebrate the exhibition with an illustrated book. Frank Pick engaged E. McKnight Kauffer to design the cover, W.B. Honey of the Ceramics Department arranged the photographs and wrote the introduction while Frank Pick and Sir Eric Maclagan jointly signed the prefatory note. This booklet now constitutes a useful record of the exhibition which ranged from studio wares by Bernard Leach and Michael Cardew to laboratory porcelain by Doulton and Worcester. It also shows a number of pieces such as an earthenware jug by C.H. Brannam Ltd and brown stoneware cooking pots by Joseph Bourne & Co. as well as bone china teaware by Josiah Wedgwood & Sons which have since made their way into the Museum's collections.

This same format of showing historic and contemporary material together was repeated just before the outbreak of war with an exhibition of tiles. The committee for this was headed by Harold Stabler with David Burton of Pilkingtons and A.S.D. Cousland of Mintons representing the Glazed and Floor Tile Manufacturers' Association, Cyril Carter of Carter & Co and W.B. Honey. Later, W.B. Dalton was brought in to represent studio tile makers.

In 1937 a second international exhibition was held in Paris and Pick's Council, as it had become known, was responsible for the selection of the exhibits, working through the Board of Trade. Plans were drawn up for the acquisition by the Museum of examples shown in the exhibition, to be arranged through the CAI. Firstly, duplicates or similar examples to those wares shown in Paris were in some cases given and in others lent to the Museum's travelling service under H.A. Kennedy and, on the closure of the exhibition, some of the actual pieces selected by Maclagan and Kennedy were also added through the arrangements set up by Frank Pick. The ties between the Museum and the Council at this time, were very close and there was regular correspondence between the various representatives.

The war brought an end to the Council's activities and Frank Pick died in 1941. After the war a new generation of Councils were set up beginning with the Central Institute of Art and Design and evolving one by one into the present Design Council. The CAI loans to the Museum were eventually absorbed into the collections in 1954, just twenty years after the major group of BIIA acquisitions.

As a direct result of the energies of these two institutions and the close relationship established with the Museum, the ceramics and glass holdings of the mid-twentieth century are extensive. The selection was probably on the cautious side and there are many gaps but as a representation of the official or government sponsored view of the best of British ceramics and glass design, these two collections are unequalled.

FIG.1 Bottle, porcelain, with a high temperature glaze, described as 'peach blow' in the BIIA records. Bernard Moore (1850–1935), St. Mary's Works, Longton. 1921, ht. 14.2cm. Given by Bernard Moore to the BIIA Permanent Collections in 1921. C.441–1934. Vase and cover, bone china with mottled 'Titanian' glaze. Carved wooden cover in emulation of the Chinese. Doulton & Co, Nile Street, Burslem, c.1920, ht. 10cm. Given by the makers to the BIIA Permanent Collection in 1920. C.494–1934. Vase and cover, porcelain, with 'Persian Blue' glaze. Bernard Moore (1850–1935), St. Mary's Works, Longton, c.1921, ht. 9.9cm. Given by Bernard Moore to the BIIA Permanent Collections probably in 1921 and described as an 'experimental piece'. C.442–1934. FIG.3 The Balloon Woman, earthenware painted in colours. Charles Vyse (1882–1971), Chelsea, 1921, ht. 22cm. Given, possibly by Charles Vyse, to the BIIA Permanent Collections. C.432-1934. The Lavender Seller, earthenware, painted in colours. Charles Vyse (1882–1971), Chelsea, 1920, ht. 22cm. Given by Charles Vyse to the BIIA Permanent Collections in 1920. C. 428–1934.

1

3

SEMPRE LO STESSO VETRO, DA MILLE ANNI.

Sempre lo stesso vetro, da mille anni
la tradizione del vetro di Murano
non cambia; sabbia, fuoco, la
mano dell'uomo e gli umori
dell'isola.
Ciò che cambia costantemente,
invece, è il nostro modo di
riproporlo, attraverso un design
raffinato ed attuale, come ad
esempio i vasi, le coppe ed i
bicchieri della serie: CARTOCCIO

® carlo moretti

NOBILITA IL VETRO.

CARLO MORETTI S.r.l. Fondamenta Manin, 3 / 30121 Murano VENEZIA
Telefono: 041/739217-736588 / Telex: 410850 EMMECI-I

Primavera

Minaudière—Cartier Paris

Floor Lamps—Sue et Mare   Lacquer Vase—Mergier and Hamanaka   Sharkskin Screen—Jean-Michel Frank   Lacquer Table—Eileen Gray

Primavera Gallery   808 Madison Avenue, New York 10021   212·288·1569

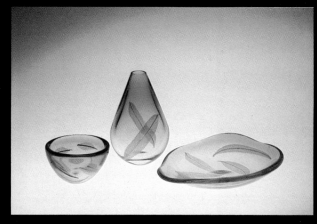

ARCHIMEDE
SEGUSO

1 ''Le piume'' Dish, vase and bowl crafted in 1955 in pale shading coloured glass with feathers.

2 ''Faccia al vento'' Face against the wind 1974.

Italy Venice Murano
Fond.ta Serenella, 18

Living with Art

'Art is an aspect of everyday life'
Eduardo Paolozzi, Great Britain.

The Artist
Eduardo Paolozzi, born in
Edinburgh in 1924, has succeeded
in defining the twentieth century in
relevant form and visual language.
He has constantly expressed our
modern environment in terms of art.

'Suomi' – Object no. 3
Paolozzi's design on the shape
'Suomi' by Timo Sarpaneva may
be regarded as an element in the
microcosm of technology –
coloured circuits brought to life like
currents in the stream of conscious-
ness. This coffee pot is one of four
limited 'Suomi' objects by Eduardo
Paolozzi which can be combined

with the unlimited service pieces in
the 'Suomi' shape.

'Suomi' combines art and design.
The limited objects are at the same
time works of art and items for
practical use.

Rosenthal Studio-Linie
For almost 30 years Rosenthal has
worked with over 100 important
artists and designers in the
development of the Rosenthal
Studio-Linie. The aim is to produce
unique works which correspond to
the spirit of our time, and to make
these available to a wide public. The
result is a collection which reflects
the variety of expression in the art of
our time.

The Rosenthal Jury
Every design for the Rosenthal
Studio-Linie is judged by an
independent jury of recognised art
and design experts. Only a positive
majority decision ensures the
acceptance of a design into the
collection.

**The Rosenthal Studio
Department**
The Rosenthal Studio-Linie
collection is found exclusively in
Rosenthal Studio Departments and
in Rosenthal Studio Houses
throughout the world.

studio-linie

LOOKING AT DOLLS' HOUSES

Anthony Burton

'Why am I bothering to look at this?' Museum curators do not often stop to ask this question about the things in their museums, since professional necessity and academic interest supply for them instant justification. Likewise, curators do not often stop to wonder how museum visitors face the same question. The visitor may hit on a quick answer, 'Because it is here, in the Museum'; but this only provokes other questions: 'Why is it in the Museum? What is it supposed to do for me?'

Most visitors to art galleries know roughly how they are supposed to react to a picture. First, they are to recognise what it represents, and then to sense that it is beautiful. Pictures, anyway, are fairly easy to cope with because they come in a standard shape and are neatly packaged in a frame. But the contents of a decorative arts museum like the V&A are more varied in form and size, and visitors are probably much less schooled in how to react to them. Most things in a museum are old, so it is a safe bet to admire antiquity. The straightforward desire to know what a painting represents is matched, before a decorative arts exhibit, by the inquiry, 'What was it used for?' Curators rarely stoop to answer either of these questions intelligibly. What 'beauty' is to a painting, perhaps 'design' is to an object of decorative art, but the latter quality seems even more insubstantial than the former to the man in the street. In the end, visitors often go round in a frankly consumerist spirit. 'I'd like one of those,' you hear them say, or (perhaps before some throne of cedarwood, amethysts and beaten gold) 'I wouldn't have that in my front room'. Audience reaction is very hard to judge in a museum.

At the Bethnal Green Museum of Childhood, we know exactly how our adult audience (whether a little old lady or a Minister of the Crown) will react. At some stage an imaginary lightbulb flashes above a visitor's head, and he says, with obviously pleasurable reassurance, 'Oh, I used to have one of those'. This response, which may be denigrated as 'mere nostalgia', is not often provoked in the V&A, because of the richness of the collections; few people used to have a throne, or even a Chippendale chair. It can be evoked in social history museums, but the exhibits there ('bygones') are often bafflingly obscure. Among designed objects, toys are exceptionally accessible, because we all had them at a time when our perceptions were intense, and they embrace a limited range of types, repeated over centuries. So they are a good way of arousing a grown-up's interest in material culture.

This should be true for children as well. Of course, children are often taken to museums to undergo an educational experience, and teachers are wont to suppose that a museum of childhood is intended to be a teaching machine. Fortunately, it is very hard to turn playthings into teaching material. The reaction of children in the Bethnal Green Museum is pure pleasure, which springs up despite the fact that the exhibits are still presented in a rather po-faced museum style, and are protected from exploring fingers by glass.

The two responses, 'Ooh look at this!' from the child, and 'I used to have one' from the adult are so simple and direct, that it seems priggish to try to work on them so as to improve a visitor's mind. (Anyway we shall eventually have some more conventionally fact-fraught and thought-provoking displays in our upstairs galleries, to be devoted to the social history of childhood and family life.) One class of exhibits, however, seems to support a

more complex pattern of response, of a kind nearer to that offered at the V&A: the dolls' houses.

Old and elaborate dolls' houses naturally find a place in a museum, since, as they become venerable, they cease to be playthings (if they ever were) and become something to be looked at and shown off: exhibits. The grandest of all dolls' houses, those made in Holland in the seventeenth and early eighteenth centuries, and surviving in the museums at Utrecht, Amsterdam and The Hague, must have been created with motives not unlike those which stimulated the creation of that Mannerist art-form, the 'Antwerp cabinet'. The Dutch dolls' houses have no exterior architecture; from the outside, they are indeed cabinets. When opened, they present, as do the Antwerp cabinets, a spectacle of minute craftsmanship, lavish intricacy, and visual illusion. But instead of an ingenious system of drawers, cupboards, niches and mirrors, they disclose a miniature domestic world: in aesthetic terms, a sort of representational version of the abstract pleasures of the Antwerp cabinet.

Even dolls' houses showing less aesthetic refinement can earn a place in a museum as examples of fine craftsmanship, objects of decorative art in their own right; and so, good dolls' houses will be found in museums in Paris, Munich, Nuremberg, Stockholm. Certainly, the expertise of the decorative arts student can be applied to the wallpaper, fabric, paint and furniture in dolls' houses. There is, indeed, a characteristic connoisseurship in dolls' houses, as demonstrated in Vivien Greene's books, with their mixture of practical information and atmospheric writing. Authentic art-historical points can sometimes be made: Leonie von Wilckens traces the interior decoration of a Nuremberg house to its source in a print, just as one

265

FIG.1 A peep into 3 Devonshire Villas, made *c*.1900: note the
conservatory with its bead curtain, and the staircase that goes
nowhere. Misc. 5–1972.   FIG.3 The Nuremberg House:
domestic interiors of 1673. W. 41–1922.   FIG.4 Mrs Bryant's
Pleasure: domestic interiors of the 1860s. Misc. 9–1955.

1

3

4

FIG.6 The Tate Baby House. An interior showing finely
detailed cornice, door-frame and fireplace. W. 9–1930.

might with a full-scale house. Yet there is a snag in approaching dolls' houses as decorative art objects. Their appeal lies essentially in the fascination of the miniature. But the kind of wonder at change of scale which we can imagine when we read fairy-tales or *Alice in Wonderland* is never truly to be found in a doll's house, because miniature objects can rarely be made to possess texture, shape and tension in a right relationship, corresponding to their full-scale counterparts. To the eye accustomed to appraise objects of decorative art, the miniature fittings of a doll's house must seem slightly false.

It is also difficult to be sure to what extent the entire mise-en-scène in a doll's house is a true or false reflection of something that once may have existed in real life. Teachers, anxious

to make our exhibits instructive, often think that dolls' houses can be treated as a reliable record of life in the past. But a moment's reflection convinces us that they are no more reliable than a picture: they may be a kind of reporting, but more likely they are an imaginative creation. Sometimes we are led to believe that a house is a deliberate copy of the home of an erstwhile owner. In our collection '3 Devonshire Villas' (Misc. 5–1972) (FIG.1) is named after the house in Kilburn High Road upon which the exterior is supposed to have been modelled, but it is obvious that its interior layout is not authentic: the staircase, for example, does not lead to the upper storey. We have, perhaps, only two houses which we know to be closely copied from real houses: a fine

mansion lent by Mrs P. Swain, and a little suburban box of the 1930s, made by an architect who followed his own plans for the full-size real thing (Misc. 34–1965) (FIG.2).

If few dolls' houses can be proved to be accurate models of a particular building, some at least can be presumed to be a studied representation of aspects of domestic life in general. Such is the case with our oldest house, made in Nuremberg in 1673 (W. 41–1922) (FIG.3). Contemporary literary sources refer to such houses as being made with an educational purpose – to instruct girls in domestic economy – so we may assume that their interior fittings have a high degree of conscious realism. The Dutch houses already mentioned are also highly realistic – presumably, however, for reasons of

FIG.5 The Tate Baby House. Georgian grace: but is it quite right for the central Venetian window to have a pediment above? W. 9–1930.   FIG.7 The Thornton Smith Baby House, with its staring windows. Misc. 145–1923.   FIG.8 Mary Foster's House. The key-hole and hinges interrupt the classical harmony of the façade. W. 49–1925.   FIG.9 Caroline Cottage, 1831. A simple box with classical trimming. Misc. 216–1923.   FIG.10 A simple box, c.1840, with Gothic trimming. W. 17–1930.   FIG.11 Mrs Greg's House, c.1830. More joinery than architecture. Misc. 44–1925.

5

7

8

9

10

11

FIG.13 Miss Barker's House, 1887. Late Victorian architecture translated into wood by a billiard-table maker. W. 147–1921.   FIG.14 A picturesque villa made by Thomas Risley, 1880. Misc. 5–1958.   FIG.2 A suburban house of the 1930s: a doll's house modelled on a real building. Misc. 34–1965.

13

14

2

adult pride. A similar feeling must have inspired a house in our collection made in 1860–5 for a Mrs Bryant (Misc. 9–1955) (FIG.4): it has exceptionally well-crafted, convincing furniture. But the house itself is hardly more than a cupboard, architecturally unrealistic and merely a setting for the furniture. A feature that it shares with other mid-Victorian dolls' houses is that its rooms are disproportionately lofty, perhaps to make it easier to see and reach inside. The disproportion may be seen also in our Gothic house of c.1840 (W. 17–1930), the Drew doll's house of c.1860–65 (Circ. 400–1953), and the Egerton Killer house of c.1835–8 (W. 15–1936).

The latter is a set of rooms created within a lacquered cabinet decorated in Japanese style, and so, like most of the Dutch houses, it has no external architecture. Most dolls' houses, however, do have exteriors with some architectural pretension, which give a visitor an opportunity for art-historical appreciation. Our collection provides a miniature history of English architecture from the late eighteenth century to the present, though yet again we must be on the alert for false notes.

The old notion that eighteenth century dolls' houses were customarily designed by 'prominent architects' surely cannot be true. In an age which possessed an accepted architectural language, a carpenter could have run up a convincing dolls' house with no more difficulty than a jobbing builder would have run up a presentable real house. Georgian dolls' houses are symmetrically proportioned, usually with a centre panel crowned with a pediment and side wings with opening fronts. Door and window frames have more or less elaborate mouldings, and architectural features such as pilasters, rusticated quoins, urns and balusters are applied to taste. The Tate Baby House, of c.1760 (W. 9–1930) (FIG.5) is an ex-

tremely fine house (an adult rather than a juvenile plaything) (FIG.6), well detailed and well preserved, surpassed perhaps only by the dolls' houses at Uppark and Nostell Priory, and the Blackett house in the Museum of London. It even has working sash windows. And yet something is wrong here, for these have no glazing bars. If the Tate house were a full-size building, we would think that its Georgian grace had been spoiled by Victorian plate glass windows.

Such an architectural solecism is even more obvious in the Thornton Smith Baby House (Misc. 145–1923) (FIG.7). Though this has the customary eighteenth century proportions, its detail is more perfunctory than the Tate's, and its cream and green colouring must surely be a repainting. Its windows are blank panes, and make it look ruinous. Yet inside, like the Tate, it has fine detail: well-moulded cornices and architraves, and good fireplaces. Once it would have had glazing bars stuck or painted on to the glass, so as to preserve the regular articulation of the façade. That this was the way Georgian dolls' house windows were

FIG.15 A late nineteenth century terrace house. The back, with its projecting kitchen, etc., is equally realistic, and the sides open variously so that a child can get at the interior. Misc. 40–1961.

made is confirmed by many examples: in our collection by the Denton Welch house, 1783 (W. 13–1949), and Mary Foster's house, c.1800 (W. 49–1925) (FIG.8).

This kind of house is designed in a kind of joiner's delayed Palladian style. The Greek and Gothick revivals and the refinements of Soane and Holland do not register on English doll's house architecture, though one feels that Nash ought to have designed a doll's house. Early Victorian dolls' houses are generally simple cupboards, divided inside into four rooms by vertical and horizontal partitions. The outside style of such houses may be vaguely classical, as in our Caroline Cottage (Misc. 216–1923) (FIG.9), or vaguely Gothic, as in W. 17–1930 (FIG.10), but there is little that is architectural about either of these. If they have an attractive texture and a venerable patina, that too has nothing to do with architecture and everything to do with the qualities of wood, paint and paper.

Dolls' houses are, after all, woodwork, and this usually shows. A pilaster on a façade may be approximated by a length of beading, tacked on, as on Mrs Greg's house, c.1830 (Misc. 44–1925) (FIG.11). Even in the high-quality house given by Lady Henriques (W. 1–1954) (FIG.12), the decoration on the pediment (which on a real building would probably be a relief in Coade stone) looks like a bit of fretwork from a chair-back. Though most doll's houses are painted to resemble brick or stone, some show off the attractions of natural wood. One such is the house made for Miss Barker by the Ashcroft billiard table manufacturers of Liverpool in 1887 (W. 147–1921) (FIG.13). Its architecture is recognisably late Victorian (a sort of Norman Shaw Tudor) but the finish is of different polished woods. Another house in our collection (Misc. 97–

FIG.16 A traditional English cottage designed by Charles Spooner. The washing-line shows that dolls live there. Misc. 9–1924.   FIG.17 Whiteladies. A dream home for bright young dolls of the thirties. W. 3–1937.

1975), of a style that is rather hard to pin down, uses a rare, reddish wood called paduk for its roof tiles, while the rest is of stained and natural birchwood.

Usually a doll's house is made shallow, one room deep, so that its back goes to the wall, and architecture is confined to the front. But sometimes a miniature house is designed to be viewed all round. The little villa made by Thomas Risley in 1880 (Misc. 5–1958) (FIG.14) might almost be an architectural model, so carefully is it made, but as Risley was only 17 when he did it, it is more likely to be a piece of apprentice cabinet-making. Another faithful model is a bay-windowed terrace house of the turn of the century (Misc. 40–1961) (FIG.15), but this certainly was a doll's house. A borderline case is an Old English cottage and garden designed by Charles Spooner, 'architect and instructor in furniture-making at the LCC Central School of Arts and Crafts' in 1923 (Misc. 9–1924) (FIG.16). While this is truly an architect's model, it was commissioned by Mrs Greg for the Museum, for the benefit of 'children hungry for beautiful things to look at', so it counts as a doll's house too.

Architecturally, it represents the end of the English vernacular tradition, which was to be so rudely interrupted by the Modern Movement. Here too, our dolls' houses supply an echo of full-scale architecture, not only in mass-produced 'Cubist' houses produced by Triang (Misc. 60–1965, Misc. 65–1975), but also in the splendid 'sun-trap' house, 'Whiteladies', designed by Moray Thomas (W. 3–1937) (FIG.17). This was intended to be a doll's house and is inhabited by wiry little figures, but it aimed also to reflect the ethos of the inter-war generation.

Later dolls' houses in our collection tend to reflect the ideas of educational psychologists (simplified forms, bright colours) rather than architecture. But the rather playful architectural climate of 'Post-Modernism' would seem particularly propitious for a revival of doll's house building. We shall see.

Not all the houses mentioned here are on view at Bethnal Green at present. Gallery re-arrangements in progress include a new area for dolls' houses, where they will be better seen together. Then perhaps, some of the questions lightly aired in this article can be raised more seriously, and the houses can be subjected to a more searching scrutiny by visitor and curator alike.

16

17

Stephen Marks
Autumn-Winter 83/4.

64/66 Great Portland Street,
London W1N 5AJ
Telephone: 01-580 2507

STEPHEN MARKS

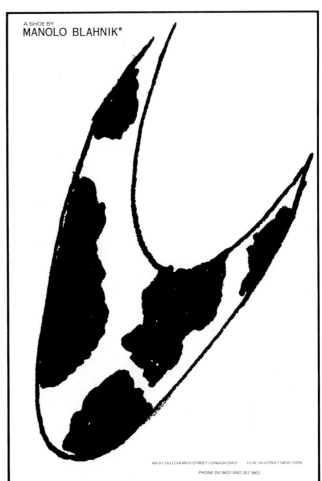
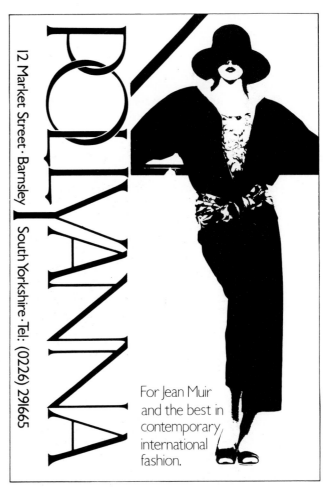

Ambers

OF AMERSHAM

AMBERS IS OUR HOME FOR FASHION

We aim to give that touch of elegance provided by the complete fashion story to make your visit to us a pleasurable experience. We can dress you from top to toe, starting with our millinery collections, through lingerie and hosiery, our own designers for that very special occasion, garments from 100 different designers and manufacturers, to shoes and leather accessories. We pride ourselves on our honest help and advice, whereby we give you that final look which is exciting, glamorous and different.

We are 25 miles from Central London, on the edge of the interesting historical town of Amersham and know you will enjoy your visit to Ambers, where the mill stream flows through the building and we have a restaurant and ample car parking for your convenience.

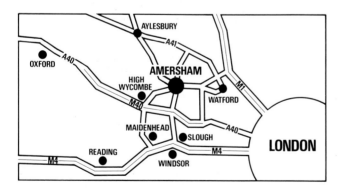

Ambers
OF AMERSHAM

THE MILLSTREAM, LONDON ROAD
AMERSHAM, BUCKS HP7 9DA

TELEPHONE: AMERSHAM (024 03) 22471

Helen Trist
Hand Painted Original Designs

Entirely original unique silk clothes, designed and hand painted to order at our studio. Personal shoppers welcome. Open 10 am–4 pm Mon–Fri. Catalogue available for mail order.

'Helen Trist'

No. 5

Dovedale Studios

465 Battersea Park Road, London SW11
Tel: 01-223 9643

. . . "who gave thee clothing of delight" . . .

anna roose

4 Station Road West	57 Pimlico Road	Love Lane
Oxted, Surrey	London, S.W.1.	Denbigh LL16 3LE
Tel: (088 33) 7788	Tel: 01-730 2867	Tel: (074571) 2431

THE FRIENDS OF THE V&A

AIMS

To help in the work and activities of the Victoria and Albert Museum and in particular:

To purchase works of art

To maintain a lively exhibition programme

To expand the Museum's training schemes and research projects

To contribute towards the cost of refurbishing the galleries

PRIVILEGES

1. Free and immediate entry to all paying exhibitions at the Museum and to Ham House, Osterley Park, and Apsley House (Bethnal Green has no entry charges).
   The membership normally admits husband/wife or other guest and Friend's children under 16.

2. Special Evening Private Views

3. Advance information on Museum activities.

4. Discounts on selected catalogues and other publications, and purchases in the Craft Shop.

5. Visits abroad and in this country, accompanied by staff from departments of the Museum.

6. Social occasions at the Museum, Ham House, Apsley House and Osterley Park.

MEMBERSHIP

Membership Fee
£15 annually

Special Fee
£10 annually
(for pensioners and those working full time in UK museums)

Corporate Fee
£100 or more annually
(with transferable membership cards)

Benefactor
£1,000 annually
A Benefactor may specify which department or project of the Museum should receive his gift

For further details and application form, please apply to:
Friends' Office
Victoria and Albert Museum
South Kensington
London SW7 2RL
01-589 4040

FIG.1 Dress and coat, jersey and wool,
Sheridan Barnet and Sheilagh Brown
T.195–T.200–1980.

A COLLECTION GROWS
The Gift of British Fashions for Winter 1979

Valerie D. Mendes

The new permanent display of four hundred years of fashionable dress (1550s to the present day) is now open in Gallery 40 and about one-third of the exhibition is devoted to the twentieth century. This seems an opportune moment to consider the significance of the important gift made to the fast-expanding twentieth century dress collection in spring 1979. It was enriched by twenty-five complete outfits from top British designers chosen by the leading fashion editor, Barbara Griggs. The generous donation was the result of a powerful combination of the designers themselves, Dr Leonard Simpson, Chairman of Simpson (Piccadilly) Ltd (who organised the exhibition of the collection and then transferred it to the V&A), and of the foremost mannequin manufacturers Adel Rootstein. The offer (via a telephone conversation with Simpson's Margaret Box) came as a complete surprise. The Museum's temporary exhibition galleries were booked solidly for almost five years save for the fortuitous one week spot in May 1979. With haste, a team led by Simpson display manager Peter Southgate and including lighting expert Arnold Dover and fashion display artist Kevin Arpino (now responsible for the compelling windows of Wallis shops), re-organised the show in gallery 48E, and with equal speed dismantled it just seven days later to make way for the next exhibition. The effort was rewarded as the exhibition proved a popular attraction seen by thousands of visitors.

The Cecil Beaton Collection of designer clothes and accessories forms the nucleus of the later twentieth century dress collection. Since it was exhibited in 1971 clothes have been systematically added to reveal annual fashion trends but among these acquisitions the extensive collection of British Fashion for Winter 1979 is unique in its precise coverage of one season's developments. It presents an almost complete picture of the various 'looks' which were offered to the well-dressed woman at the end of the decade. This detailed survey (which also includes artwork) should prove a boon to future students who will now be able to match excellent photographic records in the fashion press with the full range of actual objects preserved in the Museum. The normal life of some of these objects is all too ephemeral, as fashions are rapidly changed. It is already difficult for example to find equivalents of the patterned stockings which were current in 1979. The preparation of the exhibition in Gallery 40 has emphasised one of the chief assets of this collection – that each ensemble is complete (including mannequin)

FIG.2 Evening dress, jersey trimmed with beaded tassels, hat by Frederick Fox, John Bates
T.190–T.204–1980.

from head to toe. Numerous main items of designer clothing (even very recent designs) survive, though usually without their accessories, which entails a sometimes frustrating hunt for the correct and essential garnishings. An exact date-match is often impossible, so a compromise is reached whereby the overall appearance is correct, but the date-range of objects might be as much as five years. Happily this problem will never arise with the collection for Winter 1979. The clothes were fully accessorised by the designers – almost as if their creations had been lifted from the catwalks of live shows into Simpson (Piccadilly) Ltd, and thence into the Museum.

For the first time ever the Museum was given custom-designed, display mannequins with hairstyles and make-up to complement each outfit. These mannequins from the impressive *Whirl, Swirl, Twirl and Shadow* range (sculptor John Taylor) were presented by Adel and Richard Hopkins. Adel Rootstein is world famous for the enormous advances she has made in the art of mannequin making. Her work (in the hands of a group of talented display artists) plays a key rôle in the unrivalled success of window display in London stores. Once again recent experience reveals the significance of the gift of these mannequins. In an ideal museum world with unlimited space every twentieth century fashionable ensemble would come with its own tailor-made mannequin (in perfect condition). They would range from wax figures of the early 1900s through the stylised forms of the 1920s and 1930s to the superbly realised mannequins of the 1970s and 1980s. A mannequin which is contemporary with its clothes has the fashionable posture and gestures of the period – features which are so difficult to capture once that time has passed. Curatorially, it is a great relief to know

FIG.3 Dress and jacket, jersey and suede, Ann Buck.
T.201–T.204–1980.   FIG.4 Dress and coat, knitted wool,
cotton and lurex, clutch Cargo (Sandra Best and Alyce
Chadwell). T.193–T.194–1980.   FIG.5 Coat, blouse and
skirt, various woven wools and worsted, hat by Herbert
Johnson, Wendy Dagworthy T.225–T.236–1980.
FIG.6 Roller disco outfit, hand-knitted woollen sweater
with tights, socks and skates, Paul Howie.
T.245–T.250–1980.

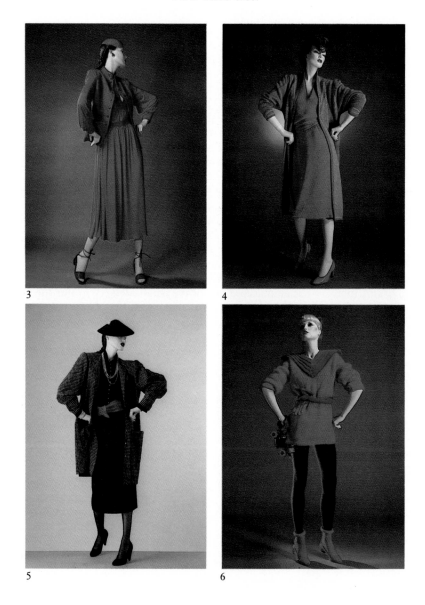

3

4

5

6

FIG.7 Blouses and footless tights, jersey and sequined jersey, Jean Muir. T.279–T.282–1980.   FIG.8 Coat, jacket, blouse, skirt, belt, umbrella, bag and hat, wools, cottons, leathers and felt, Mulberry Company (Roger Saul). T.287–T.297–1980.   FIG.9 Evening dress and cape, printed chiffon and pleated satin trimmed with beads, Zandra Rhodes. T.283–T.286–1980.   FIG.10 Evening dress and jacket, jersey trimmed with metallic thread, Janice Wainwright. T.313–315–1980.

7

8

9

10

that twenty-five Adel Rootstein mannequins of 1979 stand ready to be dressed with their own 1979 clothes which they will show to maximum advantage. The figures are from one range but skilled hairdressing and make-up creates many types ranging from a teenage blonde for Paul Howie's roller disco outfit (FIG.6) to an older sophisticate wearing John Bates's plunging evening dress (FIG.2).

Various considerations (principally the question of storage and display space, and the nature of other British dress collections) formulated the V&A's policy of collecting fashionable clothes by established designers. Thus, in 1979, the addition of work by twenty-five top designers was a timely gift bringing this specialist collection right up-to-date and providing a much needed fillip, while Gallery 40 was submerged by scaffolding and undergoing its lengthy face-lift. Some joined the collection for the first time while others – Jean Muir, John Bates, Zandra Rhodes, Yuki and Maureen Baker were already represented. The collection illustrates the immense range of fashion talents active in Britain in 1979. Unfortunately it is impossible to show all twenty-five outfits here, though, hopefully, the selection indicates the diversity of the gift. Although the Department of Textiles and Dress collects clothes which have been worn (many by those famed for their taste and elegance), it is a conservation advantage that this collection is in an unworn, pristine condition. It is interesting that the clothes have hardly dated as there has been no dramatic change in silhouette or hemline length over the past five years. Although short skirts or 'ra-ras' were introduced, they remain strictly for the young. Only the exaggerated square shoulders (harking back to the 1940s) of some of the designs suggest that they were conceived in 1978–9. Special occasion clothes

such as evening dresses tend to be cherished and offered to the Museum, whereas day wear is often worn out and discarded. It is the V&A's good fortune that here we have the entire gamut from Zandra Rhodes's evening extravaganza (FIG.9) to the Mulberry Company's practical layered outfit (FIG.8). The 1970s prediliction for disco dancing is revealed in two outfits with similar lines. Jean Muir combines a typical softly draped blouse with immaculately top-stitched details with clinging, sparkling tights (FIG.7) while Paul Howie tops black tights and roll-down socks with a bold hand-knitted sweater. Zandra Rhodes is well known for her screen-printed chiffons which are united with minutely pleated satins in her 'cascade' dress (FIG.9). The scrolling gold motif is echoed by the hair adornment. When the exhibition was transferred to the V&A a television news-crew were much taken by John Bates's audacious black evening dress (FIG.2) embellished by Frederick Fox's Bird of Paradise hat, beaded tassels and a great deal of bare flesh. Janice Wainwright's black ensemble trimmed with gold appears demure but under the jacket the halter neck dress is completely backless to the waist (FIG.10). As ever, black was popular in 1979 and Murray Arbeid, Jane Cattlin, Juliet Dunn and Yuki all contributed black dresses. Maureen Baker gave a shocking pink silk seersucker evening dress and Victor Herbert donated a pair of glistening silk velvet and lurex evening pyjamas. In addition to the five day outfits shown, Caroline Charles, Gordon L. Clarke, Chris Clyne, Pauline Wynne Jones, Roland Klein, Michiko, Celia Mortimer, Patti Searle and Daks donated day apparel. Chris Clyne's amusing bright red satin and velvet ensemble based on clown costumes is in direct contrast to the classic Daks suit and Celia Mortimer's sensible mix and match kilt, blouse,

jacket and shawl.

The collection encompasses numerous types of fine dress fabrics ranging from delicate printed silks to durable woven woollen checks. Happily, British manufacturers were responsible for a large percentage of the textiles including the heavy winter woollens and the viscose jersey, while Celia Mortimer's design uses that versatile British produce – Viyella. Light jersey knits are much in evidence, and the late 1970s revival in heavier knitted goods is manifest in Clutch Cargo's intricately constructed dress and coat (FIG.4). Ann Buck carefully handles jersey to create a long-sleeved supple dress worn under a suede jacket with punched and machine-embroidered decoration (FIG.3). Wendy Dagworthy's chic day outfit (FIG.5) comprises a straight skirt in worsted and a shirt in plain wool under a slim single-breasted, shepherd-check wool coat with interesting full sleeves and padded shoulders. In anticipation of a cold 1979 winter, Sheridan Barnet and Sheilagh Brown conceived a practical and attractive combination of a bright yellow melton coat over a simple black jersey dress (FIG.1). Additional high spots of colour are provided in the purple belt and vivid pink bow which surmounts the veiled hat. The later 1970s saw the useful layered look become modish. Various articles of clothing were assembled one over the other but the appearance of bulk was avoided by keeping the line long. Layers of harmonious plain coloured wools and cottons provide warmth in Roger Saul's ensemble (FIG.8) which is completed by the familiar Mulberry and Company leather accessories.

After the successful exhibition it was decided that when the Dress Collection re-opened, the outfits would be shown in rotation to reveal British design for 1979. At the moment the outfit by Wendy Dagworthy is on display.

orelle Chiarugi
icami Artistici

igliana - Vinci (FI) - via Raffaello Sanzio 26 tel. 0571 509363 509440

Topfloor

A fine collection of antique costume, important early textiles and decorative works, including:

European and Eastern clothing; Victorian and Edwardian 'whites'; specialist Irish crocheted garments; English farming smocks; beaded dresses; Oriental robes, skirts and wall-hangings; European woolwork, beadwork, tapestry and other furnishings.

14 Church Street
Marylebone
London NW8
(moving to 2 Church Street)

Hours 10.00am – 5.30pm
Mondays to Saturdays
(01) 723 9981

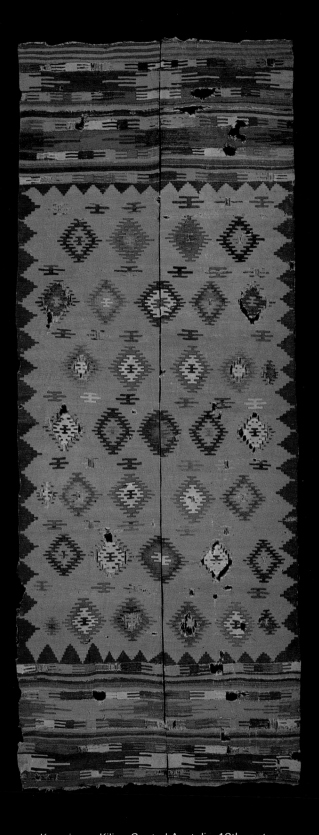

RAHIM BONAKDARIAN

"The soul of the apartment is in the carpet"

A 19th-century Bessarabian carpet, measuring 9.5 x 9.1, with an exceptionally bland and completely understated color palette. The enlarged design elements are beautifully conceived and form a voluptuously entwined pattern, which adds to the already beautiful square dimensions. Pale grey, pale peach, and ivory are set off by accents of light Delft blue and lemon yellow. This example is visually a treat, as it does not overwhelm the viewer, and if anything, it indulges our sense of fantasy.

This gallery features an eclectic array of room size carpets and small collector pieces of outstanding merit in Oriental and European weaves.

An Appointment Is Suggested

**ANTIQUE AND EXEMPLARY CARPETS
AND TAPESTRIES**
in New York
at 15 East 57th Street
212-759-3715

Doris Leslie Blau

A Dealer Interested in this Art Form in America

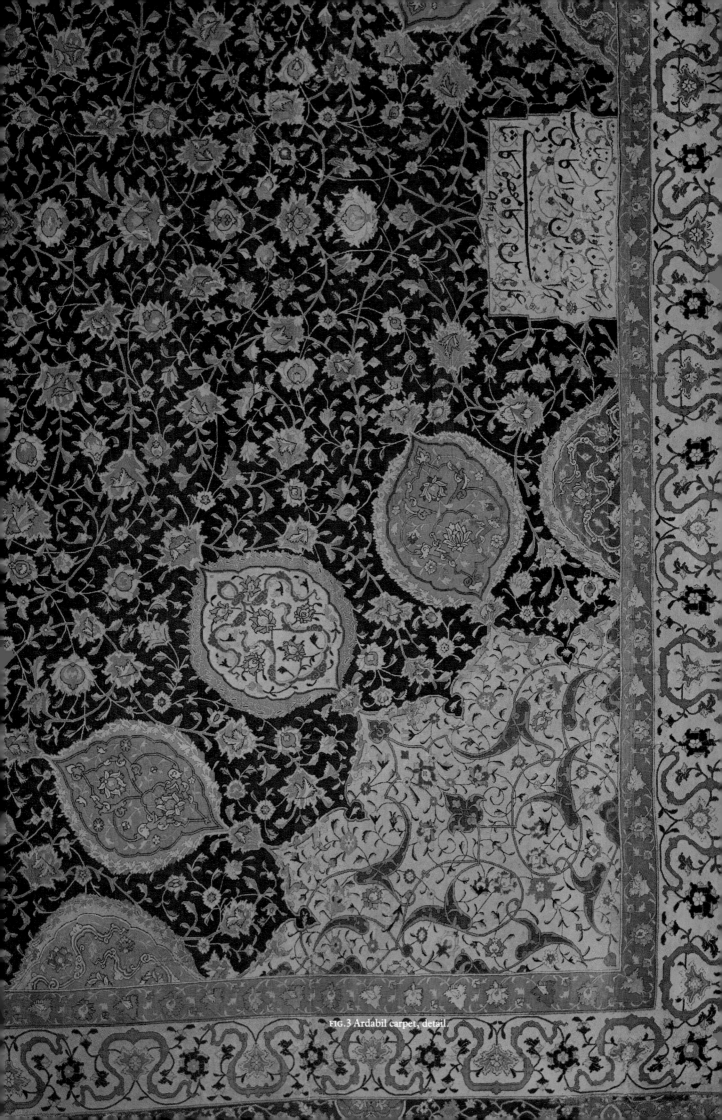

FIG. 3 Ardabil carpet, detail.

PERSIAN CARPETS OF THE SAFAVID PERIOD

Donald King

The finest of all existing carpets, as is generally acknowledged, were produced in Persia during the sixteenth and seventeenth centuries under the rule of the Safavid dynasty. Nearly a hundred years ago, before the price of such rarities rose to prohibitive levels, the Victoria and Albert Museum was fortunate enough to acquire a number of outstanding examples. This article is a brief exploration of the character of a few of these masterpieces.

In making a carpet, warp threads are stretched on a loom and weft threads are interlaced with them at right angles, as in weaving plain cloth. But after every few weft threads the weavers (on wide carpets several weavers work side by side) loop additional lengths of thread round the warp threads, forming rows of knots which stand more or less erect on the plain woven foundation. Each knot produces a coloured spot in the pile, like a cube in a mosaic, and by using threads of various colours – and here the skill of the dyers makes an essential contribution – polychrome patterns are built up which, according to the relative coarseness or fineness of the weaving, may be bold and angular or infinitely delicate and complex. Complex designs such as we are considering in this article must always be originated by professional painters or designers, but it is the weavers' skills of hand and eye which ensure a lively translation of the design into knotted pile.

Seeing a carpet displayed on a museum wall or illustrated on a printed page is excellent for studying its design, but inevitably isolates the spectator from some of the carpet's most essential qualities. The original intention was that, with the carpet lying flat, one should remove one's shoes and walk, sit or kneel on it, in direct contact with its materials and texture; looking around, within the field of the carpet, one would see the nearer parts of the design in close-up, more distant parts in sharp recession, with the shades of all the colours changing according to the direction of one's glance. None of this is possible under museum conditions, but it is always worth the effort to look closely at the details of drawing and colour, to peer into the materials and texture, and to try to imagine the tactile and visual effect of walking, sitting or kneeling within the field of the carpet.

Carpet-weaving had been practised in Persia since remote antiquity, but the patchy evidence for its history in ancient and medieval times has little relevance for our present theme. The Venetian ambassador, Barbaro, was much impressed by the carpets which he saw at Tabriz in 1474, finding them far superior to those produced in Egypt and Turkey. From carpets depicted in Persian miniatures of the second half of the fifthteenth century we know that many of the motifs found in later Persian carpets – floral scrolls, arabesques, central medallions – were already current at that period, but no surviving Persian carpets of this type can be assigned with any confidence to a period earlier than that of the first two Shahs of the Safavid dynasty, Isma'il (1502-24) and Tahmasp (1524-76). The power-base of these Shahs lay in north-western Persia and a considerable number of sixteenth century Persian carpets are attributed to that area. Their capital was initially at Tabriz but, as a result of repeated Turkish attacks, was removed in 1548 to Qazvin; these cities were obviously centres of patronage, but it is uncertain to what extent they were also centres of carpet-manufacture.

A large, incomplete sixteenth century carpet in the Museum (FIG.1) belongs to a class of north-west Persian carpets with well-marked family characteristics: cotton warp and weft, woollen pile of moderately fine texture with 156 knots per square inch (24 per square centimetre), a majestic central medallion superimposed on a stiff repeating pattern of coiling floral stems, and a border with a bold pattern of arabesque strapwork. Such a family of carpets must represent a long-continuing commercial production by a skilled work-force, in a prosperous urban environment where there was a lively demand for large, beautiful and expensive carpets for palaces and public buildings. It seems likely that the carpets were also exported to Europe. This example was bought by the Museum in 1894 for £84·10s. from the Florentine dealer Stefano Bardini and probaly came from some Italian palace or church. Many years later, in 1959, a missing piece from one end of the carpet was generously given to the Museum by the American collector Joseph McMullan, who had found it in New York. When complete, the carpet was of giant size, about 35 feet long and 13 feet wide, with a total of about 10 million knots. Even in its mutilated state, the austere grandeur of the design makes it a most impressive work.

The Ardabil carpet (FIGS.2,3), probably the most famous carpet in the world, is even larger, 34½ feet by 17½ feet, even more solemnly impressive, and at the same time a radiant and completely individual work of art. The conception is in essence similar to that of the preceding carpet, with central and corner medallions on a field pattern of two types of coiling floral stems, but here everything is designed and executed with much greater freedom and fluency. Notwithstanding the enormous scale of the work, every detail of the ornament is full of life and movement and the eye can wander indefinitely through the labyrinth without the least sense of fatigue or monotony. Warp and weft are of silk and the texture of the woollen pile is fine, about 340 knots per square inch

FIG. 1 Medallion carpet, north-western Persia, possibly Tabriz, period of Shah Tahmasp (1524–76). 326–1894.

(53 per square centimetre), making a total of about 30 million knots in all. The lamps which appear suspended at either side of the central medallion suggest that the carpet was specially designed for some sacred edifice. According to the London dealers Vincent Robinson & Co, from whom the Museum bought the carpet for £2,500 in 1893, it came from the Safavid family shrine at Ardabil, the burial-place of Isma'il, the first Safavid Shah. This provenance is confirmed by the English traveller W.R. Holmes who, visiting the Ardabil shrine in 1843, saw on the floor there 'the faded remains of what was once a very splendid carpet, the manufacture of which very much

surpassed that of the present day. At one extremity was woven the date of its make, some three hundred years ago'. Such a carpet, in such a place, might well have been commissioned by Shah Tahmasp himself, but the woven label which Holmes saw says nothing of this; instead it states that the carpet is the 'work of a slave (or servant) of the Holy Place (or court), Maqsud of Kashan, 946', ie 1540 AD. Maqsud came from the carpet-weaving centre of Kashan, but whether he was the head of the workshop that made the carpet, or the patron who commissioned it, remains uncertain. Actually, there was not just one carpet, but a pair of carpets, identical twins each with the same inscrip-

tion. The second, whose existence had not been revealed by Robinson & Co, had been cut up about 1890 to patch the V&A carpet; the major part of what remains of it is now in the Getty Museum in California. It is interesting and curious that the two carpets appear to match in every detail of the design, including a multitude of small anomalies and asymmetries which one might think accidental, were they not so exactly repeated.

The Chelsea carpet (FIGS. 4,5) is so called because it was purchased in 1890, for £150, from Mr Alfred C. Cohen of 189 King's Road, Chelsea. Nothing is known of its earlier history, but since it came to the Museum it has

FIG.2 Medallion carpet known as the Ardabil carpet, from the ancestral shrine of the Safavid dynasty at Ardabil, western Persia, possibly Tabriz or Kashan, signed by Maqsud of Kashan, 1540. 272–1893.   FIG.4 Multi-medallion carpet known as the Chelsea carpet, western Persia, possibly Tabriz or Kashan, period of Shah Tahmasp (1524–76). 589–1890.

2

4

opposite: FIG.5 The Chelsea carpet, detail.
FIG.7 Silk floral carpet in the form of an ecclesiastical
vestment, with Annunciation and Crucifixion scenes,
western Persia, possibly Kashan or Esfahan, period of Shah
Abbas I (1587–1629). 477–1894.   FIG.8 Vestment, detail.
FIG.6 Fragment of a silk floral carpet, western Persia,
possibly Kashan or Esfahan, period of Shah Abbas I
(1587–1629). T.36–1954

7

8

6

been universally regarded as one of the most beautiful, perhaps *the* most beautiful, of all carpets. Very much smaller than the two preceding pieces, though still quite a large carpet, 17 feet 8 inches by 9 feet 8 inches, it is rather closely related to the Ardabil carpet in colour and in various details of the design, such as the medallions with arabesques and the pointed oval cartouches with foliated frames. It is also technically similar, with silk warp and weft and woollen pile, here in a very fine texture with 470 knots per square inch, making a total of over 11½ million knots in all. Unlike the magnificent centralised designs of the other two pieces, however, this has a repeating pattern, on a smaller scale, and the austerity of their coiling floral stems is here transformed into a paradise-garden, with flowering and fruiting trees, natural and mythical animals and birds, fish-ponds and monumental vases. Whereas the other two carpets were conceived for great public or sacred buildings, the Chelsea carpet seems designed for private pleasure, for the luxurious apartments of some great connoisseur, probably a member of Shah Tahmasp's court, if not the Shah himself.

The next great period of Persian history and art was the prosperous reign of Shah Abbas I (1587-1629), who in 1597/8 removed the capital from Qazvin to Esfahan, which he developed as a splendid and cosmopolitan city. Most carpets of this period (FIGS.6-9) have all-over designs of large stylised blossoms, full of movement, but lacking the clear focus of the earlier medallion designs. If we may apply European terms to Eastern art, the designs of Shah Tahmasp's time show the clear divisions and sharp detail of Renaissance art, whereas those of the Shah Abbas period have the swelling forms and all-embracing rhythms of the Baroque style. The opulence of the age

and style is reflected in the sumptuousness of the materials. Many carpets (FIGS.6,7) have a silk warp and weft and a richly dyed silk pile in extremely fine textures of about 400 to 800 knots per square inch (60 to 120 per square centimetre), often supplemented by areas of tapestry-weaving in gold and silver thread. A fragment of a large carpet of this kind (FIG.6), bought from an English collection in 1954 for £2,000, has a repeating pattern of arabesque strapwork, related to the border patterns of earlier carpets; the same design recurs in a large carpet preserved at the shrine of the Imam 'Ali at An Najaf in Iraq, which may have been given to the shrine by Shah Abbas himself. Another sumptuous carpet of silk, silver and gold (FIGS.7,8), bought from Monsieur L. Marcy in London for £420 in 1894, is in the form of a unique ecclesiastical vestment which, when worn, displayed on the front the Annunciation to the Virgin Mary and, on the back, Christ crucified, with the Virgin and St. John; it was obviously commissioned for a Christian church, perhaps one of those which served the large Armenian community settled in the neighbourhood of Esfahan. This class of silk-and-gold carpets is thought to have been made both in Kashan and in the carpet-workshops which Shah Abbas founded in Esfahan itself. Many other carpets of the period had floral designs of somewhat similar character. One purchased by the Museum in 1884 from the Castellani collection in Italy (FIG.9) has a silk warp, a cotton weft and a woollen pile, which is supplemented with cotton and with gold and silver tapestry. Designs of this type, with coiling stems bearing large stylised flowers, interspersed with cloud-bands and sometimes with birds and animals, are believed to have been woven at Esfahan, at Herat in eastern Persia (now Afghanistan), and also in India. Such carpets were

exported to Europe in large numbers and are depicted in many European paintings of the Baroque period.

The design of vase carpets, so called from the vases which appear in them, also originated in the time of Shah Abbas and persisted, in modified forms, for several generations. The V&A collection is rich in carpets of this class, which are generally attributed to Kerman in central Persia. The one illustrated (FIG.10) shows a characteristic triple lattice of stems bearing stylised blooms, but the Baroque exuberance of the original concept has been tamed by the introduction of a multitude of semi-naturalistic flowering plants, producing the illusion of a flower-garden. This carpet, which was probably woven during the reign of Shah Abbas II (1642-66), formerly hung in William Morris's dining room and was bought from his widow for £200 in 1897; it is easy to see how congenial it was to his ideas as a designer.

The spirit which presided over the formation of the Museum's marvellous collection of Safavid carpets was admirably expressed in a letter written by William Morris in 1893, advocating the purchase of the Ardabil carpet. 'Next, and this is the chief reason that I wish to see it bought for the public, the design is of singular perfection; defensible on all points, logically and consistently beautiful, with no oddities or grotesqueries which might need an apology, and therefore most especially valuable for a Museum, the special aim of which is the education of the public in Art. The carpet as far as I could see is in perfectly good condition, and its size and splendour as a piece of workmanship do full justice to the beauty and intellectual qualities of the design... In short I think that it would be a real misfortune if such a treasure of decorative art were not acquired for the public.'

FIG.10 Vase carpet, incomplete, central Persia, possibly
Kerman, period of Shah Abbas II (1642–66). 719–1897.
FIG.9 Half of a floral carpet, Persia, possibly Esfahan or
Herat, period of Shah Abbas I (1587–1629). 721–1884.

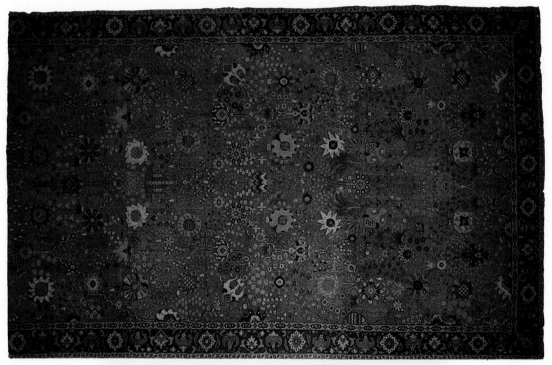

10

9

DETAIL: 17th century Flemish tapestry
Prior to restoration

Restored at Kilejian, 1983

Kurm-Kapu, Silk and Metal, 125 × 195 cm (4 × 6.5) ca. 1900

Tapestry, Gobelin, 175 × 200 cm (5.9 × 6.7) 1902-3

A very exotic Embroidery of English origin
English 1700–1750
8′ 6″ × 5′ 3″ (260 × 160 cm)

Paul Hughes

Fine Antiques and Ancient Textiles
3A Pembridge Square, London W2 4EN, England
Tel: 01-243 8598 (by appointment only)

TAPESTRIES

You Can Own One Of These Magnificent Reproduction Tapestries For Less Than $1,000.00.

THE HUNT OF THE BOAR AND THE
BEAR—d'après the original tapestry in the
VICTORIA & ALBERT MUSEUM, LONDON
(size 68" wide by 53" high)

THE LADY WITH THE UNICORN—
"TASTE"—d'après the original tapestry in
the CLUNY MUSEUM, PARIS
(size 67" wide by 52" high)

Largest Collection of Machine Woven (100% Cotton or Wool) Aubusson
and Gobelin Tapestries in the United States. By Private Showing Only.
(212) 490·0930, 356 East 41st Street, New York, N.Y. 10017.

Museum and Galleries inquiries invited.

LOVELIA ENTERPRISES, INC.
Specialists for 20 Years

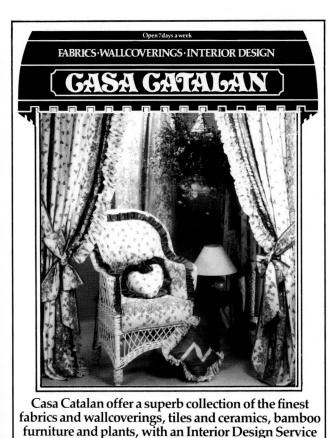

MANUEL CANOVAS

PARIS
7 PLACE FURSTENBERG 75006
TEL. 325.75.98

NEW YORK
979 THIRD AVENUE N.Y. 10022
TEL. (212) 752.95.88

EOS - Photo DANIEL JOUANNEAU

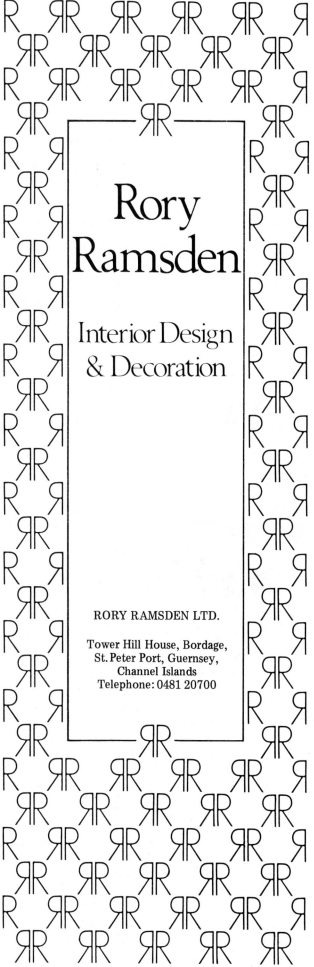

WARNER FABRICS

By Appointment to
H.M. Queen Elizabeth II
Suppliers of Silks and Furnishing Fabrics

By Appointment to
H.M. Queen Elizabeth the Queen Mother
Suppliers of Silks and Furnishing Fabrics

WARNER & SONS LIMITED

Furnishing Fabrics and Wallcoverings

7-11 NOEL STREET, LONDON W1V 4AL

"Peony" © a superb interpretation of a
classic Victorian chintz from Warner's "Personal Choice" Collection.
Available in three colourways.
Please write to us for the names of retailers specializing in Warner fabrics.

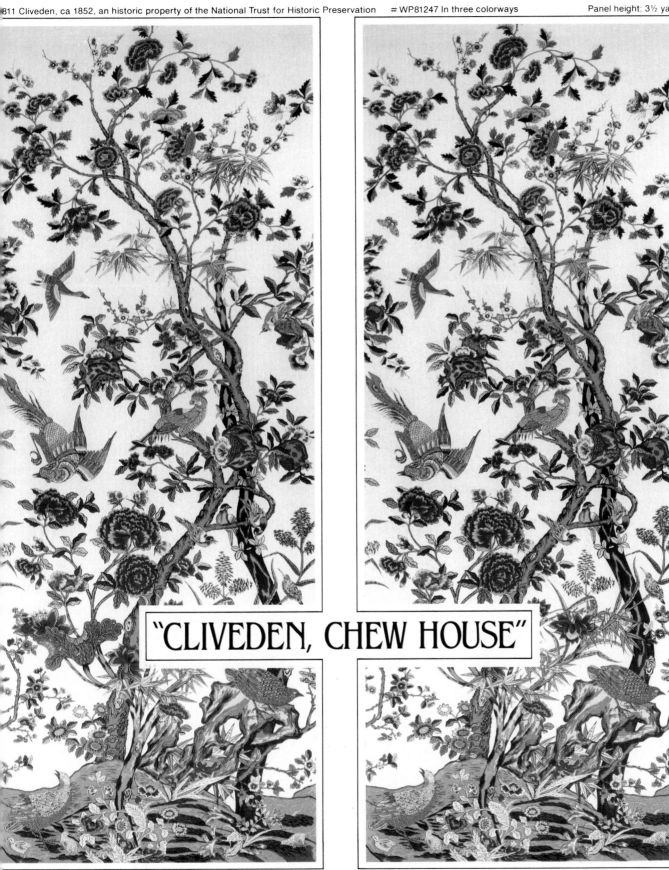

PAINTED PAPER OF PEKIN
Chinese Wallpapers in England

Gillian Saunders

Trade between Europe and China grew considerably in the 17th century, through the agency of the East India Company (established 1600) and similar Dutch and French ventures. The Chinese developed a flourishing export industry producing goods adapted to Western tastes. Silks and porcelain made up the bulk of this trade; early accounts make no mention of wallpaper for it was classed as a minor product and carried as 'private trade'. The wallpapers were created specifically for the European market in imitation of the painted silk hangings used by the rich in China. The Chinese themselves did not use elaborate papers of this kind, except as funerary and festival decorations. Father Louis Le Comte, a Jesuit missionary in China, noted (1698) the use of silk hangings, but added 'Others only whiten the chamber, or glew Paper upon it'. Later accounts by Sir William Chambers (1757) and Lord Macartney (1793) indicate that plain papers, white, crimson or gilt, were favoured.

The appearance of Chinese papers in England, from the middle of the seventeenth century, gave an impetus to the growing fashion for papering walls in imitation of more costly hangings: embossed and gilded leather, tapestry, embroidery, damask, chintz. Until the early 18th century, however, wallpaper was regarded chiefly as a cheap substitute suitable only for lesser rooms, but the Chinese papers were of a different class: the rich colours and exquisite draughtsmanship, the sheer technical perfection, were unequalled by anything produced in England at the time. They were considered appropriate decoration for the best apartments, and became much sought after. From

FIG.4 Fragment from the base of a length of paper showing a fruit tree in a pot with flowering shrubs behind, second half of eighteenth century, gouache. E. 3944–1915.

1740 to about 1790 there was a great vogue for Chinese wallpapers; with their sinuous lines and asymmetric form the designs found an echo in the prevailing Rococo style and inspired all manner of 'chinoiserie' furnishings.

A contemporary observer wrote of 'the Chinese papers so much in fashion in our great houses', and we know that many boasted a room furnished with 'painted paper of Pekin and . . . choicest moveables of China' (Madame du Bocage, *Letters on England, Holland and Italy*, 1750) for it was a feature commonly remarked upon by diarists and travellers, in letters and journals. There are frequent references to 'Japan' or 'India' papers – erroneous terms used indiscriminately for all kinds of Oriental artefacts. At that time notions of geography were vague, and the East India Company gave its name to many of the goods it imported, whatever their origin.

It is known from his accounts that Thomas Chippendale hung several rooms with Chinese papers as part of complete decorative schemes. He specified his own 'Chinese' furniture as being 'very proper' for a room hung with 'India' paper. The best method for hanging Chinese papers was to mount the sheets on canvas stretched on battens which were then fixed to the walls. This had the advantage of making these valuable hangings portable should the need arise, and was therefore preferable to lining the papers and pasting them directly on the wall.

The papers were sent from China in sets, usually of twenty-five rolls, each approximately 12 feet by 4 feet. Every sheet was different, and they could be joined to make a continuous decoration around the room, or framed as individual panels with a patterned border. Sometimes extra birds and branches were included, to cover damage or simply to embellish the paper, since

the Chinese designs, with their elegant and positive use of space, were not always sufficiently ornate for English tastes. Lady Hertford hit upon a novel way of elaborating the paper hung at Temple Newsam in the 1820s – she added birds cut from plates in Audubon's *Birds of America*.

Though printing had been known in China for centuries, the V&A has only two examples where printing has been used, for the outlines alone. The wallpapers were almost always painted by hand throughout, in gouache or tempera. They were much imitated in England and France, but as Eugène Delacroix observed (1847) 'we have nothing to equal their skill in producing fast colours . . .'.

With one or two exceptions the papers can be divided into three classes, according to their design. Most surviving examples in the V&A and elsewhere are of the so-called 'bird and flower' type in which a flowering tree climbs the length of the paper from a rocky base, its branches interspersed with birds and butterflies. The whole is silhouetted against a plain-coloured ground (FIGS.1 and 2). Individual artists introduced slight variations to this basic model; occasionally the climbing plant grows amongst stems of bamboo (FIG.3); bird-cages may be suspended from branches (a feature confined to later eighteenth century papers); ornamental balustrades, pools of water, or shrubs in pots may enliven the foreground (FIG.4).

Though the elements of the composition are stylized to a certain extent, they are executed with a remarkable degree of realism. William Whitehead (in *The World*, no. 38, 1753) described 'the richest China and India paper where all the flowers of fancy were exhausted in a thousand fantastic figures of birds, beasts and fishes which never had existence', but in fact the flora and fauna depicted are exist-

FIG.1 One of ten panels forming the complete decoration of a
room, originally hung in Eltham Lodge, Kent, second
quarter of eighteenth century, tempera. E. 2092B–1914.
FIG.2 One of seven panels from the Archdeaconry House,
Peterborough. Late eighteenth century, pen, watercolour
and bodycolour. E.3592–1922.

1

2

ing species, not fanciful inventions. The botanist Sir Joseph Banks noted in his Journal (1771) that 'some of the plants which are common to China and Java, as bamboo, are better figured there than by the best botanical authors that I have seen'. This close and accurate observation of natural forms, though stemming in part from the traditions of Chinese painting, seems to have been fostered by European tastes: 'The Chinese having found that the representation of natural objects are more in request among foreigners, they pay strict attention to the subject that may be required.' (J. Barrow, *Travels in China*, 1804) (FIG.5). Some of the later papers, however, departed from a strict naturalism in favour of more whimsical designs produced in response to a demand for variety (FIG.6).

The second class of Chinese papers show scenes of industry or daily life in China. One of the rare papers with printed outlines is of this type. Another example shows a crowd at an outdoor theatrical performance. In all these figure subjects the landscape is presented in accordance with Chinese conventions. In the upper portions of the paper are jagged mountain tops; the figure groups are composed below in 'islands' divided by rocks and trees (FIG.7). The panoramic papers were more expensive than the 'bird and flower' kind. According to a letter in the archive at Dunster Castle, 'Indian paper representing the several stages of a Chinese manufacture . . . the figures very compleat and intersperst with romantick views' cost at least seven shillings a yard, whereas those 'representing trees, birds and flowers' could be obtained at four shillings.

In the third class of Chinese papers

'bird and flower' elements are combined with figures. The flowering trees fill the top three-quarters of the sheet and form a backdrop to the lively incidents below. A particularly attractive example (FIG.8) shows a sporting scene; another, the story of tea-making. All the papers of this class date from the second half of the eighteenth century, again devised in response to demand from Europe.

Two papers in the museum's collection fall outside these categories. A fragment of a Cantonese paper (FIG.9) shows conclusive evidence of a direct stylistic influence from Europe. The decorative cartouche which frames the Chinese garden scene is taken from a design by Watteau, engraved by Gabriel Huquier, c. 1730. European engravings were commonly used as source material by porcelain painters, but it is unusual to find a wallpaper design similarly influenced. The result is a Chinese paper in the 'Chinoiserie' style, uniting Rococo motifs with traditional landscape painting.

FIG.5 Fragment from the base of a length of paper, late seventeenth century, tempera. E.1211–1922. This is closer to the restrained and subtle manner of Chinese academic painting than the eighteenth century papers which are generally more exuberant and 'obvious', the colour and detail emphasized to appeal to European tastes.

Another paper from the same house departs from the pictorial mode in favour of symmetry and 'all-over' patterning. A trellis-work of ribbons contains in the intersections a variety of motifs – flowers, fruit, insects, ceremonial pots, a mask, a fan and a *sheng* (bamboo flute) (FIG.10). It is a most unusual design and no comparable example is known amongst the Chinese export papers.

Unlike papers of native manufacture and European imports, the East India Company merchandise was specifically exempted from the taxes on wallpaper introduced in 1712 and 1773. It is therefore very difficult to date the Chinese papers precisely, since they bear no tax stamp, a feature which acts as an approximate guide for dating other papers. Some are documented in decorators' accounts or family archives, but in most cases any estimates of date must be largely based on changes in style and technique, which, given the strict adherence of the artists to a limited range of models, were minimal.

By the end of the eighteenth century when the Rococo taste had given way to the formality and restraint of Neoclassicism, both English and French manufacturers were producing papers to match the quality of the Chinese. In 1794 the import tax was extended to Chinese papers and these factors combined to kill the trade completely. A brief revival in the nineteenth century was fostered by that Chinoiserie extravaganza, Brighton Pavilion, but the quality of the papers had declined. The green-painted paper presented to Sir Walter Scott in 1828, which he hung rather reluctantly at Abbotsford, was probably the last example of this long-lived fashion.

FIG.3 One of eight panels, late eighteenth or early nineteenth century, tempera. E.31A–1912. This paper is an exception to the rule of botanical accuracy for the artist has depicted at least four different flowers growing from a single stem. FIG.6 Panel with sprays of flowers and two butterflies. Early nineteenth century, bodycolour touched with gold. E. 409–1932. FIG.7 One of three panels with hunting, boating and festival scenes, second half of eighteenth century, gouache. E.1181–1921.

3

6

7

FIG.8 One of two panels showing sporting scenes, from the
Old Brewery House, Watford, second half of eighteenth
century, gouache. E.252–1924.   FIG.9 Fragment from the
library of Hampden House, Great Missenden,
Buckinghamshire, *c*.1730–40, pen and ink, watercolour and
bodycolour. E.51–1968.   FIG.10 Paper from Hampden
House, Great Missenden, Buckinghamshire, *c*.1800,
bodycolour. E.948–1978. A fragment of a contrasting
border paper can be seen at the top.

8

9

10

COWTAN & TOUT
FINE CHINTZES HANDBLOCKED WALLPAPERS
D&D Building 979 Third Ave., New York 10022 (212) 753-4488
FLORAL BOUQUET AND RIBBON: glazed chintz.
100% SILK STRIPE

Photographer/Feliciano

SUSAN ZISES GREEN, A.S.I.D.
Interiors
500 East 77 St.
New York, New York 10021
212-249-9311

313

clarence hou

40 EAST 57 STREET NEW YORK THROUGH DECORATORS AND FI

LAURA ASHLEY

AYLESBURY BATH BIRMINGHAM BOURNEMOUTH BRIGHTON BRISTOL CAMBRIDGE CANTERBURY CARDIFF CHELTENHAM
CHESTER CHICHESTER EDINBURGH GLASGOW GUILDFORD IPSWICH LLANIDLOES LONDON MANCHESTER NEWCASTLE
NORWICH NOTTINGHAM OXFORD RICHMOND SHREWSBURY TUNBRIDGE WELLS WINCHESTER WINDSOR YORK
HOME DECORATING SHOPS WITHIN SAINSBURY'S HOMEBASE HOUSE AND GARDEN CENTRES:
BASINGSTOKE CARDIFF CROYDON GLOUCESTER ILFORD LEEDS NORTHAMPTON
NOTTINGHAM SOUTHAMPTON WATFORD

ALEXANDRA STODDARD

INCORPORATED

100 PARK AVENUE, NEW YORK, NEW YORK 10017
26TH FLOOR

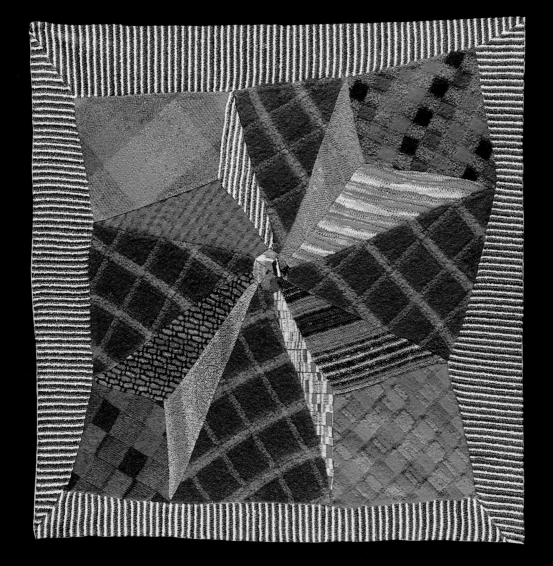

 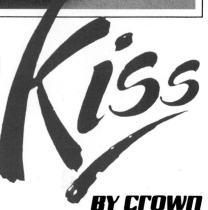

Interiors International Limited

Ann R. Musgrave Interiors, Inc.
2404 Cedar Springs • Suite 300
Dallas, Texas 75201
(214) 748-8115

ANN R. MUSGRAVE-HAYMAN
ROBERT S. DANIEL A.I.A.
VAL A. STURHAHN

W. MICHAEL BOASE
SUSAN V. CAVELL
CANDACE M. DENNEY

JANE B. ROBINSON
B. JILL WITHERSPOON
HENRIETTE C. KOZANDIS

FIG. 6 The central tower of the Victoria and Albert Museum

ASTON WEBB

Gavin Stamp

Portraits of Sir Aston Webb, the architect of the Cromwell Road portion of the V&A, show a typical Edwardian face, conventionally replete with a colossal moustache. His pupil in the 1890s, H. Bulkeley Cresswell, remembered him as 'essentially a happy little man; he gloried in his powers and nothing seemed to bother him or obstruct the fecundity of his ideas. A little man he was, alike in bodily make-up and in his conventional outlook on life and affairs in which, for him, the prominent man was the great man and the only measure of attainment was success'.

Sir Aston Webb (1849–1930) was certainly successful. He designed many important public buildings and left a significant mark on London. He was adept at winning competitions and, as H. S. Goodhart-Rendel recalled, was 'well known for his experience and common sense'. As a result, he has received comparatively little attention from historians, who tend to revere failure rather than success and who favour the progressive 'art' architect rather than the hard professional. In the great 'Architecture: A Profession or an Art' controversy of the 1890s, Webb was firmly in the professional camp and it certainly cannot be claimed that he was in any way an original designer. His buildings are derivative in style, but that does not detract from their many virtues. After all, an original architect may well not be the best architect and usually does not do the best by his client.

Hard, competent professionals like Webb and Alfred Waterhouse, architect of the Natural History Museum with whom Webb had much in common, are often more truly representative of their time and can leave behind them buildings which are successful, practical and popular.

Aston Webb is difficult to categorise. Like many architects of his generation who followed on from the break-up of the consistency of the Gothic Revival, Webb used a variety of styles in an eclectic and undisciplined way – 'bric-a-brac', as Goodhart-Rendel aptly characterised the phase. Yet, like Waterhouse, he used modern materials like terra-cotta and, as a result, although he always fulfilled his obligation to provide variety and decoration, his buildings can be hard and unsympathetic in texture. His approach to design could not be more different from that of his eponymous but unrelated senior, Philip Webb, the domestic architect and friend of William Morris, who strove so self-effacingly to use local materials and make his buildings fit harmoniously onto their site. In contrast, Aston Webb, according to Cresswell, 'rarely went on to his jobs and none of his staff ever did. His clerks of works – often from afar – came to him, reported and received his orders' in the office in Queen Anne's Gate. But Philip Webb never tackled large public buildings with complicated requirements which Sir Aston seemed to be able to plan and detail so effortlessly.

Aston Webb was born in Clapham in 1849. His father was Edward Webb, a water-colourist and engraver. Webb received his architectural education articled to Messrs Banks & Barry, ie, Charles Barry junior, the architect of Dulwich College, the Piccadilly front of Burlington House and the Great Eastern Hotel. Having won the RIBA's Pugin Scholarship in 1873, Webb set up in independent practice in London. After 1882 he collaborated with E. Ingress Bell (1837–1914) on many projects, although the relative contributions of each in this usually informal partnership is difficult to establish.

Aston Webb and Ingress Bell first achieved real success in 1886 when they won the competition for the new Victoria Law Courts in Birmingham (FIG.1). The style of the resulting buildings is a jolly and florid mixture of Tudor and Jacobean, with a French flavour given by Webb's characteristic elliptical-headed windows (FIG.2). The remarkable aspect of the design was, however, the extensive use of terra-cotta, inside and out – perhaps it had not escaped the architects' attention that terra-cotta was a favourite material of the competition assessor, Waterhouse. The exterior of the building is entirely faced in dark red terra-cotta; inside the material is of a lighter buff colour. Throughout, the building is more interestingly detailed than might be expected from the use of this repetitive washable material and, as on many jobs, Webb employed good artists to provide architectural sculpture: in this case William Aumonier, Harry Bates and Walter Crane. Apart from establishing the architects as rising stars, the Victoria Law Courts design had two local consequences: a fashion for red terra-cotta in Birmingham and an immediate strike by the city's stone-masons.

The French character in Webb's eclectic, Early Renaissance style was maintained in the Metropolitan Life Assurance Offices, built in 1890–92 in Moorgate in the City of London and whose façades still survive on the corner of King's Arms Yard. More appropriately it appears in the curious design for the French Protestant Church in Soho Square of 1893 (FIG.3). The exterior of this exotic building is faced in the rebarbative combination of purple-grey Luton bricks and red terra-cotta dressings, while the structural steelwork of the interior is concealed by more terra-cotta. This no-nonsense, industrial side to Webb received a happier expression in Mumford's Flour Mills in Deptford, a great brick grain silo which still survives off the Greenwich High Road. A very

325

FIG. 1 Victoria Law Courts, Birmingham.
(Photograph: Alan Crawford).

FIG.2 Victoria Law Courts, Birmingham (detail).
FIG.3 French Protestant Church, Soho Square.
FIG.4 St. Bartholomew-the-Great, Smithfield.
FIG.9 St. Michael's Court, Gonville and Caius College,
Cambridge.

2

3

4

9

FIG.5 Competition design for the South Kensington
Museum.   FIG.7 Victoria and Albert Museum, entrance
hall from west.   FIG.8 The Octagon Court, now the Dress,
and Musical Instruments Galleries.

SELECTED DESIGN
for the
COMPLETION OF SOUTH KENSINGTON MUSEUM.

MR. ASTON WEBB, F.R.I.B.A., ARCHITECT.

5

7

8

different sort of job of the same decade – the 1890s – was the restoration of the fragment of the ancient Norman church of St. Bartholomew-the-Great in Smithfield (FIG.4). This much abused building was surprisingly sympathetically treated by Webb, who was responsible for the present transepts, the flint-patterned west wall and for commissioning the fine metalwork by Starkie Gardner.

Such jobs are not typical, however, for it was as a designer of public and educational buildings that Aston Webb really established himself. In 1891 he won the competition for completing the South Kensington Museum up to the Cromwell Road (FIG.5), but by the time work began in 1899 on what became the Victoria & Albert Museum, the design had been transformed (FIG.6). If the long brick and stone exterior of the building in its eclectic and confused style with hints of Spain and France is still reminiscent of the 'Free Renaissance' *bric-a-brac* of the winning scheme, the grand interior vistas of domes and vaults (FIGS.7,8) owe much to the unsuccessful entry by John Belcher. Unfortunately, the effect of Webb's galleries has been spoiled by later alterations and, as John Physick demonstrates in his recent book *The Victoria and Albert Museum: The history of its building*, Webb was obliged to comply with instructions from his clients which have proved impractical.

The V&A interiors reflect the growing enthusiasm for the Grand Manner, a taste for a less confused Classicism in which Belcher was a pioneer. Architects began to look back to Gibbs and to Wren and Wren was the dominant influence on Webb's design for the Royal Naval College at Dartmouth of 1897. But for the new buildings for Christ's Hospital at Horsham, begun in 1893, Webb chose an earlier, more Elizabethan style with hints of the old

school buildings in London. Webb was nothing if not eclectic and catholic in his borrowings. For the new University of Birmingham he created a sort of Byzantine-cum-Tudor style for the blocks which are arranged on a semi-circular plan radiating from the tall Chamberlain Tower, or *campanile*. Intriguing from a distance, the hard shiny red brick used for these buildings makes them utterly repellent on close inspection. Perhaps Webb did not much care; 'They've swallowed the lot!' he announced to his office on returning from presenting his designs. Yet at about the same time, during the early years of the new century, Webb designed two delightful buildings in Tudor Gothic for Cambridge: one for Caius (FIG.9) and one for King's. Both are very well detailed and faced in stone; perhaps by this date the ever-alert Webb had employed assistants who were inspired by the Arts & Crafts movement.

The Reign of Edward VII saw Aston Webb at the top of his profession. To him fell the opportunity of trying to make London emulate Paris and Berlin, and make the capital into an Imperial City. This was a rare attempt at national architectural grandeur which was inspired both by the taste for the Grand Manner and by the Imperial mood and the cultural inferiority complex induced by the South African War. The result was Aston Webb's transformation of the Mall into a great ceremonial route; he rose – almost – to the occasion.

Soon after the death of the old Queen in 1901, a competition was held for a Queen Victoria Memorial to be erected in front of Buckingham Palace – the house which she had hated. In conjunction with the sculptor Thomas Brock, Webb won, but his design was not universally admired. Lutyens commented in 1902 that 'The Queen's Memorial is horrid as far as I have seen

it, Aston Webb has got it all inside out and far too small in detail and too funny for words . . .' However, the Memorial which was eventually unveiled in 1911 had been redesigned (FIG.10). Instead of a semi-circular forecourt to the Palace enclosed by colonnades, Webb created a very Parisian *rond point* with the Memorial in the centre. Around the circumference are monumental gate piers bearing the names of distant parts of the Empire. But Lutyens's criticisms remain valid: the florid sculpture by Brock is out of scale with the architecture and the style of the whole suggests a gauche attempt at the sugary French Beaux-Arts style of 1900.

Rather better is the structure which Webb designed at the distant, opposite end of the Mall. Until Edward VII's reign, the Mall was a comparatively secluded ride, with no direct access from Trafalgar Square – Queen Victoria's Diamond Jubilee Parade had to reach the Mall from Whitehall through the Horseguards. In 1905 Webb was asked to create a suitably ceremonial gateway from Trafalgar Square. The old houses around Spring Gardens were cleared away and in 1910 Webb's tripartite arch was completed. In style it is a competent essay in the more geometrical and disciplined Mannerist Classicism fashionable in the early twentieth century – the County Hall by Webb's former assistant, Ralph Knott, is another example. More important, perhaps, is that the Admiralty Arch is a supreme example of Webb's practical cleverness. Not only does the building also provide accommodation for Admiralty clerks – the British Treasury were not going to pay for something so useless as a mere arch – but the change in axis between the Mall and the Le Sueur's statue of Charles I is brilliantly concealed by making each front of the Arch concave in plan (FIG.11).

The final completion of the Mall

FIG.11 Admiralty Arch, from the north-east. Design, 1909,
drawn by Robert Atkinson. (Courtesy of the British
Architectural Library/RIBA). FIG.12 Edward Blore's
façade to Buckingham Palace, with Aston Webb's piers and
gates. (Courtesy of the National Monuments Record).

11

12

FIG.10 The Victoria Memorial, with Buckingham Palace in
the background (Photograph: André Goulancourt).

awaited another monarch but again the architect was Aston Webb. When the Queen Victoria Memorial was unveiled, Buckingham Palace behind presented a forlorn appearance as the Caen stone on the façade, designed by Blore for the Prince Consort (FIG.12), was badly decayed. Webb designed a new façade in Portland stone in 1912 but the design as executed also owed much to King George V, whose narrow, nautical tastes despised frills. A drawing at the RIBA shows that the King vetoed Webb's urns and sculpture and the result is something more Louis XIV than the Third Republic of the Memorial. The job was a triumph of organisation. The King did not wish for a single window to be altered and for the work to be carried out while he was away, so the new façade was applied in just three months, from

August to October 1913, with the contractors working at night under arc lamps as well as by day. The architectural solution, a pragmatic response to taxing conditions, is typical of Aston Webb, who was a Late Victorian eclectic trying to be Grand, and not really understanding how. As Goodhart-Rendel's complained, the unsatisfactory proportions and clever botches in the façade 'are distressing consequences of a cavalier treatment of neo-Classical obligations, such as never could have occurred in the first house of any land in which neo-Classicism was generally valued and understood.' But Sir Aston Webb was the man of the moment, and his age.

Cresswell's judgement seems fair: 'His contentment was sumptuous, his demeanour modest to admiration; he was widely esteemed both personally

and professionally, and he was truly an artist . . .' As a result he was knighted in 1904, awarded the Royal Gold Medal of the RIBA in 1905 and in 1907 became the first English recipient of the Gold Medal of the American Institute of Architects. As President of the RIBA in 1902–04, Webb did much to heal the breach between the Artists and the Professionals after the quarrels of the 1890s, and in 1919 he became the second architect President of the Royal Academy. He was no inconsiderable figure. And of all his many works, the enlargement of the V&A, if not the best, is certainly the most accessible and is still a tribute to Sir Aston Webb's skills in creating richly sculptured, decorative and enjoyable public architecture.

ARTS ANCIENS

Service d'estimation, de vente et d'étude du marché des objets d'art

2022 BEVAIX CH
☎ 038 46 16 09
Banque UBS NE
CCP 436 235 05 U

Maurice de Vlaminck 'Paysage' / huile sur toile / 53 × 64 cm /

- Organisation de ventes et expositions thématiques.

- Ventes aux enchères annuelles à Genève, Hôtel des Bergues.

- Service d'estimation, de vente et d'étude du marché des objets d'art.

- Gravures, peintures suisses, livres sur la Suisse.

- Art russe, art chinois, art japonais.

- Argenterie ancienne.

- Peinture ancienne et moderne.

- Livres anciens, livres illustrés modernes, manuscrits autographes.

Ensemble d'argenterie Française XVII et XVIII ème

When it comes to architectural antiques, the world comes to The Wrecking Bar.

For over a decade, Wilma Stone, owner and president of The Wrecking Bar of Atlanta, Georgia, along with her staff, has actively pursued a singular commitment: To travel the globe, seeking out, preserving, and restoring for use, authentic examples of the world's rich ornamental history.

She invites you to contact The Wrecking Bar, and discover more about its three million dollar inventory of architectural masterpieces. All showcased within the Victor Kriegshaber Home, itself listed on the National Register of Historic Places.

THE WRECKING BAR *of Atlanta*

292 Moreland Avenue, N.E.
Atlanta, Georgia 30307 U.S.A.
(404) 525-0468

Antony Embden

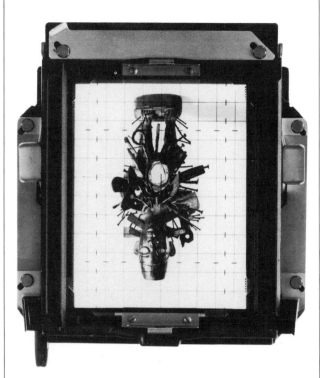
336

Frith 3563, Luddington Village.

THE FILES OF FRANCIS FRITH

Valerie Lloyd

About 1954 or 1955 the V&A had a 'phone call from F. Frith & Company, the postcard firm in Reigate, Surrey, asking if the museum would like the file set of prints of the company's earliest views. John Physick, on behalf of the museum, accepted all of them, and since then they have lain rather neglected and forgotten in filing cabinets in the print room store. One can see why: at first sight they look quite unattractive, the crumbling cardboard on which they are mounted spreads yellow dust throughout the drawers, and the large, handwritten serial numbers and titles which adorn most of them are generally in the skies, being the lightest part of the picture, making it difficult to assess them pictorially. Additionally, many of them are very faded and there are no dates or photographic credits. However, to dismiss them as uninteresting would be a great mistake.

The name of Francis Frith is well known to any student of photography, particularly for his Middle Eastern views taken in the late 1850s; but he is also known to a wider public for his later tourist views of Great Britain, and various other countries, many of which were still reproduced as postcards until recently by the Frith company. Apart from one biography of Frith by Bill Jay (1973), who was instrumental, when the company ceased to trade, in distributing the rest of the Frith company material, negatives and prints, including the Bedford archive, very little study has been made of Frith's work except for the Middle Eastern photographs. Considering that by the time Frith left for Egypt in September 1856 he was one of the most technically accomplished photographers in Britain and must have produced quite a large body of work, and considering the size of his more commercial operation at Reigate from 1860 onwards, including the printing and publication of many other photographers' work, this is rather surprising.

Although Bill Jay tells us quite a lot about Frith's personal life and the management of the company, information mainly culled from Frith family archives and Frith's own diaries, many of the questions concerning his photographic career remain completely unexplained. Julia Van Haaften in her introduction to *Egypt and the Holy Land in Historic Photographs* . . . (1980) has answered some of these. Liverpool, where Frith was a partner in a grocery firm from 1845 to 1850, when he established his own independent printing firm in the same city, was one of the main centres of photographic activity, with Manchester, which is close by, in the early years of the medium. Several well known names had been experimenting with photography from the moment it was invented, particularly J.B. Dancer in Manchester. Bill Jay says that Frith started photography in 1850, in which case he must have learned the calotype process, using paper negatives. There is no evidence for this, although later he was clearly familiar with the technique. It is more likely that he started with the wet-collodion-on-glass negative process invented by Frederick Scott Archer in 1851, which was free of patent restrictions. In March 1853 Frith was one of the founder members of the Liverpool Photographic Society, enrolled with the membership status of 'professional' at the Society's first meeting. Later, however, in 1856, a local reviewer described Frith's contribution to the Photographic Society's exhibition in London. 'The best portraits are those by our member, Mr Frith, an amateur.' William C. Darrah, in the *World of Stereographs* (1977), describes stereoscopic photographs by Frith issued before his departure for Egypt in 1856; scenic views of England and Wales mounted on thin lavender cards with the titles handwritten by Frith. One of the discoveries in the Reigate premises when the company closed was a box of five 16×20 inch, 'mammoth plate' negatives signed by Frith and dated 1856. Now in the collection of Janet Lehr in New York, three of the negatives are of ecclesiastical ruins (probably abbeys) and two are of new railway bridges, one, Stephenson's Britannia Bridge over the Menai Straits, constructed in Egyptian Revival style. These would probably compare closely with the work of Roger Fenton, who documented extensively British cathedrals and abbeys, the landscape, and various industrial subjects, including the Saltash Bridge, between Devon and Cornwall, under construction, during the same period and using almost equally large negatives.

Frith left on his first expedition to Egypt in September 1856. He took glass plates and apparatus for making negatives in three sizes: stereoscopic, whole-plate (8×10 inches) and the mammoth plates. He sailed to Alexandria and went up the Nile from Cairo to Abu Simbel, photographing all the main sites and antiquities. During this period archaeology was becoming increasingly popular and respected, and the general interest in Victoria's reign in antiquities, the natural sciences and travel, as well as the fact that Frith was a committed Christian, must all have contributed to his choice of the Middle East. Egypt and Palestine had increasingly become ultimate destinations for travellers on the 'Grand Tour'. Several French photographers visited the region in the 1840s and 50s and the British photographer-surgeon C. G. Wheelhouse made some very notable views in 1849–50. However, no photographer went as far as Frith, or was as thorough. He was accompanied on this first journey by the mechanical and

1 Frith No. 1014, Bheels.   2 Frith No. 398, Ancient Church,
Hitterdal.   3 Frith No. 3110, Delhi. Railway Bridge, River
Jumma.   4 Frith No. 1355, Tomb of first Ming Emperor,
China.

1

2

3

4

1 Frith No. 1485, Tunbridge Wells.   2 Frith No. 2469,
Torrent Walk, Dolgelly.   3 Frith No. 2413, Festiniog
Valley.   4 Frith No. 3328, Ely Cathedral.

optical engineer, Francis Wenham, who designed the steam-powered yacht they used for transportation up the Nile and advised Frith on optics and other matters. It was probably through Wenham's influence that Frith was able to send back one hundred stereoscopic negatives to Messrs Negretti and Zambra in London, in advance of their return. These were published as glass slides by Negretti and Zambra in the autumn of 1857. On his return from the first trip in July 1857, Frith was acclaimed for his accomplishments and made arrangements with the printsellers, Thos. Agnew and Son, to handle the large views, and with the publisher James S. Virtue for the serial publication of the wholeplate size views, and for published folio albums of the large plates. Although he was not employed or commissioned by any of these firms, it is almost certain that he would have had at least informal arrangements for similar transactions before leaving on his second expedition only three months later. This time he went on, via Jaffa, to Palestine and Syria, visiting Jerusalem, Mount Sinai, Damascus, Baalbeck and the Cedars of Lebanon. Once again the stereoscopic views obtained on this trip were published by Negretti and Zambra, again as albumen-on-glass slides in the first instance, and James Virtue issued views from both trips in twenty-five parts containing three photographs each, with an extra self-portrait of Frith in Eastern costume with the first issue, during 1858–59. Frith would not have made any of the prints for these publications, although at various times it is possible that he supervised them. This time he was home for more than a year, and he met his future wife, Anne Rosling. In 1856 when Frith had sold his printing business for a good profit, and become a gentleman of private means able to undertake expeditions to

the Middle East, he had moved nearer to London. It is possible that he went then to Reigate, but at any rate he was there by 1860, when he set up his own photographic printing firm, and determined to marry and settle down.

Many British photographers had photographed abroad in the 1850s, particularly in India. Exceptionally gifted photographers such as Linneaus Tripe and Dr John Murray produced large views of great beauty and sophistication, using the waxed-paper negative method, easier to handle than collodion-on-glass in very hot climates. Frith's comments in the *Art Journal* of 1859 about the calotype, or paper negative method are interesting: '[the calotype] is chiefly employed by artists and amateur travellers who are not so much anxious to produce fine pictures, as to carry away suggestions and remembrances, its portability and cheapness being great recommendation.' Certainly some of the greatest albumen prints ever made were produced from Frith's glass negatives, and the quality of the prints from his Reigate firm was consistently excellent as far as we can tell from surviving prints. His preference for the glass negative might be further explained by another passage in the same article: '[photography's] *essential* truthfulness of outline, and to a considerable extent, of perspective and light and shade, . . . This quality has a *moral* dimension, as truth in the "very foundation of everything that is lovely on earth and in heaven", and hence will prove a beneficial influence on the morals of people.' – thus linking his perception of photographic 'reality' with his spiritual commitments. In this way his dissatisfaction with the calotype method is clearly linked to the physical interference of the paper texture, the lack of clarity, in prints from paper negatives, as if this softness or texture (very visible, and aesthetically

utilised in Tripe's prints of India and Burma) deprive the viewer of part of the truth, the visible essence, of the objects before the camera.

Frith returned in 1860 from his third and final journey up the Nile, when he claims to have travelled into the sandy desert above the sixth cataract, further than any other photographer, and over ten years before the Livingstone–Stanley expedition discovered the source of the Nile. He saw this trip as 'one more grand spell of sunshine, and so finally brace up soul and body for the great events of life'. He married Anne Rosling, who like Frith was from a Quaker family, in Reigate. She was probably the daughter of Alfred Rosling, a well known photographer some of whose photographs Frith later published. Frith began to publish photographic prints in earnest, and the output from the Reigate firm in the following years was enormous. His own wholeplate Egyptian photographs were reprinted by the firm and published by William Mackenzie, in similar volumes to the Virtue ones, but with a new text, not by Frith, and a re-ordering of the plates into geographical sequence. One hundred stereo views of Egypt were published as a book, in similar sequence to that of Negretti and Zambra, by Smith and Elder, in 1862, with a text and drawings by Bonomi and Sharpe. These publications indicate the continuing demand, but the critical response to these re-issues was now waning in its enthusiasm as the public turned its attention to further distant and more exotic places.

The early 1860s mark a kind of turning point for photography. Many of the great photographers of the 1850s stopped working, and turned back to their previous pursuits. The large fine prints of the '50s were produced no more in Britain, possibly due to their costliness and lack of a large enough

1 Frith No. 385, The Confessional, by Frank M. Good.
2 Frith No. 1847, At Erment.   3 Frith No. 4539, Bed of
Marie Antoinette, Versailles.   4 Frith No. 4023,
Philadelphia, Independence Hall.

public. Frith seems to have sensed the particular mood of the times, and seen his opportunity.

His views, in their various packages had always been more popular than most commercially, probably due to his choice of topical subject and the combination of informative letterpress descriptions with the prints. With the progress of the industrial revolution, there existed a more prosperous middle class, and many more people could afford to travel both in Britain and abroad. Frith set out to photograph every town and site of interest in the British Isles, and also went on trips to the Rhine, Switzerland, the Italian Lakes, Rome and Norway in the 1860s, producing views which were then printed in large quantities at Reigate. Various publications followed, including an illustrated version of *The Holy Bible*, 1862–3; *Gossiping Photographer on the Rhine*, 1864; *Gossiping Photographer at Hastings*, 1864; *Pictures from Switzerland and the Italian Lakes* n.d.; illustrations to *Liverpool; Its Public Buildings, Docks, Churches, etc.*, n.d.; Longfellow's *Hyperion*, 1865 and *The Book of the Thames*, 1867. These were just some titles, in addition there were series of prints obtainable in albums or portfolios on any of the subjects in store, which could be ordered.

Interestingly, Frith did not limit his publications to his own photographs. Apart from offering a printing service for amateur photographers, as well as lessons in photography, he appears to have bought up various photographers' negatives, most notably Fenton's. The last great publishing gesture in the large fine photographic print field in Britain was Frith's publication of two folio albums of Fenton's large plate views. One was devoted to English cathedrals, the other to landscapes, and they were handsomely bound with a specially designed Frith

title page in each, incorporating a Fenton view. They are magnificent prints, and provide, together with the original prints by Fenton, a great insight into the diverse possibilities in printing obtainable from one negative. Where Fenton's prints are subtler, a mellow golden colour, with rich browns, even in the least faded prints, Frith's are clear, cold, virtuoso prints, the whites clean and the gold toning very apparent in the reddish-purple colour of the images. This general colour holds true for most of the prints which came out of the Frith company, and unless they have been adversely affected by environmental conditions, they are very permanent. Frith also published wholeplate views by Fenton, Rosling, Eaton, Francis Bedford, Frank Good, Thomas Sutton and others, in *Gems of Photographic Art*, n.d., and in his English and Foreign Series; prints issued separately on mounts, available singly, in portfolios or bound into albums. During these early years of the company, prints in these series were scrupulously credited as to photographer. However, it seems that as the stocks grew, and the control of the company by Frith himself diminished, and the demand for views became more a mechanical choice of location rather than anything else, this kind of nicety was forgotten. In about 1886 the firm began to catalogue the series as to location, and alphabetical catalogues were published, first of the English (British) series, and in 1892 the complete English and Foreign Series containing up to date appendices in each region. None of these views are credited as to photographer. These catalogues are now in the hands of the Francis Frith Collection, in Buckinghamshire, which administers the negatives extant from the Reigate firm as a picture library. It seems that few, if any, of these negatives date

before about 1890. Frith's policy was to keep his views 'updated', so these early series, in most cases, would have fallen into disuse. All the prints in the V&A collection are definitely pre-1890, and the numbers do not correspond to any on the published list. However, also in the Frith Collection in Buckinghamshire, is a manuscript catalogue of all the earlier prints, and these serial numbers do correspond to the manuscript numbers on the prints in the V&A. There is no doubt that the collection contains work by other notable British photographers, I turned up *The Confessional*, by Frank M. Good, fairly quickly. It also contains Frith's own prints taken abroad, and many others he either commissioned or bought in, from places which we know he never visited, as well as many of his Middle Eastern views. There is an extensive series on India, published probably in the 1870s, as *Frith's India Photo-Pictures*. The portfolio contained about one hundred albumen prints, of 'extensive architectural and topographical surveys and a unique set of groups of various Indian castes and tribes'. The photographer of these is unknown, as are those in America, Algeria, China, Japan and Russia, as well as many of the European views. So far, even with the manuscript catalogue there is no clue to the credits for this early section, but the file prints in the V&A provide the opportunity of tracing many images from that period, by photographers whose work is not readily available. It is also quite possible, since William Darrah claims that stereoscopic images from pre-1856, by Frith, were reissued by him later from Reigate, that other wholeplate views dating from the first half of the 1850s, by Frith, are among the many views of Britain.

ALBERT ANKER, "Young Girl Knitting", ca. 1901, oil on canvas, signed. 39 × 34.5cm. Sold for 355,000 SwFr ($168,250; with premium, $185,000) in our spring 1983 auction — more than double its estimates of 100,000/150,000 SwFr.

SALES BY AUCTION

SPRING AND AUTUMN

GALERIE KOLLER ZÜRICH

GALERIE KOLLER, RÄMISTRASSE 8, 8024 ZÜRICH, TELEFON: (01) 475040/475262, TELEX: 58500
BUREAU DE GENÈVE: GALERIE KOLLER, 2, RUE DE L'ATHÉNÉE, 1205 GENÈVE, TÉLÉPHONE: (022) 210385
OFFICE NEW YORK: GALERIE KOLLER ZÜRICH, P.O. BOX 1100 NEW YORK, N.Y. 10021, PHONE (212) 775 0066, TELEX: ITT 620562
KONTAKTADRESSE IN DEUTSCHLAND: CASPAR N. TAMMS, NICOLAISTRASSE 4, D-8000 MÜNCHEN 40, TELEFON (089) 349687

GEORGE BICKHAM JUNIOR
Master of the Rococo

Michael Snodin

Rococo. What images does that strange word conjure up? They may include the pink, white and gold of a south German pilgrimage church, Boucher's Miss O'Murphy, and perhaps a silver coffee pot by Paul de Lamerie. Almost certainly none of these images will be a print, yet prints were not only often the ambassadors of the style but also very frequently its most characteristic expression.

The decorative style known as rococo grew out of the baroque of the seventeenth century. Its fully developed form in France, known at the time as the *genre pittoresque*, began in the 1720s. Its first use seems to have been in the metalwork of the French court designer Juste Aurèle Meissonnier, but its truest expression was the fantasy landscape, which had begun to appear in French prints by 1734. English decorative art, which had escaped the earlier phase of French rococo, began to be affected by the *genre pittoresque* in the very early 1730s, at first, as in France, in metalwork. The next stage, the use of the style in prints, has been connected with the arrival in 1732 or 1733 of Hubert Gravelot, a French engraver and draughtsman. There can be no doubt that his easy and elegant figure style gave a new rococo flavour to English art, but his purely ornamental work, while being entirely rococo after the mid 1730s, rarely reflected the full force of French *genre pittoresque* prints. The first clear indiction of this influence is a silver-gilt dish made by George Wickes in 1735, the decoration of which is derived from a set of cartouches by Jacques de la Joue, prob-

ably published a year earlier. This, however, is an isolated example. The chief evidence for the presence of these prints in England lies in the work of an obscure engraver, publisher and expert plagiariser of other men's works, George Bickham junior (1706?–1771).

Bickham junior was the son of a writing master and engraver, unfortunately also called George (1684?–1758) and in consequence a good deal of confusion surrounds their publications and working relationship. Bickham senior's greatest fame and skill was undoubtedly as an engraver of calligraphy, of which a contemporary wrote:

One plate of thine's of universal use,
And do's a thousand offspring soon
   produce,
For no engraver's work compared with
   thine
Could ever yet with equal glory shine.

His best known work is *The Universal Penman*, published in a collected edition in 1741. Some of the decorative head and tailpieces are signed by his son. The first, datable to 1734, is a partial copy of a print after Antoine Watteau, the greatest artist of the early French rococo. His own independent career as a copyist had in fact begun by 1731, with *A New Drawing Book Consisting of Various Kinds of Birds*, containing copies after Francis Barlow. Bickham junior's major contribution, however, was to *The Musical Entertainer*. This collection of 100 song sheets is divided into two volumes, but was sold in parts or 'numbers' of 3 or 4 sheets, apparently published twice a month between 1737 and 1739. Its first appearance was advertised as 'select Italian, English and Scotch songs . . . the whole to be curiously engraved on copper plates, and embellished not only with all variety of penmanship, and command of hand; but with headpieces, in picture-work, and other

decorations, as landskips adorned with figures expressive of each subject'.

One of the most popular settings for the performance of these songs is shown in FIG.1, an end-of-season scene at Vauxhall Gardens, engraved by Bickham junior after Gravelot. Gravelot and his friends were much involved with Vauxhall, and this is one of 14 plates in the *Entertainer* after Gravelot, most of them by Bickham junior. They are, however, almost the only plates traceable to English sources. Of the rest which are traceable nearly all can be connected with French prints. By far the most (at least 30) are after Watteau. The first true *genre pittoresque* print to be copied was for 'The Coquet' of 1737, taken from prints by Jean Mondon published in 1736. Mondon's prints, with those of Meissonnier, de la Joue and François Boucher, were the first to show the *genre pittoresque* in France.

The headpiece of 'Silvia to Alexis' (FIG.2) is typical of the approach to such sources, in this case Mondon's 'L'Amoureux Guerrier' (FIG.3), here shown in the form of a German copy. The two figures are separated, leaving Alexis gesturing but empty-handed and Silvia leaning backwards unsupported. The *rocaille* background is taken from another, unidentified, source, but the title cartouche is a direct lift from de la Joue's *Receuil Nouveau de Differens Cartouches*. The tailpiece is also taken from de la Joue. The second use of 'L'Amoureux Guerrier' is Bickham junior's headpiece for 'The Soldier's Free Mistress' of 1738 (FIG.4). This almost has the feeling, as so often in these adaptations, of a private joke, in this case on the perhaps slightly desperate words of the song:

No jealous cares attend my mind,
Tho' she's enjoyed by all mankind,
Then drink and never spare it,
'Tis a bottle of good claret.

FIG.1 George Bickham junior after Hubert Gravelot, 'The Adieu to Spring Gardens', headpiece from *The Musical Entertainer*, vol.1, 17 August 1737, engraving. Vauxhall Gardens were also called the New Spring Gardens. The orchestra and singer can be seen in the building on the right. V&A Library.

FIG.2 George Bickham junior (?), after Jean Mondon and
Jacques de la Joue. 'Silvia to Alexis', headpiece from *The
Musical Entertainer*, vol.1, 1737, engraving. V&A Library.
FIG.4 George Bickham junior after Jean Mondon, 'The
Soldier's Free Mistress', headpiece from *The Musical
Entertainer*, vol.2, 1739, engraving. V&A Library.

2

4

FIG.5 George Bickham junior after François Boucher, 'Mad Bess', headpiece from *The Musical Entertainer*, vol.1, 1738, engraving. V&A Library.   FIG.7 George Bickham junior (?), after Juste Aurèle Meissonnier, 'Moor Circulating the Cheerful Glass', headpiece from *The Musical Entertainer*, vol. 2, May 1738, engraving. V&A Library.

5

7

FIG.3 Anonymous German after Jean Mondon, 'l'Amoureux
Guerrier' after pl.6 of Mondon's *Troisieme Livre de formes
Cartels et Rocailles*, 1736, published in Augsburg by
J.G. Merz, engraving. Dept. of prints and drawings,
E.314–1889.   FIG.6 Claude Duflos after François Boucher,
'Leda' from the set of screen panel designs, engraving. Dept.
of Prints and Drawings, 13685.1.   FIG.8 Laureolli after
Juste Aurèle Meissonnier, A fountain in a fantastic landscape,
from *Livre d'Ornemens*, 1734, engraving. Dept. of Prints
and Drawings, E.940–1905.

3

6

8

Mondon's girl has accordingly been replaced by a bottle, and the stag inn sign, which in Mondon presumably refers to the girl's cuckolding of her husband is here made to refer to her cuckolding of the soldier.

François Boucher is of course best known as the quintessential French rococo painter, but his influence was very largely spread by prints after his work, of which over 1500 were produced. His elegant illustrations to the 1734 edition of Molière, which also seem to have influenced Gravelot and his circle, were used in the *Entertainer* in 1737, in one case combined with a figure after Watteau. Boucher's designs for screens were also used, principally for the headpieces of 'Mad Bess' of 1738 (FIG.5). As usual Bickham is not content to lift his source unaltered, and combines the shell from Boucher's 'Leda' (FIG.6) with a figure from another screen design, the 'Triomphe de Pomone'. In this case Bickham junior's poor prints serve to date the hitherto undated fine French originals.

Meissonnier was the principal originator of the *genre pittoresque* in the 1720s, but prints after his designs did not appear until 1734. The *Livre d'Ornemens*, one of the few suites of his prints known to have been published at this early date, was used in the *Entertainer* in 1738 and 1739. The example shown here (FIG.7) combines Meissonnier's typical fantasy landscape (FIG.8) with very solid figures in theatrical costume of the day taken from another source. The same print was used by Bickham in 1748 as a firework design to celebrate the peace of Aix-la-Chapelle. The problem of the authorship of the decorations for the *Entertainer* is considerable. Many plates are unsigned, but the names George Bickham and George Bickham junior appear elsewhere. What is certain, however, is that of the named plates,

those by Bickham junior are by far the most imaginative and include all those connected with *genre pittoresque* prints. An indication of the breadth of his activities is given in a list of his prints bound into a copy of *The Oeconomy of the Arts* of 1747. Included are music sheets for the opera 'Flora', engraved by him after Gravelot, but not the *Entertainer*, although 'Six folio songs new decorated with pictures' are listed. Most of the prints are satirical, but the list concludes with artist's materials and 'all the newest prints as they come out: old prints bought and sold'. In his advertisement of 1738 he undertakes to engrave 'all sorts of curious works, viz history pieces, heads, landskips, architecture, maps, tickets, coats of arms, cyphers and shopkeepers bills, with their proper decorations . . . as also all sorts of writing'.

Further evidence of this wide-ranging activity is the undated title-page of *The Drawing and Writing Tutor* (FIG.9). It shows a room, presumably intended to be Bickham's own, lined with books. Before the window is a light-diffusing screen of the type used by engravers. The portfolio on the engraver's table bears a list of work similar to that of his advertisement, but with the addition of 'rooms, ceilings, fitted up with paper, in the English and Chinese taste of a new invention'. The books of prints on the shelves bear general titles and the names of artists from Dürer onwards, including Meissonnier, Boucher and de la Joue. The only English names are Smith (presumably John Smith the great mezzotinter), Bickham senior (which establishes the engraver as his son) and Blakey, an obscure contemporary book illustrator. Most appropriately, the title is carried on a mirror design taken from a print by Gabriel Huquier after Meissonnier. Here, then, is apparent proof of Bickham junior's library of sources.

Unfortunately, this is yet another example of the plagiarist at work. Mr Peter Fuhring has kindly drawn my attention to a drawing at the Ecole de Beaux Arts in Paris which lies behind the title page. The whole image is present, except for the mirror, the 'boete aux couleurs' on the right, and some small details, the inclusion of which has forced Bickham to stretch the design horizontally. The drawing is, in effect, a trade card for the great Parisian print dealer, engraver, publisher and collector, Gabriel Huquier (a slightly different drawing, also at the Beaux Arts, is dated 1749). The portfolio is inscribed with Huquier's advertisement and above the book shelves is the inscription 'Estampes differentes pour l'etude du dessein' which also appears in Bickham. Of the 64 book titles, most of which are reproduced by Bickham, many refer to Huquier's own engravings. Bickham omits Michelangelo, Natoire, Oppenord, Jouvenet and several general categories such as 'orfévrerie'. Added by Bickham are Bickham senior and Blakey, but also La Bas (ie J.-P. Le Bas the great French teacher of engraving) and 'desseins Engleis' (sic). We cannot, of course, be sure of the significance of the additions without seeing an impression of the print which was very probably Bickham's source, of which no example seems to have survived. We can, however, be sure that Bickham was aware of the importance of Huquier as a print dealer and publisher of the works of Watteau, Boucher, de la Joue and Meissonnier. Might we suspect here another joke? It is certainly the most outrageous of George Bickham junior's many borrowings of other men's clothes.

Rococo: art and design in Hogarth's England, the Museum's major exhibition in 1984, will run from 16 May to 30 September.

FIG.9 George Bickham junior after Gabriel Huquier and
others *The Drawing and Writing Tutor*, title page, after
1749, engraving. V&A Library.

French & Company inc.

ONE OF THE MOST BEAUTIFUL COMMODES
IN THE WORLD

Pierre Langlois made six almost identical commodes: Two are at Windsor Castle,
Two are at Buckingham Palace and One is at the Huntington Museum, California.
This is the sixth and last in the world.

Height: 33 inches · Width: 61 inches · Depth: 25½ inches
(84cm. x 155cm. x 65cm.)

This commode was made circa 1760.

FIG.6 The Prince Consort inspecting the design for the
memorial to the 1851 Exhibition. Watercolour by Anthony
Stannus, A.L. 7851.

A QUARTIER LATIN OF A DIGNIFIED AND POPULAR SORT

Prince Albert's own contribution to South Kensington

Hermione Hobhouse

The Great Exhibition of the Works of Industry of All Nations closed on 15 October 1851. Queen Victoria herself was not present to see the closing meeting chaired by Prince Albert, the Chairman of the Royal Commissioners.

'To think,' she wrote sadly in her Journal, 'that this great and bright time is past like a dream, after all its success and triumph, and that all the labour and anxiety it caused for nearly two years should likewise now be only remembered as "a has been" seems incredible and melancholy.'

Fortunately, the Exhibition was not only a great triumph on its own account, the first international exhibition, a resounding financial success, a defeat for all the prophets of doom, but through the energy of a small band of enthusiasts it also left behind a lasting monument in South Kensington. The leader in this project was Prince Albert, Queen Victoria's German husband and first cousin, who at the age of 32 was beginning to be recognised as a powerful and influential figure. Lord John Russell wrote to the Queen after the Exhibition, observing that 'it is to his energy and judgement that the world owes both the original design and the harmonious and rapid execution'. The concept of a quarter in London devoted to education, and the arts and sciences, does seem to have been very much his own idea, more so than the exhibition itself, where others can be seen to have come to him with the project. The concept of a learned quarter clearly owed something to the complex of university and museums at Munich laid out by von Klenze; in its breadth of scale and comprehensive nature it was much grander than any other contemporary scheme for an educational foundation in England. Unfortunately it was never fully realised, largely owing to the Prince's early death. The beginning was propitious and many of the institutions

have survived, but the removal of the Prince's coordinating hand was fatal to the town-planning aspects of the scheme, and the story is one of the great London 'might-have-beens'.

The ultimate surplus from the Exhibition was £186,000, doubled in due course by the Government, and used for the purchase of some 86 acres in Brompton, then a convenient suburb, as yet undeveloped due to a series of land-holding problems. (FIG. 1. *Map of Estates in Kensington and Westminster Purchased by the Commissioners, 1853*, from the Third Report, 1856). The intention was to ensure 'maintenance of the pre-eminence of Great Britain as the centre of the industry of the world', which it was felt, was threatened by a 'want of system' in the promotion of Science and Art. In addition, the Commissioners wanted to establish the juxtaposition of the numerous institutions, 'whether dependent on government or private support, which have in view the advancement of Science and Art in their private branches . . . especially in respect of the practical application of Science and Art in their various branches'.

The Prince was busy on the project even before the Exhibition closed. In a memorandum prepared in August 1851, he proposed that the surplus should be used to further the objects of the Exhibition, which he thought to have been:

'. . . the promotion of every branch of human industry by means of the comparison of their processes and results as carried on and obtained by all the nations of the earth, and the promotion of kindly feelings of the nations towards each other by the practical illustrations of the advantages which may be derived by each from the labours and achievements of the others.'

In practical terms the Commissioners decided that what was most needed

was an 'Institution which should serve to increase the means of Industrial Education, and extend the influence of Science and Art upon Productive Industry'. Such an institution, they pointed out in a carefully argued report was much needed in England, as a focus for the provincial Schools of Design and other local teaching institutes, and further afield, the Madras Museum of Economic Geology and the Royal Dublin Society. Polytechnic institutes for the training of mechanics were already well organised in France and in Germany where 'even small states support them at great expense'. The lack of them, the Commissioners warned, was nullifying much of the effort spent in this country on the promotion of Science and Art.

The Prince's own concept was altogether grander in scale, and he circulated a rough plan and a memorandum in August 1853, setting out his views and asking for comments. They were sent out to the Commissioners, particularly to allies like Lord Granville and Henry Cole, and also to such public figures as Charles Barry, and to leaders of the artistic community like Edwin Landseer. The site stretched from Hyde Park southward to the small community of Brompton, centred on the Brompton Road, and the recent church of Holy Trinity. There were relatively few buildings, the only substantial group being Brompton Park House on the eastern side near the church, so a grand symmetrical layout on the centre of the site was possible.

The dominant building would have been the National Gallery, with a frontage of 800 feet, and a total of 190,000 square feet, some seven times larger in area than the existing Gallery in Trafalgar Square, then much under attack for the damage being done to the pictures by the 'vitiated' and polluted air of central London. It was to be

FIG.1 The Estates purchased by the 1851 Commissioners
(from their *Third Report*, 1853).

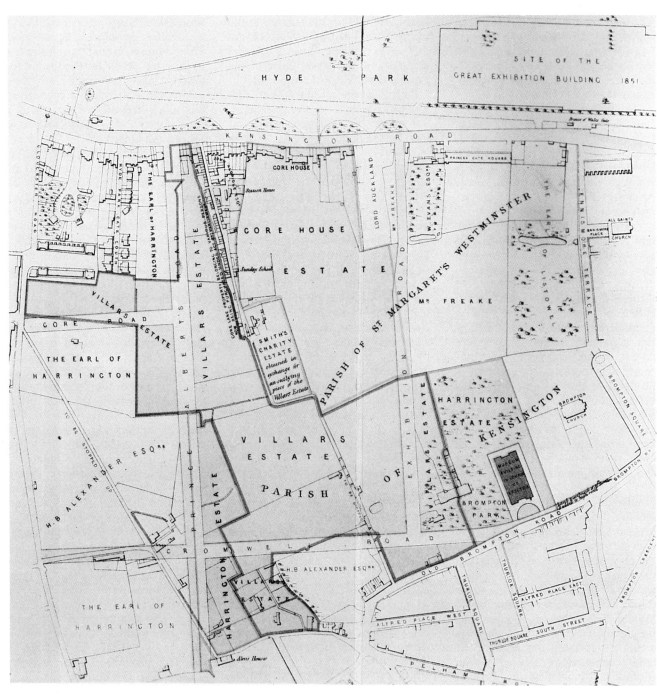

FIG.2 The Horticultural Gardens in 1863, looking northwards to Hyde Park. The Conservatory at the top was designed by Francis Fowke, and the major part of the arcades by Sydney Smirke. The two bandstands on either side are now at Southwark and on Clapham Common. Below them, in the centre, is the Memorial Fountain to the 1851 Exhibition, surmounted by the statue of the Prince Consort. Note the embroidery beds, the maze, as designed by W.A. Nesfield, and the statues and other sculpture as advocated by the Prince. (Courtesy of the Royal Horticultural Society).

FIG.3 Project for completing the Royal Horticultural Society arcades, showing the Gardens in 1868. On the left is the Conservatory, with the site of the Royal Albert Hall. On the right is the proposed building to complete the Gardens on the south. Beyond can be seen the South Kensington Museum, with the Science Schools, then under construction. Etching by Robert Collinson, coloured by hand, A.L. 7225.

2

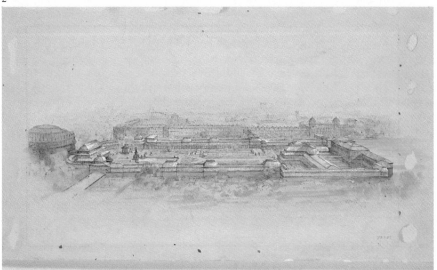

3

FIG.4 H.R.H. F.M. P.A. at it again. Cartoon in *Punch*,
12 July 1856. (Photograph: R. Todd-White).

reached from the Cromwell Road through a triumphal arch by a three hundred yard long approach between architectural gardens. These would contain ornamental fountains, and statues, and monuments erected to men distinguished in Art, Science and Industry. The gardens were to be flanked by buildings housing the Museums of Industrial Art, Patented Inventions, Trade Museums, etc . . . The site now occupied by the Albert Hall was intended for the Colleges of Art and Science. A number of official residences, other institutions, and private houses would occupy other land belonging to the Commissioners, and by 'their architectural lines . . . materially add to the harmonious effect of the whole . . .'.

'I should be glad' concluded the Prince, 'if these suggestions were considered on the spot, and looked into by competent persons, and also if Artists would sketch out the Elevation which might be best suited to give them effect.

'I should myself incline to an Italian or Palladian style of architecture, as admitting variety of outline and invention with symmetrical architectural lines . . .'.

Sadly, no full scale architectural competition was held at that time, though a number of ideas were contributed by the leading architects of the day. Certainly no Belgravian group of public buildings filled the grand quadrilateral between Hyde Park and the Cromwell Road, flanked by Exhibition Road, and Prince Albert's Road (now Queen's Gate).

Topsy-like development began almost at once on the Brompton Park Estate, immediately taken as the headquarters of a detachment of Engineers, and later for offices by Henry Cole, Richard Redgrave and Dr Lyon Playfair, who in 1852 had taken over the running of the Department of

Science and Art. In the course of the 1850s this became the site of the South Kensington Museum, later to be renamed the Victoria and Albert Museum. A number of buildings were erected on the site largely to the design of Francis Fowke, an Engineer officer, who was resident architect until his death in 1865. Some were temporary, like the Brompton Boilers, some more permanent, like the Sheepshanks Gallery and the North and South Courts. The opportunism and persistence of Henry Cole and his allies, badgering the Government of the day for money, and spending it swiftly to house diverse collections, secured for the nation its greatest museum of applied art. The Patent Museum and the educational collections purchased after the 1851 Exhibition started the museum off, to them were added the Sheepshanks collection of contemporary paintings, the Soulages collection of majolica and other ceramics. Both science and art were catered for, and in due course art students moved in from their temporary quarters at Marlborough

H. R. H. F. M. P. A. AT IT AGAIN!
Policeman, "ONLY MOVING THE PICTURES TO KENSINGTON GORE! SUPPOSE YOU LEAVE 'EM WHERE THEY ARE, EH?"

House, and science students from the College of Chemistry and the Museum of Practical Geology in the West End.

On the central part of the site only part of the scheme was ever carried out. The first problem was that the National Gallery, the jewel in the South Kensington crown, would not move. 'H.R.H. F.M. P.A. at it again' growled *Punch* (FIG.4), and despite the dirt, the traffic, and the lack of room, the nation's pictures stayed in Trafalgar Square. More room was found by giving the learned societies Burlington House, but the lack of space for expansion has been a perennial problem.

The southern site bordering on the Cromwell Road was the home of the 1862 Exhibition, whose building was originally intended to be a permanent enhancement of the area (FIG.5). Through jealousy of Cole and Fowke, and in the absence of a powerful co-ordinator like Prince Albert, the demolition of the substantial buildings was insisted on, and in due course, the Natural History collections from the British Museum were housed on the site.

South Kensington did in fact attract more scientific institutions than artistic ones, as indeed Charles Barry had predicted.

The South Kensington Museum split to become the Victoria and Albert Museum, and the Science Museum, which was given an independent director in 1893, though its independent building was not opened till 1928. Imperial College was set up in 1907, uniting three earlier institutions, two of which were connected with Prince Albert. The first of these was the Royal College of Science, the descendant of the College of Chemistry of which the Prince had laid the foundation stone in 1846. An even greater service had been the appointment of A.W. Hoffmann as professor for the new institution,

FIG.5 The 1862 Exhibition building, from Cromwell Road,
5 May 1861.   FIG.8 Francis Fowke's great conservatory
under construction.   FIG.10 The Royal Horticultural
Gardens in about 1862.

5

8

10

FIG.7 The Prince Consort Gallery in the South Kensington
Museum in 1876. Drawing by John Watkins, No. 8089.1.
FIG.9 The opening of the Royal Horticultural Gardens by the
Prince Consort, 5 July 1861, in the Conservatory.
Watercolour by E. Walker, P. 37–1976.

7   9

which had only been done through the Prince's personal intervention. The Royal School of Mines, the second institution, was descended from the Museum of Practical Geology in Jermyn Street, in which Prince Albert had also taken an interest, and where he had attended its evening lectures for working men. The Prince Consort's work for scientific education has thus been continued though it might be argued that it is not quite as united to artistic education as its founder intended.

The Museum of Practical Geology also moved to South Kensington, just before the Second World War, reinforcing the idea that teaching institutions and collections should be side by side, one of the basic concepts of the South Kensington Museum.

Prince Albert saw the architectural gardens as the central town-planning feature of the site, a retreat where 'the student and the amateur might retire to refresh themselves, when fatigued by their labours'. He failed to arouse enough interest and public money to create them however, and he had to fall back on doing this through the agency of a private society, an ingenious compromise which only really worked in his lifetime, and under his personal supervision. This was the Horticultural Society of which the Prince became president in 1858. It was an old-established institution which had fallen on hard times, finding itself unable to support either its headquarters or its existing gardens at Chiswick. The Prince Consort accepted the presidency and launched a scheme by which money would be raised through debentures and a campaign for prestigious life memberships to fund the development of gardens and offices.

With surprising speed the money was raised and the gardens laid out. The architectural skeleton of arcades and offices was designed by the ageing Sydney Smirke (FIGS.2,11) with a conservatory of great magnificence (FIG.8) and a Board Room for the Society contributed by Francis Fowke. Other designs reflecting the South Kensington preoccupation with terracotta and mosaic came from Godfrey Sykes, and other members of Henry Cole's design team. The gardens themselves which included symmetrical canals, and the central dominant Memorial Fountain, commemorating the Great Exhibition, were laid out by W.A. Nesfield, and his designs were personally approved by Prince Albert. Formal bedding schemes were much in evidence, including an 'embroidery garden' of box hedges and gravels, and an extensive maze occupied one of the parterres.

A number of statues were purchased or donated to embellish and enrich the area at the Prince's especial insistence, and these contributed to the magnificence of the design, which made the gardens the largest and most important formal gardens ever to be created in London. The buildings were opened by the Prince on 5 June 1861 (FIG.9), though much remained to be done. The Prince was much involved with the finishing touches to the garden, throughout 1861, the last year of his life, an interest which seems to have been resented by the Queen. Even so, immediately after the Prince's death, at the end of December, the Queen wrote to the Society saying that she would like it to be considered 'as under her peculiar patronage and protection', an acknowledgement of her husband's almost obsessional interest in the gardens.

They served as a most agreeable and attractive focus for South Kensington (FIG.10), being opened to visitors to the 1862 Exhibition, and to the series of minor exhibitions staged throughout the 1870s and into the 1880s. How-

ever, even royal patronage could not make it possible for a small private society to run a large public garden, and friction over the matter of rent developed with the Commissioners of the 1851 Exhibition. As the Society's historian observed, 'with the Prince-President seems to have passed away also . . . the Commissioners' friendliness'. The Gardens passed under the direct management of the Commission in 1882, and in due course, with remarkable short-sightedness, the site was used for a series of unrelated buildings, first the Imperial Institute in 1887, and then the Royal College of Music destroyed any hope of keeping a north-south axis. The arcades to the gardens survived as the Western and Eastern galleries housing collections from the South Kensington Museum, and were only demolished in the final rash of building in the 1970s.

Almost the only real relic of the Prince himself in South Kensington is the monument to the 1851 Exhibition, a lesser-known memorial to the Prince which stands on the south of the Albert Hall, on the axis of the better-known National Memorial (FIG.12). The proposal to commemorate the Exhibition by a statue of the Prince came very soon after the closing of the Exhibition, and was the suggestion of the Lord Mayor of London of the day. The Prince was hesitant about it, and was warned firmly by Granville not to be tempted to allow his statue to be put up. Perhaps somewhat hurt, the Prince replied:

'I can say, with perfect absence of humbug, that I would much rather not be made the prominent feature of such a monument, as it would both disturb my quiet rides in Rotten Row to see my own face staring at me, and if . . . it became an artistic monstrosity, like most of our monuments, it would upset my equanimity to be permanently laughed at and ridiculed in effigy . . .' He

FIG.11 Design by Sydney Smirke for a pavilion for the
Horticultural Gardens. (Courtesy Royal Horticultural
Society)   FIG.14 The Commissioners' Estate in 1910.
(Photograph: R. Todd-White).

11

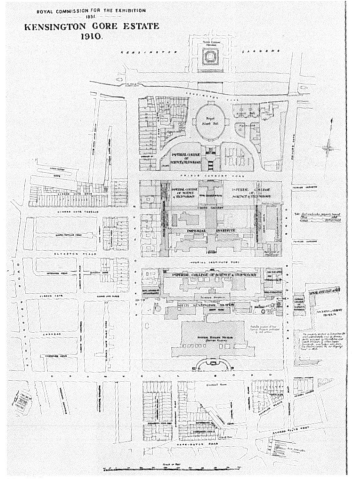

14

FIG.12 The Albert Memorial, Kensington Gardens.
FIG.13 The Memorial to the 1851 Exhibition, south of the
Royal Albert Hall.

pointed out with perfect justice that the monument was to 'commemorate the *fact* of the Exhibition of 1851 over which I presided – which fact will remain unaltered were I to turn out a Nero or Caligula.'

The Prince's own suggestion that the site of the Palace itself should be marked in Hyde Park, and that any balance should go towards museums or travelling scholarships was ignored, and a committee of leaders of the artistic establishment was formed to organise fund-raising and a competition. A statue of Britannia was agreed upon, surrounded by groups representing the continents. Joseph Durham won the competition, and a site was found in the Royal Horticul-

tural Society's Gardens. The Prince took a great personal interest in the project, and designed a clasp for America's mantle himself. He inspected the statue very carefully, having it set up at exactly the right angle in the South Kensington Museum. In July 1861, the Committee decided that a statue of the Queen would be more appropriate, but the Prince's tragic death brought another change. The Prince of Wales wrote in his own hand to say that his mother would prefer a statue of the Prince Consort: '. . . it would be most hurtful to Her feelings were any other statue to surmount this Memorial, but that of the great, good Prince, my dearly beloved Father, to whose honor (*sic*) it

is in reality raised.'

The statue was unveiled on 10 June 1863, and presided over the gardens until they were finally dismantled when it was moved to its present position (FIG.13). It is ironic that the view spread before the Prince is so far from that which he worked so hard to create, and one can only deplore the lack of leadership from the Commissioners in the late nineteenth century which allowed this destruction (FIG.14).

An exhibition, 'Albert His Life and Work', sponsored by the *Observer* with the Midland Bank Group, is being held in the Royal College of Art from 11 October 1983 until 22 January 1984.

12

13

V&A SHOP
some present ideas

NE OF A PAIR OF GILDED ARMCHAIRS
MADE TO ORDER FOR THE BALLROOM
F LIONEL DE ROTHSCHILD'S HOUSE
T 148 PICCIDILLY LONDON ADDING TO
N 18th CENTURY SET OF EIGHT
TTRIBUTED TO NICHOLAS HEURTAUT.
HE CONTENTS OF THE HOUSE WERE

SOLD IN APRIL 1937 BY SOTHEBY'S
FOR VICTOR ROTHSCHILD. IN 1967
THE 18th CENTURY SET OF EIGHT
WERE SOLD AGAIN BY SOTHEBY'S
FOR £26,000 ($72,600). THE 19th
CENTURY PAIR ARE NOW IN OUR
POSSESSION IN TORONTO.

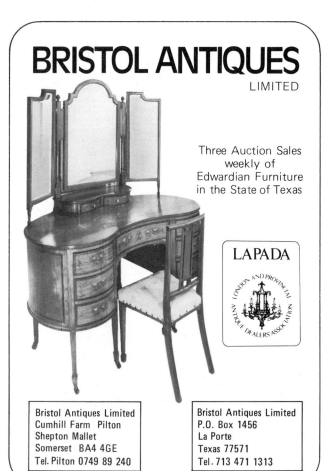

Britain's leading provincial auction house

FINE ARTS RECEPTION

Our highly skilled team provides a very unprovincial service to the fine arts and antiques world – conducting weekly specialist sales in purpose built salerooms with valuers and advice constantly available.

Our offices throughout the north of England give personal contact to clients from coast to coast, worldwide.

Henry Spencer & Sons

HSS 1840

Henry Spencer & Sons Ltd, 20 The Square, Retford, Notts. Tel: 0777 708633. Telex: 56212.

Antique Furniture Restoration

MARQUETRY ● BOULLE ● IVORY WORK
TURNING ● CARVING ● WAX POLISHING
COPY CHAIRMAKING ● UPHOLSTERY
CANING ● FURNITURE HAND MADE TO
CUSTOMER'S REQUIREMENTS

Private enquiries welcome

Collection and delivery

Overseas enquiries invited

CLIFFORD J. TRACY
6–40 Durnford Street,
Seven Sisters Road,
London N15 5NQ
Telephone: 01-800 4773/4774

Cyril Humphris

*EUROPEAN SCULPTURE,
PAINTINGS
AND OTHER WORKS OF ART*

Please note that early in 1984
we shall be moving from

23 Old Bond Street

our new address will be

8 Pembroke Walk
London W. 8.

Telephone: 01-937 1719

PARISH-HADLEY ASSOCIATES, INC.
305 EAST 63RD STREET   NEW YORK, N.Y. 10021

FIG.5 Spur set in a root, steel and wood, said to
have been found on the field of Agincourt.
(M464–1927).

NOBLE WORKS
OR BASE DECEPTIONS?

Some Victorian Fakes and Forgeries

Malcolm Baker

During the 1860s and 70s the energy, knowledge and flair of the South Kensington Museum's curators – notably John Charles Robinson – led to the acquisition of many of the Museum's outstanding examples of decorative arts and sculpture. This same period saw the development and enrichment of the collection of plaster casts, taken largely from originals of Medieval and Renaissance date. Quite apart from their own aesthetic and historic significance, acquisitions in both these fields have today a considerable interest as an index of High Victorian taste. Such taste also found expression in another category of material that tends – in museums at least – to receive less attention: fakes and forgeries.

A permanent exhibition of copies, pastiches and fakes in the styles of the Middle Ages and Renaissance has recently been mounted in the corridor between the two cast courts, complementing the casts to which it is adjacent. Both in their different ways provide us with a Victorian view of the Middle Ages and Renaissance. The corridor has been redecorated in its original colours of 1873 and the mosaic floor, Henry Cole's 'opus criminale' laid by the women prisoners of Woking jail, restored. In keeping with this setting, the objects are displayed in original cases of 1870 (dated on the locks) and mounted to simulate, at least approximately, the richly crowded displays of the 1870s.

The definition of a fake is both difficult and tendentious and the objects included in this display have been shown to represent the widest range of possible interpretations. They stretch from the straightforward and honest copy to the sophisticated simulation of an authentic object produced with the intention of deceiving for profit. At one extreme is an enamel roundel of Julius Caesar (FIG.1) which was directly copied from a sixteenth century enamel already acquired by the Museum in 1875, and is boldly signed '1882 L's Dalpayrat South Kensington Museum'. Louis Dalpayrat taught enamelling at the South Kensington Art School and executed a number of copies for the Museum, including another roundel copied from a 'coloured photograph' and produced to complete a set from which the Museum already had the other pieces. The enthusiasm of the 1870s for the same French Renaissance style is also reflected in the ewer produced by Minton in imitation of that exceptionally sophisticated earthenware decorated with strapwork and arabesques, known as St. Porchaire ware. This, like the Limoges plaque, was purchased as a modern work. At the other extreme is a superbly made pastoral staff (FIG.2) with a cast copper-gilt group of the Virgin and Child and its stem enriched with enamels and filigree decoration in the style of the thirteenth century. This was probably produced for the dealer, Louis Marsy, who during the 1890s supplied many finely made examples of goldsmith's work, supposedly of twelfth and thirteenth century date, for those wealthy collectors who vied with each other to obtain medieval objects of great sumptuousness.

Between the two poles represented by the Limoges plaque and the pastoral staff lie many intermediary positions. Although the term forgery implies an intention to deceive, this was not necessarily the motive of the craftsman who produced an object. A pastiche employing various motifs from different Renaissance works, for example, may have been produced completely honestly and only subsequently presented by a later owner to a prospective purchaser as an authentic sixteenth century object. Such was the case with perhaps the most impressive of all the fakes shown in the gallery; the oratory

(or *coretto*) by Edgardo Minozzi. Acquired from an English private collection as an exceptionally fine example of fifteenth century marquetry, it resembles the well-known oratory of 1460 formerly in the Chapel of the Castello di Torrechiara in Parma. However, reading a report of the acquisition in an Italian newspaper, the maker's son recognised it as a copy made from old materials by his father in 1912. Only a year later it had been sold as an authentic piece by the Parma dealer, Brassi, to an English collector.

In other cases, an object may be in part authentic but have had alterations or additions made to it to render it grander in appearance and therefore more saleable. A standard late sixteenth century morion, for example, could in the nineteenth century be embossed with an elaborate combination of allegorical figures and strapwork so that what was a relatively ordinary helmet now masquerades as part of a glamorous Mannerist parade armour (FIG.3). Refurbished and upgraded arms and armour figured prominently in the contents of the Spitzer sale and it was from this source the Museum acquired in 1893 a goblet with a fluted stem (FIG.4). This was purchased as Venetian, late fifteenth century, an attribution still considered correct for the bowl. The foot, on the other hand, is an addition by Spitzer, a *marchand-amateur* who evidently employed a considerable number of craftsmen in different media to turn his stock into something more glamorous than when it first came into his hands.

An addition of a different kind is seen in the case of the 'Agincourt' spur (FIG.5), where a perfectly authentic object has been given a fanciful provenance intended to appeal to the late nineteenth century taste for romantic historicism. A root was soaked in water and then bent around a fifteenth century spur; to this was then attached a

FIG.1 Plaque, Julius Caesar, painted enamel, by Louis
Dalpayrat, signed and dated 1882. (1519–1882).

FIG.2 Pastoral staff, copper gilt set with pastes and enamels, French, late nineteenth century in the style of the thirteenth century. (434–1895).　FIG.3 Morion, steel, embossed and damascened, Italian, late sixteenth century, decorated in the nineteenth century. (M14–1921).　FIG.4 Goblet, glass, the bowl Venetian, late fifteenth century, the stem and foot, late nineteenth century. (698–1893).　FIG.7 Casket, tin-glazed earthenware; nineteenth century in the style of the tenth century. (640–1875).

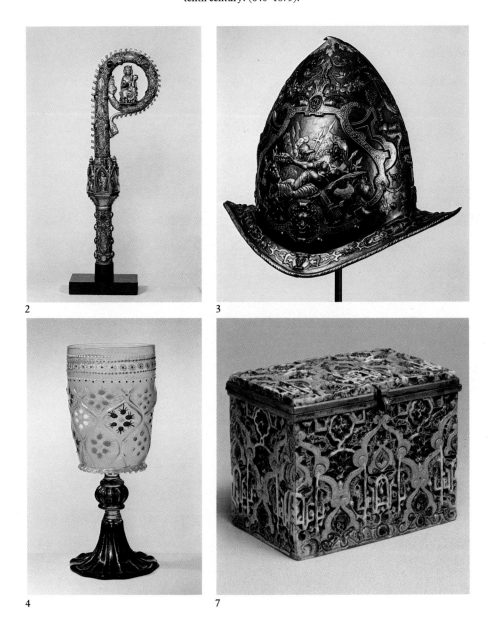

2

3

4

7

FIG.8 Allegorical figure, boxwood, probably French, late
nineteenth century in the style of the sixteenth century.
(343–1885).

brass plate richly engraved with the inscription, 'From the Field of Agincourt Fought on the Day of Crispin Crispianus 25th Oct 1415'. Here, as in the examples already discussed, we see the tastes and attitudes of a period determining the nature of the 'fakes' that were produced for its collectors.

If one of the attractions of fakes is their interest as a reflection of the taste of their period, another is the way in which their true nature is revealed. Here too we encounter ambiguity. Sometimes, however, the development of certain scientific tests has led to some clearly decisive answers. The analysis of a sample of terracotta by thermo-luminescent techniques can establish the approximate date at which the clay was fired. By this method it was revealed that the imposing – if somewhat garish – Italian maiolica busts of Roman emperors, were fired not in the seventeenth century but around 1860. Subsequently, they were linked with copies produced by Angelo Minghetti, working in Bologna in the 1860s.

Often, however, the scientific data has to be interpreted together with the art-historical evidence and still some puzzles remain. For example, a splendid terracotta portrait bust (FIG.6) depicting a German burgher of the type painted by Dürer and Cranach has been cited in a standard account of German sculpture as an important work by an early sixteenth-century Augsburg sculptor. Others, however, have regarded it as a nineteenth-century pastiche. The T.L. test, on the other hand, indicated a firing date of about 1780 so that it is now tentatively described as a historicising portrait of the late eighteenth century. It was bought by the Museum at a period when Robinson and Cole were eagerly acquiring both original examples and casts of German Renaissance sculpture.

Analysis of metals may sometimes, like T.L. tests, produce conclusive evidence about dates of manufacture. Often, however, a fake is revealed only by anomalies in its use of materials, function or style. Thus, a polychromed glazed earthenware casket (FIG.7), decorated with Hispano-Moresque ornament and acquired in 1875 as 'Oriental', strikes a wrong note in that it copies a form familiar only from eleventh-century ivory versions. Equally revealing is the way in which fakes often have no evident function. The popularity of French Gothic in the nineteenth century encouraged a wide and eager market for ivory reliefs in a fourteenth-century manner. But in copying panels of the Crucifixion or the Coronation of the Virgin, for example, many fakers overlooked the fact that most authentic panels originally formed one of a pair, hinged to make up a diptych. Therefore the absence of hinge holes on a panel that was usually paired immediately prompts suspicion.

Occasionally a faker will misunderstand his model in such a way that it is impossible for the object to be of the date that it purports to be. An example of this can be seen in a delicately carved ivory of Christ Blessing with the four evangelist symbols at the corners. A tenth century ivory of this subject in the Wallerstein collection at Maihingen had been recognised as an important early medieval work during the nineteenth century and plaster casts were made of it. The carver of our ivory was evidently working from one of these as the details of the lion of St. Mark, which became blurred on the plaster cast, are reinterpreted to form a second eagle of St. John.

Sometimes the source used can be surprisingly obvious but remains unnoticed nonetheless. A bronze group of Hercules and the Centaur was acquired as seventeenth-century German and

attributed to Hubert Gerhard. However, despite the apparent similarity of its surface chiselling to German bronzes of this period, its direct dependence on the large marble group by Canova that dominates the staircase in the Kunsthistorisches Museum, Vienna, makes it clear that it cannot date from before the nineteenth century. Often several models are combined. An exquisite silver-gilt triptych employs translucent enamels in the International Gothic style of around 1400 with leaf decoration of the late fifteenth century. Rather less inherently contradictory are the sources used by the carver of a boxwood allegorical figure (FIG.8) acquired as sixteenth-century French in 1885, when the Museum was buying its casts of French Renaissance sculpture. The main part is derived from one of the figures from the Chasse of St. Germain, celebrated in the late nineteenth century as the work of the sixteenth-century French sculptor Germain Pilon. Since this lacks arms, however, these are adapted by the carver from a standard antique figure, known in countless casts and copies, the Callypigian Venus.

Although some dealers and collectors have been mentioned, the identity of most of the craftsmen who produced these works remains unknown. A few, however, have emerged from the shadows, usually when their works have been exposed. Perhaps the best known is the Florentine Giovanni Bastianini (1830–1868) who as well as being an accomplished sculptor in his own right, produced a series of remarkable portrait busts in Quattrocento style. His most famous work, which eventually led to his exposure in 1867, is the bust of Girolamo Benivieni in the Louvre but some equally intriguing examples are on display at the V&A. The most imposing is that of the religious reformer, Savonarola (FIG.9).

Based on a notable medal, this portrait was carefully coloured and aged, the bottom part broken and then repaired with plaster. It was then planted in an old villa at Fiesole, and shown in a charity exhibition where it was drawn by an admiring Lord Leighton. Leighton, along with Alma-Tadema and Poynter, recommended it for purchase by the Museum. But when it was eventually purchased in 1896 it was as a modern work by Bastianini and as 'a very extraordinary instance, not only of modelling a bust from life, but also of the method of colouring sculpture, which is very much in vogue now, and of which we have very few good specimens'.

As the Director in 1896 recognised, Bastianini's work cannot be dismissed as worthless, even though it was originally produced to deceive. Many of these works thus raise challenging questions of both connoisseurship and aesthetics. How, for instance, should we regard the ivory relief of the Naming of St. John the Baptist by Richard Cockle Lucas? Lucas was responsible for various fakes, among them the celebrated Leonardo 'Flora' wax in Berlin, but this piece was presented to the Museum by the artist himself as a straightforward copy of the honestone relief bearing Dürer's monogram in the British Museum. Here, however, a faker was himself duped since the British Museum relief has now been reattributed to the seventeenth century Nuremburg sculptor, Georg Schweigger, working after a Dürer engraving. The final irony of this riddle only became apparent two years ago when the plaque bearing Dürer's monogram was taken off to reveal Schweigger's signature and the date 1642.

Nowhere is the ambiguity about the status of fakes better illustrated than in the changing fortunes of an agate cup and cover, mounted in silver-gilt (FIG.10), purchased at the Hamilton Palace sale in 1882 for £535-10-00. When it was acquired at one of the most important sales of the late nineteenth century it was regarded as a particularly fine example of Italian sixteenth-century goldsmith's work. But by 1897, when the Director was closely questioned about it by the Select Committee on Museums of the Science and Art Department, its hallmarks had been identified as those of 1815 and the piece regarded as an 'ordinary modern Indian agate cup, worth a few pounds only', mounted in a 'nondescript debased modern style'. Banished to store for seventy years, it re-emerged a few years ago as a remarkable, pioneering example of English historicist silver. An object that would without doubt have been included in an earlier Fakes and Forgeries gallery, today enjoys pride of place in the nineteenth-century English Primary display.

FIG.6 Bust of an unidentified man, terracotta. German, perhaps late eighteenth century based on a sixteenth century model. (222–1865). FIG.9 Girolamo Savonarola, pigmented terracotta, by Giovanni Bastianini, Italian (Florence), 1865. (31-1896). FIG.10 Cup and cover, agate with silver-gilt mounts, made for William Beckford of Fonthill Abbey, maker's mark of James Aldridge, English (London), 1815–16. (428–1882).

6

9

10

Contributors

Michael Archer *is Deputy Keeper of the Department of Ceramics. He specialises in English and Dutch tin-glazed earthenware and has a particular responsibility for the Museum's collection of stained-glass. He is a Fellow of the Society of Antiquaries, a member of the Redundant Churches Board, and is an author and lecturer.*

Malcolm Baker *is an Assistant Keeper in the Department of Sculpture and is responsible for sculpture, other than Italian, from 1300 to 1900. His areas of specialist interest are late Gothic German sculpture, eighteenth-century English sculpture and Baroque ivory carving. He is currently preparing the sculpture section of the forthcoming English Rococo exhibition, planning the Gothic Primary gallery and working on a catalogue of Baroque ivories.*

Anthony Burton *was Assistant Keeper in the V&A Library for ten years, after which he transferred to an administrative post in the Directorate, also acting as Assistant Secretary to the Advisory Council 1979–83. In 1981 he became Curator of the Bethnal Green Museum of Childhood.*

Shirley Bury, *Keeper of Metalwork, joined the V&A in 1948 and has principally specialised in silver and jewellery from the eighteenth century to the present day. Liveryman of the Goldsmiths' Company; member of the Hallmarking Council; President of the Society of Jewellery Historians; Fellow of the Society of Antiquaries. Her* Jewellery Gallery Summary Catalogue *was published by the V&A last year.*

Caroline Davidson *is the author of* A Woman's Work is Never Done: a History of Housework in the British Isles 1650–1950, *and has recently been specialist advisor to the Department of Furniture and Woodwork on the restoration of the kitchen at Ham House.*

Joe Earle *has been Keeper of the Far Eastern Department since October 1982. He has recently published a translation of a book on the Japanese sword and is presently engaged on research in the history of Japanese lacquer which will take him to Japan in September and October this year.*

Professor Charles Foster *is Emeritus Professor of Cell Biology and Histology, University of London. His wife, Mrs Anne Foster, is Senior Lecturer in Clinical Microbiology at St. Mary's Hospital Medical School, London. Both are Friends of the V&A.*

Dr James Fowler *carried out postgraduate research in Shakespeare and seventeenth-century drama before working in professional theatre and in adult education. He joined the Theatre Museum as Assistant Keeper in 1979, and has edited* Images of Show Business *(1982).*

Christopher Frayling *is Professor and Head of the Department of Cultural History at the Royal College of Art. The author of numerous books and articles on the highways and byeways of modern culture, he is responsible for the new Master of Arts course on the* History of Design and Decorative Art – *which involves both the Victoria and Albert Museum and the Royal College of Art, re-establishing the historic links between the two institutions.*

Sir Alexander Glen, KBE, DSC, *was Chairman of the British Tourist Authority from 1969 to 1977. He has been Chairman of the Advisory Council of the Victoria and Albert Museum since 1978.*

Hermione Hobhouse, MBE, *was Secretary to the Victorian Society from 1977 to 1982 and has written* Thomas Cubitt: Master Builder *and* Lost London. *She is a Fellow of the Society of Antiquaries and is organising the Prince Albert Exhibition being held at the Royal College of Art from October 1983 – January 1984.*

Donald King *is a former Keeper of the Department of Textiles and Dress. He has recently been the organiser of the Arts Council's exhibition,* The Eastern Carpet in the Western World, 15th–17th centuries, *held at the Hayward Gallery, 1983.*

Lionel Lambourne, *who is Assistant Keeper in the Department of Paintings, has had a varied career within the V&A and at leading Regional Galleries. His interests range from the visual history of Sport to the Arts and Crafts Movement, Caricature and Popular Art. Publications include* Utopian Craftsmen; Derby Day 200; Ernest Griset; *and two books in the* Introduction *series –* Victorian Genre Painting *and* Caricature. *He is currently organising the Dickie Doyle centenary exhibition opening on 30 November 1983.*

June Lennox *has been on the staff of the Museum for ten years, and she is the Chief Conservation Officer with responsibility for stained glass. As a designer, among her windows is one in the church of St. Botolph-without-Aldgate, London.*

Valerie Lloyd *is a photographic consultant and the former Curator of Photographs of the Royal Photographic Society. She has written many articles and has organised exhibitions for the Arts Council and the Victoria and Albert Museum.*

The Countess of Longford, CBE, *historian and author, was a member of the Museum's Advisory Council from 1969 to 1975. Among Lady Longford's books are –* Victoria R.I., Wellington: Years of the Sword *and* Wellington: Pillar of State.

Valerie Mendes *is an Assistant Keeper in the Department of Textiles and Dress with special responsibility for the twentieth century collections.*

Jennifer Hawkins Opie *is in the Department of Ceramics and specialises in the nineteenth and twentieth centuries. She has lectured on ceramics of this period and is author of* The Poole Potteries, *London, 1980. She has worked on a number of exhibitions including 'Keith Murray', 'Teaspoons to Trains, the Work of Frank Pick' and the major exhibition 'Thirties: British art and design before the war'. At present, she is assembling the ceramics and glass section of the twentieth-century primary gallery.*

John Physick *joined the staff of the V&A in 1948 and is the Deputy Director and Keeper of Museum Services.*

Gillian Saunders *is a curator in the Department of Prints, Drawings, Paintings and Photographs. She is researching aspects of the wallpaper collection.*

Michael Snodin *is a Research Assistant in the Department of Prints and Drawings. His particular concern is with the architectural and older design material in the Department. He is the principal organiser of the 1984 Rococo exhibition.*

Anna Somers Cocks *is Assistant Keeper in the Metalwork Department. She specialises in the Continental collections, and at the moment, especially in German silver and Renaissance jewellery.*

Gavin Stamp *is an architectural historian and journalist. He is the author of* The Great Perspectivists *and* Temples of Power *and is the Chairman of the Thirties Society.*

Simon Tait *has been a journalist for 17 years. He worked on local, regional and national newspapers for the first nine, and joined the public information service in 1975. He became the V&A's press officer in 1980.*

Andrew Topsfield *is Assistant Keeper in the Indian Department since 1978. Publications include* Paintings from Rajasthan in the National Gallery of Victoria *(1980) and* An introduction to Indian court painting *(forthcoming). At present, working on a study of the Udaipur school of Rajasthani painting.*

Clive Wainwright *has worked in the Museum since 1966 and in the Department of Furniture & Woodwork since 1968. He is particularly interested in nineteenth and twentieth century furniture and interiors. He has published extensively and has made a particular study of Pugin and his work at the Palace of Westminster.*

Rowan Watson *is Assistant Keeper in charge of manuscripts in the Library. Among his projects is the preparation of a catalogue of illuminated manuscripts dating from before 1600.*

Paul Williamson *is Assistant Keeper in the Department of Sculpture, with responsibility for Early Medieval and Byzantine sculpture, and is a member of the Working Committee for the exhibition '1066–1200: English Romanesque Art', to be held in London in 1984.*

Most of the photographs reproduced are the work of the Museum's studio, and grateful acknowledgement is made to Peter Macdonald, Stanley Eost, Philip Barnard, Graham Brandon, Sally Chappell, John Hammond, Ken Jackson, Michael Kitcatt, Dominic Naish, Brenda Norrish, Hugh Sainsbury, Christine Smith, Philip Spruyt de Bay and Ian Thomas.

THE FRIENDS OF THE V&A

AIMS

To help in the work and activities of the Victoria and Albert Museum and in particular:

To purchase works of art

To maintain a lively exhibition programme

To expand the Museum's training schemes and research projects

To contribute towards the cost of refurbishing the galleries

PRIVILEGES

1. Free and immediate entry to all paying exhibitions at the Museum and to Ham House, Osterley Park, and Apsley House (Bethnal Green has no entry charges).
   The membership normally admits husband/wife or other guest and Friend's children under 16.

2. Special Evening Private Views

3. Advance information on Museum activities.

4. Discounts on selected catalogues and other publications, and purchases in the Craft Shop.

5. Visits abroad and in this country, accompanied by staff from departments of the Museum.

6. Social occasions at the Museum, Ham House, Apsley House and Osterley Park.

MEMBERSHIP

Membership Fee
£15 annually

Special Fee
£10 annually
(for pensioners and those working full time in UK museums)

Corporate Fee
£100 or more annually
(with transferable membership cards)

Benefactor
£1,000 annually
A Benefactor may specify which department or project of the Museum should receive his gift

For further details and application form, please apply to:
Friends' Office
Victoria and Albert Museum
South Kensington
London SW7 2RL
01-589 4040

Jean Max Cassel

Fine paintings

356, rue S.ᵗ Honoré,
75001 Paris

Tél. 261.02.01 +
parking Place Vendôme

Baron François Gérard
Portrait half-length of Constance Ossolenska Lubinski. Painted 1813/14
Oil on canvas 65¹/₂cm × 52¹/₂cm

Provenance: Anc. Collection Lubinski, Warsaw.
              Leupert, Zurich.
              Baszanger, Geneve – 1948.
              Priv. Coll. Switzerland.

Bibliography: A. Ryszkiewicz
              'Francusco Polskie Zwiazkiartystyczne'
              – Warsaw, 1967; Fig. n. 62

              Will be reproduced in the 'Complete
              catalogue of the works of Baron
              Gérard' – Prepared by Alain
              Latreille, Paris.

The age of elegance has not passed.

Empire Razor 1929

WILKINSON
SWORD

Royale Razor 1983

Index of Advertisers